MIKE HAILWOOD

THE FAN'S FAVOURITE

Drawing by David Boarer.

MIKE HAILWOOD
THE FAN'S FAVOURITE

MICK WALKER

First published in Great Britain in 2005 by
The Breedon Books Publishing Company Limited
Breedon House, 3 The Parker Centre,
Derby, DE21 4SZ.

Paperback edition published in Great Britain in 2012 by The Derby Books
Publishing Company Limited, 3 The Parker Centre, Derby, DE21 4SZ.

Dedication

This book is dedicated to my love of Scotland, where in
Caithness and later in Edinburgh the manuscript for Mike
Hailwood: The Fans' Favourite was written.

ISBN 978-1-78091-214-1

Printed and bound by Copytech (UK) Limited, Peterborough.

Contents

"I am privileged to have access to the Mortons Motorcycle Media Archive, which I consider to be the finest in the world and a national treasure."
MICK WALKER

Every so often a unique snapshot of times gone by is discovered in a dusty vault or in shoeboxes in an attic by an enthusiastic amateur photographer. They are living history. Each and every one of us cannot resist the temptation as we marvel at the quality of the images, to let our mind drift back to the good old days and wonder what it was really like.

We at Mortons Motorcycle Media, market-leading publishers of classic and vintage titles, own one of the largest photographic archives of its kind in the world. It is a treasure trove of millions of motorcycle and related images, many of which have never seen the light of day since they were filed away in the dark-room almost 100 years ago.

Perhaps the biggest gem of all is our collection of glass plates – almost two tons of them to be precise! They represent a largely hitherto unseen look into our motorcycling heritage from the turn of the century. Many of the plates are priceless and capture an era long gone when the pace of life was much slower and traffic jams were unheard of.

We are delighted to be associated with well known author Mick Walker in the production of this book and hope you enjoy the images from our archive.

Terry Clark,
Managing Director,
Mortons Media Group Ltd

Preface

THIS, the third in a series intended to eventually encompass the careers of the world's greatest motorcycle racing champions, covers the man who, almost a quarter of a century after his untimely death in a road accident, is still a hugely popular figure who is respected and loved all round the world.

Following on from biographies of John Surtees and Giacomo Agostini, *Mike Hailwood: The Fans' Favourite* is the story of an extraordinary career, which saw someone born into a wealthy and privileged background go on to become the most popular rider of all time – not because of his background, but because of his abilities on the race circuit. Unlike some of today's sporting prima donnas, Mike Hailwood was a shy person at heart, but someone who enjoyed life. He did not just win races and break lap records – everyone loved Mike.

Many books have been written about Mike Hailwood over the years. *Mike Hailwood: The Fans' Favourite* seeks to add to this existing and appreciated earlier work.

Being born a couple of years after Mike has meant that my own motorcycling career has kept me in touch with the events that shaped his life. I even visited the Hailwood and Gould motorcycle dealership in my role as British Ducati representative in the late 1970s.

In compiling *Mike Hailwood: The Fans' Favourite*, I have been fortunate in having so many friends in the world of motorcycling. In this respect I should like to make special mention of the following: John Surtees, Tommy Robb, Nobby Clark, Steve Wynne, John Armstrong, Jim Scaysbrook, Bill Stone, Mr and Mrs Hampton, David Boarer, Kathy Nutt (formerly Smith), Dan Shorey, Pat Slinn, the late Ing. Fabio Taglioni, Graham Eckersley, the late Arthur Wheeler, Livio Lodi, Paul Smart, Pamela Lawton and Phil Read.

Photographs have come from various sources, including: Bill Innoles, Richard Pentelow, Peter Reeve, Trevor Turner, Brian Silver, Breese Stamp Company, Ian Welsh and last, but certainly not least, the Morton's Motorcycle Media archives, which houses those including the *The Motor Cycle* and *Motor Cycling* collections.

Just how and why Mike achieved the greatness he did is contained within the following pages, from his first race on a borrowed 125cc MV Agusta at Oulton Park on Bank Holiday Monday 22 April 1957, right through to his last ride on a Dunstall GS1000 Suzuki at Mallory Park on Sunday 10 June 1979. I just hope you, the reader, have as much enjoyment reading Mike's story as I have had in writing it.

Mick Walker, Wisbech, Cambridgeshire

Chapter 1

First steps

S.M.B. (Stanley Michael Bailey) Hailwood was born on 2 April 1940, just as Hitler's armies were about to invade the Low Countries and France, with the Battle of Britain to follow. Michael, as he was then known, joined an older sister Christine (who preferred simply Chris) in a well-off family. Michael and Christine's father was S.W.B. (Stanley William Bailey) Hailwood, a self-made millionaire businessman and the man behind the success of the King's group of motorcycle dealerships, which was the biggest such organisation in Great Britain.

More simply known as Stan, Hailwood Senior was to play a pivotal role in his son's racing career, at least in its formative years. Another chapter on him is included, not only reveal to the reader what sort of a man Stan was, but also to explain clearly why and how he is so important to any biography of his son, Mike-the-Bike, the most popular racing motorcyclist in the history of the sport and today an Elvis Presley-type legend, who unlike others has an ever-growing fan base, even though he has been dead for almost a quarter of a century.

Early schooling

Mike spent two years at nursery school near his home at Goring-on-Thames before going to boarding school at Purton Stoke, near Newbury. This meant that, from the age of only six, Mike lived largely away from home. His sister Chris says that this was because their father had to go to the United States on business and he didn't want the housekeeper to have the responsibility of looking after the children. Mike and Chris's mother, the first Mrs Stan Hailwood, had left the family home, never to return.

This incident has never been fully explained, but suffice to say that it happened and eventually Stan married Pat, who all deeply loved. Chris was also packed off to boarding school, as she recalls, 'near Ipswich in Suffolk'.

In *Hailwood*, compiled by Ted Macauley and Mike himself, and first published in 1968, Mike had this to say:

...at six years of age I was living away from home at this boarding school, trying to do all the things that were supposed to shape me as a future gentleman, ready to ease myself into high social circles. I had piano lessons and learnt to ride!

He says he 'struggled through his eight years at Purton Stoke.'

There is no doubt that Mike's schooling was not an easy experience, although, in retrospect, it served to toughen him up for his future life.

First motorcycle

At seven years of age, his father bought Mike a Royal Enfield mini-bike powered by a 100cc two-stroke engine. Stan removed the kick-starter so Mike would have to learn how to bump start. Mike rode this machine on the lawn of the family's home. He was also given a child's car (again powered by a 100cc engine) and, in time, the use of an ex-Royal Air Force Link Trainer (a ground-based flight simulator, used to train pilots).

By now the Hailwood family had moved from Goring to Highmore Hall, Nettlebed, near Henley-on-Thames. Situated on the Berkshire/Oxfordshire border, this 10-bedroomed house (best described as a mansion) was a large residence with 52 acres of ground, having been built in the reign of Charles II. Even today, it's an imposing residence.

At 14 years of age, Mike entered Pangbourne Nautical College in the Upper Thames valley near Reading, Berkshire. Actually, before joining Pangbourne, Mike had a vision of himself as a seafaring man, but all this was soon to change. The official aims of the Pangbourne Nautical College are: to promote self-reliance and a smart and alert bearing, and to prepare its pupils for careers as officers in the Royal and Merchant Navy.

Even though Mike had previously professed a liking for the naval way of life – and had loved going up to London to be fitted out with his uniform – he actually hated Pangbourne as soon as he arrived.

As Christopher Hilton recalls in his book *A Man Called Mike* (MRP):

...at sixteen Michael asked if he could leave the college (Pangbourne) and Stan agreed. Michael went to his room, packed and simply got in the car. He didn't look back. The future, whatever it was, would not be cold showers, iron discipline, and at least one beating he would remember all his days.

Although at the time Mike disliked Pangbourne intensely, he was later to acknowledge it had bred in him a feeling of independence. While there his only real interests were music and boxing. In the latter, Mike represented the College and in 14 bouts he won 13 times – and shared a split decision in the other. At Pangbourne he had been given the nickname 'oilwood', because, as he once described, of 'the mixture of cockney and Northern' in his accent. Interestingly, the nickname was dropped when he started to be successful in the boxing ring! Mike also considered that not only was he 'never fitter in my life' than at Pangbourne, but also that his will to win really began there.

Something to look forward to

While at Pangbourne, often on a Sunday, after the regimental church parade, Stan (or stepmother Pat) would drive to the college, collect Mike and take him home to Highmore Hall. There he would ride in an eight-acre field, often for several hours at a time. By then the little Royal Enfield had given way to a full-size 197cc Villiers-engined James Commando trials bike. One day, unobserved, Stan noticed that Mike had laid out a miniature trials course and that his son was showing some considerable ability in his riding. It was also during these Sunday 'home visits' that Mike learned to drive a car – thanks to his stepmother allowing him to drive her Jaguar XK120 sports car. Stan didn't know about this until much later!

A working life

After Pangbourne Mike had a spell working in the King's Oxford branch, but this didn't work out as Stan had hoped. As Mike himself explained:

The Hailwood family home during the 1950s was Highmore Hall, Nettlebed, near Henley-on-Thames. Situated on the Berkshire border, this 10-bedroomed mansion was a large residence with 52 acres of ground. Built during the reign of Charles II, Highmore was once owned by Admiral Jellicoe, First Sea Lord during World War One.

I knew he [Stan] was fairly well off, and I thought I'd be able to sponge off him for a few years until I had made my mind up what I wanted to do.

But Stan had other ideas. He had a myriad of contacts throughout the motorcycle industry and organised a job for Mike at the Triumph factory, based in Meriden near Coventry in Warwickshire. However, as Mike recalled: 'it wasn't the usual sort of old pals act. I didn't even get half way up the ladder – I was stuck right down at the bottom end of it'. Actually, the truth is that Stan had organised it this way, so Mike got all the worst jobs: cleaning floors and toilets, running errands and making the tea! After that Mike was placed on the assembly line, of which he said: 'a more boring tedious job I cannot imagine'.

When Mike was seven, his father Stan bought him a specially commissioned Royal Enfield mini-bike to ride around the extensive grounds of Highmore Hall.

Mike certainly did not live a life of luxury away from the factory either, staying at first in a cheap hotel, then in digs, and using a battered old pre-war 250cc AJS to commute to work.

Although during his time at Triumph Mike helped assemble many engines and complete motorcycles, he freely admitted that at the end it still 'remained a big mystery'. Mike was never really interested in mechanical engineering, unlike, say, John Surtees. In fact, Triumph tester Percy Tait, a successful racer in his own right, recalls Mike during his time at Triumph as 'a youngster who simply wanted to go racing'.

Seeing his son's interest in racing, Stan set about making his wish a reality. At that time Mike was still almost totally unversed in the sport and would have been hard pressed even to name any riders or give details of their bikes.

How was Mike's introduction to competitive riding to be achieved? Here the reader must realise that being the parent of a son (or a daughter) who wants to take part in a potentially dangerous sport like racing is like being torn in two opposite directions. On the one hand you want them to do well, but on the other hand you always worry about the safety issue.

At first then, Stan opted for a small, not too powerful machine. He contacted his friend and fellow dealer Bill Webster of Crewe in Cheshire. 'Weberstini' was himself a racer of no mean skill. He was also a close friend of Count Domenico Agusta, and thus had access to that company's racing

Mike (left) aged 15, while on holiday at the TT in June 1955. He went with employees from King's motors, his father Stan sending the youngster 'to mix with the lads'. It is also thought that this was the first time that Mike rode a motorcycle on the road.

wares. However, as Bill explained to Stan, he could not sell him a bike, as he was on strict instructions from the Count that the bikes could only go 'to top riders'. Bill told Stan that he would lend him a 125cc sohc MV single. This, the two decided, should be limited by means of overjetting (to give an over-rich mixture and thus less performance) and also be overgeared – again to restrict performance.

D-Day: 22 April 1957

Mike's debut day was to be Easter Monday, 22 April 1957, at the Oulton Park circuit near Tarporley, Cheshire. This of course was only a few miles from Webster's base in Crewe. Looking decidedly out of place, Mike arrived as a passenger in his father's gleaming, and very costly, white Bentley Continental. Having celebrated his 17th birthday exactly three weeks earlier, the youngster was entering a world which, although he would soon come to know and love it, was, on this spring day, a totally alien experience. With Stan and Bill Webster in attendance, Mike changed into his brand new-for-the-day riding garb and readied himself for his practice session. In truth he could remember little of this by the time his race came around. The event was a six-lap race for machines of up to 150cc. *Motor Cycle News* reported that:

> *...a day of continuous rain in the Oulton area gave way to ideal racing weather on Bank Holiday Monday, when the Wirral Hundred MC ran its traditional Easter meeting over the 2.761-mile road circuit, considered, by many, to be the finest on the English mainland.*

Dave Chadwick

Born in Lancashire in 1931, David Vincent Chadwick was Mike Hailwood's first real racing friend, and in fact Mike was Dave's best man at his wedding shortly before the latter's death in spring 1961.

Dave began his motorcycling career in 1949 with a 125cc BSA Bantam. Then in 1950 he rode in his first competitive events – trials and scrambles – using another 125cc Bantam machine.

His first road race came at the short, narrow Rhydymwyn track in North Wales, and riding Velocettes and Nortons in 1951 and 1952 Dave competed all over England.

Then came his first break when he was spotted by Manchester dealer/entrant Reg Dearden and in 1953 a partnership was formed, which was to last for the rest of his life.

In 1954, riding a Dearden Featherbed Manx Norton, Dave scored his first major success, finishing runner-up in the Junior Manx Grand Prix.

Besides the Norton, Dave Chadwick was a very successful rider of Lightweight machines, including MV Agustas for British importer Ron Harris and works Ducatis. But before this he had ridden the LEF (Lewis, Ellis and Foster of Watford, Herts) Special to fifth place in the 1956 Ultra-lightweight TT, with only works MVs and Montesas in front of him. Then in 1957 he had gone even better with a superb fourth in the 125cc Ulster GP on an MV – and capped this with runner-up in the 250cc race, behind world champion Cecil Sandford's factory FB Mondial.

He also finished sixth in the Lightweight (250cc) TT, again on a single-cylinder MV. But his Norton performances should not be overlooked, with a fifth in the 350cc Ulster race.

These results obviously influenced Ducati to sign Dave for 1958. In the seven-round 125cc World Championship series he was third in the Isle of Man and in Ulster, fourth in Belgium and Italy and fifth in Holland; ending the season fifth in the championship table.

Some nine years older than Mike, Dave Chadwick was the former's first real racing pal, and Mike was Dave's best man. Dave is seen here at Aintree in 1958 aboard a 196cc MV Agusta.

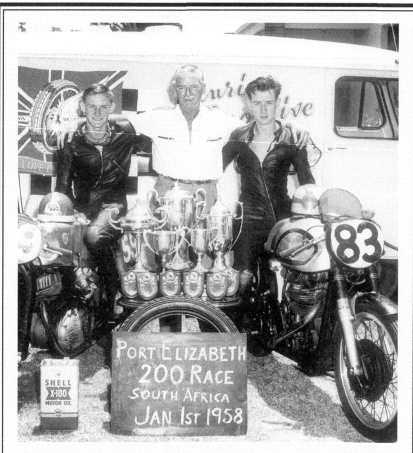

1 January 1958. Dave (right) is seated on his 350 Manx Norton, while Mike and father Stan have the ex-Surtees NSU.

Then in 1959 he was sidelined for most of the season, following a crash during the 125cc Isle of Man TT, when, as *Motor Cycle News* described: 'he was putting up a typical Chadwick effort on a slow MV, challenging much faster machines'.

This crash meant that Dave didn't ride at all for the remainder of the European racing season.

For three winters running Dave Chadwick went out to race in South Africa, in 1956–7, 1957–8 and 1958–9. And, as related in the main text, he was often accompanied by Mike Hailwood. In fact it would be true to say that Dave was largely responsible for Mike's activities while the pair were in South Africa. Not only this, but there is no doubt that Dave successfully coached Mike and helped him on his rise to stardom.

In February 1960 came news that the East German MZ factory had signed Dave to join existing rider Ernst Degner. When not able to ride an MZ, Dave would continue riding for Reg Dearden.

Then, on 23 March 1960, Mike Hailwood was best man at the wedding in Hazel Grove, near Stockport, Cheshire, of Miss Judith Stoney and Dave Chadwick. Also in attendance were Reg Dearden and Paddy Driver, together with their wives.

The newly-wed pair then left for Spain for their honeymoon, with Dave taking in the Spanish Grand Prix on 3 April at Montjuich Park, Barcelona. And on his Dearden Norton Dave was fastest in practice – having his first competitive outing since his TT injury of the previous year. As *Motor Cycle News* reported:

> *...a beautiful start by last year's winner Ferbrache riding an ex-Bob McIntyre Norton as his new Matchless is not ready. He rockets away in the lead but Dave Chadwick makes a bad start and only gets away at the back of the field.*
>
> *...yes, it's Ferbrache a full hundred yards in the lead to complete the first lap. Jim Redman is second closely tailed by Johnny Lewis and Remo Venturi on the MV 'four' and Dave Chadwick is through to fifth place already. Fantastic!*

But then Dave hit what were termed 'costly mechanical problems' and was forced into retirement. But in their 4 May 1960 issue, *MCN* ran the headline: 'Clear margin for Chadwick'. The event was the Austrian Grand Prix, held on 1 May. The report stated:

> *Dave Chadwick (Norton) made a return to top form to win the 500cc class after beating off determined challenges from Dickie Dale (Norton), John Hartle (Norton), John Hempleman (Norton) and Frank Perris (Norton).*

Other riders included Ernst Hiller and Fumio Ito (BMWs), plus Jim Redman (Norton).

The following week, on 11 May at the Saar GP, held over the tricky 2.35-mile St Wendal street circuit, Dave at last made his MZ debut, but to no avail as a broken rear brake cable put him out of the 125cc class. Then, in the 350cc race, he finished a superb runner-up behind Australian Tom Phillis; both were riding Nortons. Then came that fateful day, when at the international road race meeting on the famous five-mile circuit at Mettet, Belgium, on Sunday 18 May 1960, Dave Chadwick suffered a fatal accident, while leading the 500cc race with only two laps to go. Earlier in the day Dave had finished runner-up and set a record class lap in the 350cc race.

Motor Cycle News described the accident:

> *Chadwick was in great form and he pulled away from the field until with two laps to go he had a winning lead. It was when he was lapping Bill Sawford on one of the straights that the fatal crash occurred. For some reason the machines became locked together and in the crash Chadwick was flung with his machine into the crowd, one of whom was also fatally injured. Sawford escaped with a broken leg.*

And so Mike, together with the whole motorcycle racing fraternity, lost a true friend. One journalist described Chadwick thus:

> *...although a forceful rider well able to mix it with the best in the world, Dave was one of the few top-class racing men who I can safely say had no enemies in the game. His cheerful disposition and sense of sportsmanship avoided the clashes common between those of equal calibre but of a less even temperament.*

An MV Agusta 125 Competizione of the type used by Mike in his very first race, at Oulton Park, on Easter Monday, 22 April 1957. He finished 11th.

Mike rather fluffed his start (even though from his earliest days he had been encouraged to perfect the technique). And then he was off. Stan had drilled into him: 'ride your own race, don't worry about other riders'. This Mike found a sensible approach as when he attempted to keep up with the fastest riders he found he was making too many mistakes. So in the end he settled on 'riding to finish'. And that was exactly what happened. He eventually crossed the line in 11th spot. The race was won by Cecil Sandford who, riding a works FB Mondial, also set a new class lap record at 73.30mph. Second was future close friend Dave Chadwick (MV), while Bill Webster brought his MV home fourth.

Castle Combe

If no one except close friends and family had noticed Mike's performance at Oulton Park, the same could not be said for his next meeting, which came a mere five days later, at Castle Combe, Wiltshire, on Saturday 27 April 1957. By now, Stan and Bill Webster had decided to let the youngster have a level playing field – not only was the 125cc MV now set up correctly, but there was also the use of a larger 175cc model from the same stable.

The *Motor Cycle News* report dated 1 May 1957 sets the scene:

In spite of a cold wind and overcast skies, not to mention petrol rationing [caused by the Suez crisis] *a record number of enthusiasts*

The MV 125 Competizione was a single overhead cam version of his successful 123.55cc (53x56mm) early 1950s works model. It produced 12bhp at 10,000rpm and could reach just over 90mph.

turned out to support the stout efforts of the Wessex Centre who went ahead with the organisation in spite of a heavy financial loss last year and the withdrawal of car racing from the circuit. Officials estimated the crowd at around the twelve thousand mark and this will go a long way to ensuring that racing continues at this popular – if bumpy – 1.84-mile circuit.

When the races came, they were to be something of a shock to everyone connected with the Hailwood camp. Mike took fourth in the 125cc and, perhaps even more surprising, a fifth in the 250cc event. *Motor Cycle News* described the 125cc race as follows:

Another of Mike Hailwood's early racing machines was the 49cc Itom two-stroke.

...the 125 race was the expected MV benefit with the streamlined models of Mike O'Rourke and Dudley Edlin coming home first and second, with O'Rourke well ahead and obviously in a hurry for he broke the lap record by a fraction. The two streamliners were followed home by the naked models of S. Rees and S. Hailwood [note the S instead of M!], who provided the excitement by dicing for third place throughout the race.

125cc Castle Combe – 5 laps – 9.2 miles
1st   M. O'Rourke (MV Agusta)
2nd   D. Edlin (MV Agusta)
3rd   S. Rees (MV Agusta)
4th   M. Hailwood (MV Agusta)

O'Rourke took his larger MV (a 203cc model) to victory in the 250cc race, ahead of John Clark on Ian Telfer's Norton (earlier in the decade ridden by John Surtees), third going to the experienced Jack Murgatroyd riding a Beasley-Velocette.

250cc Castle Combe – 6 laps – 11.04 miles
1st   M. O'Rourke (MV Agusta 203cc)
2nd   J. Clark (Telfer Norton)
3rd   J. Murgatroyd (Beasley-Velocette)
4th   J. Hamilton (NSU)
5th   M. Hailwood (MV Agusta 175cc)

Besides the 125 MV, Mike also raced a 175 MV *Disco Volante* (Flying Saucer).

Scottish Six Days Trial

Another early Mike Hailwood sporting venture was of an entirely different nature to road racing. His previous off-road experience was put to the test when Mike competed in the Scottish Six Days Trial, which in 1957 started from Edinburgh's Cattle Market on Sunday 5 May. Some 173 riders set out on the 75-mile road run via the Kincardine Bridge, Menstries and Lochernhead to Glen Ogle Hill, the first observed section. This slippery, rock-dashed surface climb, divided into eight sub-sections, was followed by a lunch check at Tyndrum, then further observed sections at Altnafeadh, Conduit, the infamous Mamore and finally Town Hall Brae in the centre of Fort William – the headquarters of the trial until the following Saturday morning.

In 1957, Mamore was not observed at the bottom and riders had to cover some two miles of the old Mamore military road – built by General Wade in the 17th century as a short cut for his troops between Kinlochleven and Fort William – before coming to the first of the four sections, all of which had rocks as their main ingredient.

Mike's machine for the six days event was a standard road-going Triumph Cub, a 199cc ohv single with unit construction engine and four-speed gearbox. This was an obvious choice, given his job at the Triumph factory. The only alteration to the machine's specification was the fitment of more suitable knobbly tyres.

Unfortunately for Mike and the other competitors the weather, at least for the beginning of the week, was what *MCN* described as 'unpleasant'.

The magazine described the second day in the following terms:

> *...it was dull, cold and overcast at seven thirty – half an hour earlier than usual – the first man set out on the longest run of the week. And, not only has it been the longest run – 167 miles – but it must surely prove to be one of the toughest.*

Included in the route for the first time was an almost unbroken 25-mile stretch of rough moorland and mountain track, which began a few miles after the lunch check at the foot of Kinlochrannoch and continued over hills and dales to the main road near Roy Bridge which led back to Fort William at Ben Nevis and Town Hall Brae.

Mike was confronted by grease-covered boulders, deep mud, hidden holes and a multitude of rocky stream crossings – made even more treacherous by poor visibility caused by a mixture of mountain mist and a steady drizzle, even snow at times. And so came the third day and with it Mike's retirement. When interviewed by Bob Curry at the end of 1959, Mike commented that 'trials riding was not entirely my cup of tea!' Actually, he found the Scottish going tough and simply wanted to get back to racing.

Back to the safety of the tarmac

After the rigours endured in Scotland, turning out at Brands Hatch on Sunday 12 May must have been a big relief – at least there was a relatively flat track with tarmac everywhere! A wet morning and a cold blustery wind kept the number of spectators down to around 4,000 and the meeting was organised by the Gravesend Eagles Club. With a 200cc event in the programme, Mike raced his single overhead cam 175cc MV, bringing it home behind the 125cc MVs of Michael O'Rourke and Dudley Eldin.

Then came a very special day when Mike scored his very first victory. This was on Whit Monday, 10 June 1957, at Blandford Camp in Dorset. Mike rode in three races that day, the 50, 125 and 250cc: on 49cc Itom,

The larger MV single was later converted to 203cc.

One of Mike Hailwood's first competitors was the Shrewsbury rider/dealer Fron Purslow, who is seen here on his NSU at the British Championships, Thruxton, on 1 August 1958.

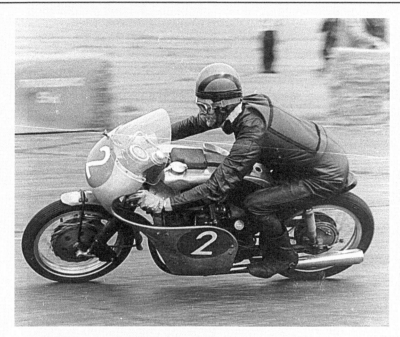

NSU Sportmax

The NSU Sportmax was one of the motorcycles which shaped Mike Hailwood's early career and, as explained in the main text, came via John Surtees, who had already enjoyed considerable success with the very same bike.

The prototype of what was to emerge as the Sportmax was first seen towards the end of 1953 during the Spanish Grand Prix in Barcelona. Thereafter, development continued apace both on the track and in the test shop at the NSU Neckersulm works. There were several actual race tests during the 1954 season at events such as Hockenheim, the Swiss Grand Prix and the Italian Grand Prix; riders included Georg Braun and Kurt Knopf.

All these early development machines were essentially similar to the production version, but employed a smaller diameter front brake and a few other minor differences. Dipl. Ing. Karl Kleinbach was responsible for the Sportmax's development. The word 'development' was used rather than 'design' because after all it was derived from the existing Max roadster series. Although it has to be said, the Sportmax was no lightly tarted-up street bike!

There has always been controversy about just how many genuine Sportmax machines were actually constructed. NSU publicity chief Arthur Westrup stated that 17 examples had been built, while other well-informed sources go as high as 34. In addition, a number of other examples were built from spare parts when the race shop was sold to the Herz family in the late 1950s. Finally, there were a large number of converted Max, Special Max and Super Max roadsters, some of these being crude to say the least – they not only utilised the series production roadster cycle parts, but were also often to be found with poorly-made replica Sportmax tanks and seats.

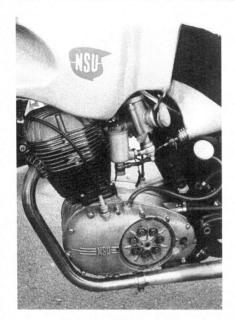

The genuine Sportmax or Type 251 RS (250cc one-cylinder Rennsport) had a displacement of 247cc (69x66mm) and a compression ratio of 9.8:1, giving 28bhp at 9,000rpm (maximum safe revolutions being 9,500). The piston was a forged Mahle-made, 3-ring type and there was an Amal GP 1³⁄₁₆ inch carburettor with remote float chamber. The distinctive 22-litre (4.84 imp gall) fuel tank was in hand-beaten aluminium. Both wheels were shod with 18-inch tyres – a 2.75 front and 3.00 rear section. With a dry weight of 112kg (246lb), maximum speed was 124mph and there were a wide variety of gearbox and rear wheel sprockets available for changing the gearing. Compared to the 1954 prototype bikes, the production models built from early 1955 featured an increase in front brake size from 180 to 210mm drum diameter.

The 247cc (69x66mm) sohc single-cylinder Sportmax engine with alloy cylinder head, iron barrel, unit construction and dry clutch.

The Sportmax proved even more successful than NSU could ever have hoped for. During the 1955 Grand Prix racing season, not only did Hermann Peter (Happy) Müller win the 250cc World Championship title, but a Sportmax also provided John Surtees with his first GP victory in Ulster during August of that year.

Other riders who went on to achieve success with the Sportmax included the likes of Hans Baltisburger, Georg Braun, Pierre Monneret, Horst Kassner, Jack Murgatroyd, Eric Hinton, Sammy Miller, Tommy Robb and, of course, the hero of this book, Mike-the-Bike.

Leading link front forks and massive drum brake from the German NSU.

125cc MV and 175cc MV machines, the Itom having been purchased the week before for £90. Blandford, at that time, was an event which attracted the big names in British short circuit racing. *Motor Cycle News* journalist Roger Maughfling commented: 'winner of the 125 race was eighteen year old SMB Hailwood (MV) riding in what was only his fourth race – his first at Oulton Park on April 22nd'. To add to his historic victory, Mike also placed third on the Itom and fifth in the 250 class. His main opposition that day was none other than Fred Launchbury (later to become renowned as a rider/tuner of BSA Bantams), Fred winning the 50cc race on an Itom and coming home second behind Mike in the 125cc event on the GTS (George Todd Special – a Bantam in disguise!).

Crashing at Scarborough

Just a few days after his Blandford success, Mike was given a sharp reminder that racing has its bad days as well as its good ones, when he was one of a number of riders who crashed at Oliver's Mount, Scarborough over Friday and Saturday 14 and 15 June 1957. As *Motor Cycle News* reported:

> *...one of the riders to come off on the top section and only slightly hurt himself was young Mike Hailwood who had won the 125cc class at Blandford on an MV a few days earlier at only his fifth-ever meeting.*

Mike had collided with another competitor, dislocating a thumb as well as suffering a gashed arm and knee.

A doctor had suggested a six-week lay-off, but Mike was back in action in half that time, appearing at the BMCRC (British Motor Cycle Racing Club) Silverstone Trophy Day on Saturday 6 July. This was an annual event and, although there was no prize money, the race awards varied from a silver cup for a first place to a Bemsee shield for the fourth man home. This meeting was run on the short 'club' circuit. Mike rode his MV (now enlarged to 203cc) in both 176 to 250cc races, finishing runner-up to a two-fifty Moto Guzzi on each occasion – with different riders, Jim Baughn and Dudley Edlin. *MCN* said: 'S.M.B. Hailwood got away to a real flying start in the 250cc event, and showed that his MV has a real turn of speed'.

First 250cc victory

Eight days later the fast-improving Mike gained his first 250cc victory at the Snetterton Combine's Norfolk airfield meeting on Saturday 14 July 1957, riding the 203cc MV Agusta single.

250cc Snetterton – 5 laps – 13.90 miles
1st   M. Hailwood (MV Agusta 203cc)
2nd   T. Thorp (BSA)
3rd   D. Shorey (Norvel)
4th   P. Tucker (Norvel)

In the 125cc event, Mike finished runner-up to Jim Baughn on another MV. A week later Mike once again finished runner-up to Jim Baughn at the Greenwich M & MCC Brands Hatch meeting on 21 July. The event was the 200cc race, Mike riding his 175 MV, while the winner and third-place man Dudley Edlin were both on 125cc MVs.

In winning both heats and finals in the 125 and 250 races (125 and 203cc MVs) over the short and narrow Rhydymwyn circuit in North Wales on Saturday 27 July, Mike brought his total of places to four firsts, three seconds, three thirds and three fourths since he began racing just over three months earlier. It was also his first double (finals) victory at the same meeting. And he was by now beginning to be noticed by the press, with *Motor Cycle News* founder Cyril Quantrill mentioning Mike's Rhydymwyn success in his Gossip column.

A return to Oulton Park

Next Mike returned to Oulton Park on Saturday 3 August. This event was his biggest yet, a national meeting organised by the BMCRC. Many of the top stars of the day were there, including John Surtees, John Hartle, Jack Brett, Alastair King, Bob Brown and Cecil Sandford. After finishing runner-up (to Fred Launchbury) in the 50cc event on his Itom and third in the 125cc (behind Sandford and Edlin), Mike then took his 203cc MV to the line for the 250cc race. There he was faced with Cecil Sandford (FB Mondial), John Surtees (NSU) and Bob Brown (NSU), among others. However, Mike crashed heavily, breaking his collarbone. As Mick Woollet says in his book *Mike Hailwood A Motorcycle Racing Legend* (Haynes):

> *…this injury threw a spanner in Stan's carefully laid plans, for Mike had already gained enough points from his race successes to qualify for an international racing licence and was entered for his first classic event – the Ulster Grand Prix!*

As the Ulster meeting was the very next weekend, the entry had to be scratched. As it was Mike was out of action for five weeks and didn't return until 8 September, the venue being Brands Hatch. There he won the 200cc

Crystal Palace; length 1.39 miles.

Brands Hatch, c.1957, before the extended GP section was introduced. Length 1.24 miles.

on his 203cc MV with the capacity reduced to 196cc and, on the same bike, he also finished runner-up in the 250cc race to Dick Harding (Velocette).

Yet another 'first' in what was quickly turning out to be a sensational first season was recorded when Mike went north to compete in his first international meeting, the Gold Cup at Oliver's Mount, Scarborough, on 12 to 14 September. There was such a large entry for the 250cc race that there were

Castle Combe; length 1.84 miles.

two heats and a final for this event. The *Motor Cycle News* race report dated 18 September 1957 says:

> *...the second heat was more exciting for Mike Hailwood (MV) made a fine start and led after a lap with Horst Kassner (NSU) and Dave Chadwick (MV) closing up. On the second lap, Chadwick used his five speed MV to advantage and passed both Kassner and Hailwood to take the lead that he held to the end. Kassner came through to take second place with Hailwood third.*

The first heat had been won by Fron Purslow (NSU) from J.G. Horne (NSU) and Herbert Luttenburger, on a ex-works Adler two-stroke twin, came third after a poor start.

Saturday's programme started with the 250cc final. Again, Mike made a good start to lead from Purslow into Mere Hairpin ahead of Chadwick and Kassner, while Luttenburger was unable to continue after colliding with another competitor at the start. At the end of the 12-lap race Chadwick won, with Kassner second and Mike third.

Surtees is impressed

John Surtees, who had been racing his private Nortons at Scarborough

Oliver's Mount, Scarborough; length 2.7 miles.

(including winning the main 500cc race) was so impressed by the way Mike rode his essentially standard MV (with only four speeds) that he offered the youngster his NSU Sportmax for the big Hutchinson 100 meeting at Silverstone the following Saturday.

However, Mike was unable to take advantage of the loan bike, because during midweek practice at the Northamptonshire circuit he crashed, breaking his ankle. This not only ruled him out for Silverstone, but also the remainder of the British season.

In fact, when an advertisement appeared in the 23 October 1957 issue of the *Motor Cycle News* by King's of Oxford offering his MVs for sale, several people thought Mike was on the verge of retiring! In fact, this was as far from the truth as could be. Mike and Stan were planning an expansion of their racing schedule for 1958 and Mike was getting ready to leave for South Africa (he departed on 21 November 1957) to do a winter's racing.

Chapter 2

Ecurie Sportive

*E*CURIE SPORTIVE – *For the Love of the Sport* was to be the Hailwoods' war cry – or at least that is how Stan Hailwood thought to promote his son's racing effort, by emblazoning the words on the sides of the impressive race transporter that he had purchased.

The general view on young Mike's first (1957) season was that he had been remarkably successful, with several victories and rostrum places to his

Mike pictured during 1958 with his crash helmet inscribed with the Ecurie Sportive motif and the Union flag.

credit. But, as the late Bob Curry recalled in *The Motor Cycle* during October 1959:

> *Mike was trying to run before he could walk and, in addition to the silverware, he collected a broken collar bone, broken ankle and sundry abrasions through sheer over-exuberance. Obviously he needed a good deal more experience.*

Following the sun south

Racing in England had come to an end, but the sun shone in South Africa. So, like the birds, Mike migrated south, where there was a winter's racing to be had with Dave Chadwick, an experienced racer from whom Mike would learn much. This would enable him to fast-track his career, so that when he finally returned to Great Britain in the spring of 1958, he had, effectively, jumped a season. But what machinery to take? Well, the South Africans didn't have 125 or 200cc events, so, as explained in the previous chapter, Stan put Mike's MVs up for sale.

Remembering the offer made by John Surtees for Mike to race the NSU Sportmax at Silverstone in September 1957 (abandoned due to a practice session crash a couple of days before the race), Stan Hailwood telephoned John and asked him whether Mike could borrow the NSU to use in South Africa that winter? John said yes. A few days later, Stan was on the telephone again asking to 'borrow' the spare engine, which was also in the Surtees workshop. Again the answer was affirmative. Most pundits have, wrongly, assumed that Stan purchased the bike (and engine). But the correct term is 'borrowed', says John, and he should know.

Stan also acquired a virtually new three-fifty Manx Norton (which he did purchase), and so, armed with two competitive bikes, Mike was ready to leave with his full-time mechanic John Dadley and Dave Chadwick, the group sailing from Southampton to Durban on 21 November 1957. Mike's broken ankle was by now fully healed.

A winning debut

At the beginning of December the ship docked at its destination. The first race meeting was at the Roy Hesketh circuit at Pietermaritzburg, near Durban. As Mick Woollet described:

> *Mike made an immediate impression on fellow competitors there, including future world champions Gary Hocking and Jim Redman, by winning the 250cc class first time out on the NSU.*

Watched by some 7,500 spectators, the event was held in lovely sunny, warm conditions. Besides the British visitors, riders from the Transvaal and Southern Rhodesia also congregated and, reported *MCN's* South African correspondent Ernest Cartwright, 'amongst the machines seen for the first time at Durban were a Mondial, a Ducati, two Puch two-strokes, NSUs and MV Agustas'.

The Port Elizabeth 200

South Africa's premier event, the Port Elizabeth 200, held on New Year's Day, 1 January 1958, had Englishmen as its oldest (Frank Cope, 60) and youngest (Mike Hailwood, 17) competitors. Stan Hailwood had flown out from England especially for the event, and Mike didn't disappoint his father. Even though he was forced to hold his carburettor in place for the last lap, he still won the 250 class, and in the process shattered race and lap records, putting them up to 88.68mph and 90.76mph respectively. Travelling companion Dave Chadwick also broke class, lap and race record on his 350 Norton.

On Sunday 19 January, it was back to Pietermaritzburg, with Mike and Dave following up their class wins in the Port Elizabeth 200 by again winning their classes at the Roy Hesketh circuit.

Mike featured in a particularly exciting race, the 250cc scratch event, which he won from Borro Castellani, the South African champion (FB Mondial). The field was already well away before Mike could get his NSU fired up, but once the Englishman did, he made up for lost time in truly brilliant style. Cutting through the tail-enders, Mike pulled up within striking distance of the home hero, and after slip-streaming the Italian machine for a number of laps Mike seized his opportunity to take the lead. But, as the *Motor Cycle News* race report declared: 'Castellani wouldn't give up without a fight but couldn't master sufficient urge from his mount to seriously challenge the leader'. Mike completed the more than 45-mile race distance in 40 minutes 11 seconds. By putting in a lap at 71.45mph he also set a new class record.

350cc debut

Next came another 250cc victory on the NSU at the Grand Central circuit (between Johannesburg and Pretoria). It was also here that Mike made his debut on a 350cc machine.

But it was not a happy occasion: Mike was forced to retire from the race with a broken connecting-rod on the Norton's engine. Many have wondered why it took Mike so long to move up. Actually, in the author's opinion, this

Mike Hailwood and engineer Bill Lacey with one of the Ecurie Sportive NSU Sportmax machines, spring 1958.

was all part of his father Stan's master plan – for Hailwood Senior realised that by restricting his son (remember that very first Oulton Park meeting in April 1957), he was protecting him, as much as he could, from the inherent dangers racing imposed. Mike 'graduated' to the 500cc class eventually, but not before Stan thought it was prudent to do so.

On 16 March, at the St Albans Aerodrome outside Port Elizabeth, the Norton failed again. Dave Chadwick, meanwhile, won both the 350 and 500cc races on his Nortons. There was no 250cc class that day.

The following news story appeared in Mick Woollet's *Motor Cycle News* 'Paddock Gossip' column, dated 12 March 1958:

> *Stan Hailwood, who has been out in South Africa enjoying the sunshine and acting as manager for Mike and Dave Chadwick, flew home the other day. He was greatly impressed by the tremendous enthusiasm of the riders out there and had obviously enjoyed every minute of his stay. On the phone he told me that Mike and Dave*

planned to fly home in time for the Easter meetings. The John Surtees NSU Sportmax that Mike had ridden so well out there will follow by sea... Meanwhile, Stan is busy looking for a Sportmax to buy.

Actually, the previous week *MCN*, dated 5 March, had carried an advertisement for just such a machine.

Sportmax NSU: one of the latest. Incorporating all modifications carried out. Complete with streamlining. This machine is almost new and all spares and information will be available to the purchaser. Clear of all duty and tax. Offers? – Box No. 1035 MCN.

It would be interesting to know who was selling this bike – and also who ultimately bought it – as genuine Sportmax machines were rare and in short supply. The answer came in *MCN* dated 19 March:

Stan Hailwood writes to tell me he bought the NSU Sportmax that was advertised in our 'Classifieds' a fortnight ago. This is now being prepared for the season by Bill Lacey, and they are confident that all will be ready for Mike when he flies in from South Africa a few days before Easter. Just to make doubly certain, Mike will bring the engine/gearbox unit that he has been using in South Africa with him by air – cost for excess baggage £125!

As John Surtees's machine and spare engine were never returned (the story behind this is related in Chapter 4), Mike actually had the use of some two and a half Sportmax bikes for the 1958 season (the recently purchased bike plus the Surtees model and spare engine).

As one journalist put it:

...the English Ecurie Sportive finished their extremely successful South African tour on Saturday 29th March with first and second places in handicap in the Van Riebeech Handicap on the Easter River circuit, Cape Town.

Dave Chadwick was the victor, and took the 350 scratch class on his Norton. Mike, on his Surtees NSU, was the Lightweight class winner. Both shattered their respective displacement record. Two days later Mike, on 31 March, left by air for London, the plane touching down in England the following morning, 1 April. Dave Chadwick and mechanic John Dadley,

Bill Lacey

Bill Lacey with his legendary Grindley-Peerless JAP, c.1928.

Born at the turn of the 20th century, C.W.G. (Bill) Lacey was a key player in Mike's early success. Stan Hailwood hired him to take overall charge of the preparation side of things, appreciating what a skilled engineer and tuner Bill was. But Bill's own career went back much further. He was an important competitor himself at the famous Brooklands circuit in Surrey. For example, in August 1928, Bill had covered 103 miles in one hour at Brooklands on a JAP-engined Grindley-Peerless, with an ohv twin-port power unit. He thus won *The Motor Cycle* Trophy as the first rider to record the magic hour at an average speed in excess of 100mph on a British circuit. Three years later, Bill pushed the same record up to around 110mph on a Norton at Montlhéry; and 10 months earlier, sharing the riding with Wal Phillips, he had helped put 306 miles into three consecutive hours with the same model at the same venue. Perhaps most impressive of all, Bill Lacey had tuned these bikes himself. Priority number one in Lacey's opinion was 'reliability'.

Years later, when talking about the dohc Norton engine, he said: 'what you have to remember is that the Manx Norton is a production engine, I can get flash power, but too much boosting can lead to trouble'. He reckoned that bottom-end trouble was unlikely, but that the Achilles heel was the highly stressed drive-side main bearing. This Bill Lacey modified 'as a matter of course'. The crankcase was bored out to take a flanged bearing housing – his own design. The case was heated to above the working temperature and the housing inserted by hand, so that the 4-inch diameter flange fitted hard up to the inner crankcase wall and was retained by four flush-fitting socket-head screws. Outside, the housing was screwed left-hand and fitted with a locking ring. Not that Lacey underrated the advantages an expert could gain from experimenting. Indeed, he tried coil ignition, twin plugs, larger valves and chromium cylinder bores on the Hailwood Nortons. Even so, he was a great believer in first obtaining the very best performance from a standard specification by meticulous attention to detail. This, he considered, was the most significant aspect of tuning.

His daughter Ann was also an integral part of the Lacey tuning establishment, which at the time of his involvement with Ecurie Sportive was based in Slough, some 15 miles from the Hailwoods' Nettlebed mansion. Ann was more than capable of stripping and rebuilding any racing engine to a higher standard than the vast majority of men.

Although it was Stan Hailwood who recruited Bill to Ecurie Sportive (Stan having known Bill since the late 1920s), it was ultimately Mike who was responsible for Lacey's continued involvement. As at one stage Bill had enough of Stan and simply walked out on the Hailwood équipe.

Bill Lacey was involved with the team from 1958 until late 1961. Besides Mike, the Lacey touch was also to be found, at various times, in the engines of John Hartle, Phil Read, Bruce Daniels, John Lewis and Brian Setchell. He was also heavily involved in the preparation of many successful car racing engines over the years.

together with the bikes and their equipment, left South Africa by sea on Friday 4 April.

Back in action at Brands

Mike was back in action straight away at Brands Hatch on Good Friday – the same day his comrades were leaving South Africa. Racing enthusiasts flocked to watch the racing over the 1.24-mile Kentish circuit, which was blessed with fine, sunny weather.

After a day of what *MCN* described as 'tremendous dicing', the 'King of Brands', Derek Minter, emerged the victor, but he had to fight all the way against three men.

First there was Mike, fresh from his triumphant South African tour. After scoring a win in the first race of the Brands season – the 200cc event (on an MV) – he challenged Minter all the way in the 250cc race.

250cc Brands Hatch – 15 laps – 18.6 miles
1st   D. Minter (REG)
2nd   M. Hailwood (NSU)
3rd   D. Shorey (Norvel)
4th   J. Hamilton (NSU)
5th   A. Pavey (NSU)
6th   T. Thorp (TTS)

The men to provide problems in the larger classes were Laurence Flury and Jim Redman.

Having just celebrated his 18th birthday, Mike was interviewed the following day, Easter Saturday, by BBC radio and the television programme *In Town Tonight*. He recounted some of his racing experiences in South Africa. Dubbed 'The fastest teenager on earth', Mike said he had never seen a tortoise run so fast as those who trundled out of his path on the race-track! This was the very first time the public were to experience his great sense of humour, which was to help him win so many fans in future years.

Winning in South London

Next port of call for Mike was the Easter Monday meeting held over the 1.39-mile Crystal Palace circuit in south London, in 'near Arctic conditions'. Even so nearly 20,000 spectators turned out to see some superb racing, the stars being Derek Minter, Jackie Beeton and Mike. With Minter (Norton) winning the 350 and 500cc classes, Beeton the side-cars and Mike taking the 200cc (196cc MV) and 250cc (NSU) races, in the smaller class Mike set a new lap record of 68.55mph.

Geoff Duke was an early admirer of Mike's abilities on the race circuit. Geoff is seen here towards the end of his career in 1959 at Oulton Park aboard his 499cc Norton.

Six days later Mike was at Mallory Park, Leicestershire, where besides finishing runner-up to Fron Purslow (NSU) in both the 250cc heat and final, he made his UK debut in the 350cc class aboard a Manx Norton and his 500cc debut (again Norton mounted). Both machines, incidentally, had been purchased by Stan from John Surtees.

But in the bigger classes things were none too easy. In the 350cc final Mike was beaten by Ray Fay, Bob Anderson, Peter Faerbrache and Alastair King. In the bigger class Mike was unplaced. At this stage in his career the opposition were simply too strong. For the record, the 500cc race at Mallory was won by Bob Anderson (Norton).

The annual and popular *Motor Cycling*-sponsored Silverstone Saturday meeting of 19 April 1958 was held under sunny skies. Close to 30,000 spectators lined the 2.92-mile Northamptonshire circuit, a few miles from Towcester.

The 125cc event was the first after the dinner break. From the start Arthur Wheeler took his recently acquired ex-works FB Mondial into the lead. As *MCN* said: 'this phenomenally fast machine was soon well clear of the field!' But Mike (MV) was soon in an equally secure second place. However, last lap drama struck Wheeler when his Mondial blew up with a puff of smoke from the exhaust and Mike took the flag with Dave Moore and Gary Dickinson (both MV mounted) second and third respectively.

125cc Silverstone – 10 laps – 29.2 miles

1st   M. Hailwood (MV Agusta)
2nd   D. Moore (MV Agusta)
3rd   G. Dickinson (MV Agusta)
4th   B. Webster (MV Agusta)
5th   D. Allen (FB Mondial)
6th   W. Smith (MV Agusta)

In the 250cc race Mike retired on one of his NSU machines.

Castle Combe

Next came the first of the Wessex Centre's national meetings for 1958, at Castle Combe. A mixture of sunshine, occasional light squalls and a blustery wind kept down race speeds, but in spite of the not too promising skies of the early morning, some 5–6,000 people lined the 1.84-mile Wiltshire circuit to watch Mike (MV and NSU) romp home an undisputed victor in the 125 and 250cc races – and put up some pretty fast laps with a brace of Nortons in both Junior and Senior races (Mike came sixth in the 350cc and fifth in the 500cc events – both of which were won by Derek Minter). Castle Combe was notable as it was the first time that Mike had contested all four classes in a single meeting.

The titanic struggle which ensued between Tommy Robb (103), Mike (111) and Sammy Miller (101) during the Irish North West 200 on Saturday 17 May 1958. All three were riding NSU Sportmax machines, and the finishing order was: Sammy, Mike, Tommy.

Bob McIntyre

Robert Macgregor (Bob) McIntyre was born on 28 November 1928 in Scotstown, a suburb of Glasgow. His father had worked as a riveter, building ships on the shores of the River Clyde.

Bob's first job was in a large motor garage near his home and his first motorcycle was a 16H Norton of 1931 vintage. After completing his national service, the young McIntyre returned home and purchased an Ariel Red Hunter and it was upon this bike that Bob began his competitive career at a scramble event at Auchterarder, near Perth.

After competing in bike events for some months and getting hooked on motorcycles, Bob found a job with Glasgow dealers Valenti Brothers. His work involved servicing and repairing touring bikes, the firm having little connection with the sport at that time.

After watching his first road race at Kirkcaldy, Bob borrowed a friend's 350 BSA Gold Star and entered his first race at Ballado. Riding pillion to the airfield circuit on the bike, they then removed the silencer and lights. His rivals were mounted on pukka racing bikes, including KTT Velocettes, AJS 7Rs and Manx Nortons, but the track was covered in loose gravel and Bob's scrambling experience came to the fore. The result was three wins in four races – and the only reason Bob didn't win that one too was because he fell off!

At that time, 1950–1, there was very little trade support for racing in Scotland. However, in 1952 Bob was asked to ride for dealers Cooper Brothers from Troon, Ayrshire, in the Junior Clubmans TT in the Isle of Man on a ZB32 Gold Star. As Bob was later to recall, 'that race made me'. He finished runner-up behind the winner Eric Housley and set the fastest lap (a new class record) at 80.09mph. A couple of days later he also finished second in the Senior Clubmans on the same bike.

That September he returned to the Island, this time to ride an AJS 7R in the Junior Manx Grand Prix. Bob not only won, but riding the same machine he also finished runner-up in the Senior!

From then on he mixed it with the big boys and after a spell working for London-based AMC (Associated Motor Cycles – the makers of AJS and Matchless), he began a highly-successful spell with tuner Joe Potts in Bellshill, Glasgow. Besides a famous 250cc Manx, Bob also rode 350 and 500cc Manx models for the Potts stable, as did his close friend Alastair King.

By the end of 1956, the McIntyre reputation had become international. The result was that when Geoff Duke was injured at the

Bob McIntyre, probably the greatest-ever motorcycle racer never to win a world championship, is pictured here in 1954 as a member of the works AJS team.

beginning of 1957, Bob was signed to race the factory four-cylinder Gileras. He proved his worth by scoring a famous double TT victory in the Jubilee races that year. He also broke the one-hour speed record (on a 350cc Gilera) at Monza later that year, after Gilera quit GP racing. In fact, when Mike Hailwood finally bettered Bob's hour record at Daytona in February 1964 it caused considerable controversy – even Mike saying that Bob's achievement in setting up his record on the bumpy Monza speed bowl in the autumn of 1957 had been 'an incredible feat of endurance and guts'.

Later Bob rode works bikes for the likes of Bianchi and Honda, but it was on the British short circuits that he continued to make his mark. And it was during this period of the late 1950s and early 1960s that he was to duel with Mike on many occasions, and in the process they became good friends.

Then came that fateful day at Oulton Park in August 1962, when, riding his Joe Potts-tuned 499cc Norton, Bob crashed heavily in torrential rain (after aquaplaning), receiving serious injuries from which he died nine days later.

The Motor Cycle dated 23 August 1962 carried the following tribute:

...though we mourn, we can be proud that the sport he graced and those who were privileged to enjoy his friendship are richer for his impact. ...a life of adventure was as compulsive to Bob as flying is to a bird. Challenge and conquest were food and drink to his spirit.

Bob McIntyre with his Joe Potts-entered AJS 7R, Silverstone, April 1959.

At Brands Hatch on Sunday 4 May 1958 Mike scored a trio of victories, including his first 350cc win. Notably in this race he beat none other than Derek Minter, the acknowledged master of the Kent circuit. Mike's other wins came in the 200cc on the 196cc MV and in the 250cc race on the NSU.

The final race of the day was the 1000cc Invitation. John Holder took the lead on the third lap from George Catlin, but Bob Anderson was catching him fast when Holder fell at Paddock Hill Bend on the seventh lap. With Anderson now leading, Derek Minter was second from Bob Rowe holding third. Mike, lying in sixth, then dropped his larger Norton at Druids Hill Bend. But before this he had clearly shown that he was getting to grips with racing the Norton singles.

A wet Aintree

Referring to the awful, wet conditions endured by all the riders at the Red Rose Trophy meeting at Aintree, Liverpool, on Saturday 10 May 1958, one competitor said: 'it was good racing, but a pretty horrible day'.

The handful of spectators not only saw Scot Alastair King win the 350, 500cc and Handicap races, but also saw Fron Purslow chalk up a 'double' by beating Mike in the 200 and 250cc events, on 124cc Ducati and 247cc NSU machines respectively. In the smaller event, Mike was riding his 196cc MV, whereas he rode an NSU in the 250cc race. And it certainly wasn't a day for race or lap records – just soaking wet leathers!

Then came a journey to Ireland for the Cookstown 100 meeting, held on Wednesday 14 May. Run over the Cookstown–Orroto–Drum road course, the meeting preceded the annual North West 200 International meeting later that week. The meeting, held under what were described as 'ideal conditions' by Billy McMaster, opened with Mike Hailwood making his Irish debut in the 200cc race over four laps (some 32 miles). This race was a handicap, and as the scratch rider, Mike had to set about retrieving the lead he had conceded to the 28 other starters. This he did in great style and, with one lap to go, he had only George McAdam (197cc Panther) and a gaggle of 50cc machines in front of his 196cc MV. All of these were disposed off during the final circuit.

When the 100-mile race got under way Noel Orr (Matchless G45) and Bob Ferguson (499cc Norton) set about each other in the 500cc class, Ralph Renson and Sammy Miller (Norton) competed in the 350cc class, while Mike (now NSU mounted) and Sammy Hodgins (Velocette) disputed the 250cc class. However, Mike was forced out on the second lap with engine trouble.

Australian Bob Brown (9) leads the 18-year-old Mike during the 1958 Lightweight (250cc) TT, held over the Clypse circuit. Both rode NSUs – Mike finished third behind the works MVs of Ubbiali and Provini, Brown was fourth.

The North West 200

The real purpose behind Mike's Ulster visit was the famous North West 200, which took place on Saturday 17 May 1958. Non-delivery of new machines was the most popular reason for no-arrivals, which reduced the entry of 92 to a starting line-up of 73 riders for this Irish classic.

In the 250cc class, Mike faced Ireland's top stars: Sammy Miller, Tommy Robb and David Andrews (all, like Mike, riding NSU machinery). And what an incredible race it turned out to be, with these riders and Bob Anderson on Geoff Monty's famous GMS all contesting matters strongly. At first Anderson led, challenged by Robb and Hailwood. Then the latter two were joined by Miller, and after Anderson retired, the three NSU riders were always close together, until Robb made a mistake. In the closing stages, Miller began to shadow Mike and as they began their last lap, Hailwood led, with Miller little more than a length behind. When they reappeared, with only a quarter of a mile to go, the positions were identical with Miller in Hailwood's slipstream, and in this order they descended the hill into Port Stewart, aiming for the right-hander just before the finishing line. Mike reached the bend first and, as he banked to take it, Sammy suddenly left his slip-stream, took a more acute line and gave his NSU the gun past Mike to get the decision by mere inches. As the *Motor Cycle News* race report said: 'only once before, in 1949, has such a close finish been seen at Port Stewart and on that occasion it was between Freddie Frith and Harold Daniell'.

Mike with his Bill Lacey-tuned Norton, which finished 12th in the 1958 Senior TT.

250cc North West 200 – 16 laps – 200 miles

1st	S. Miller (NSU)
2nd	M. Hailwood (NSU)
3rd	T. Robb (NSU)
4th	D. Andrews (NSU)
5th	R. Grey (Moto Guzzi)
6th	H. Stanford (Norton)

Despite having to make his Isle of Man TT debut (he never competed in the amateur Manx Grand Prix series), in all four classes (and over two different circuits!), Mike dashed back to Brands Hatch to ride in the Kentish venue's Whitsun Weekend meeting, held on Monday 26 May. At Brands, he decided to give the 200cc race a miss and instead entered the 250, 350 and 500cc races. Besides winning the 250cc race, he also won the 350cc event and was runner-up to Bob Anderson in the 1000cc class, prompting *Motor Cycle News* to comment: 'already a star in the Lightweight classes, Mike Hailwood is making rapid progress in the larger classes'.

TT debut

Then came Mike's stiffest test yet in his fledgling racing career: four TT rides. The machines he would use were a 124cc Paton, a 247cc NSU, and 348 and 499cc Nortons. The two Lightweight races would be over the 10.79-mile Clypse circuit, while the Junior and Senior races would be over the longer 37.73-mile Mountain circuit. It was to be the 1958 Isle of Man TT which was to finally prove that here, really, was someone with a great future, one with real skill and, ultimately, who was able to rise above the claims that it was purely his father's money that had been responsible for his early successes.

Someone once said:

...practice week in the Isle of Man is like some huge fly-wheel, at first barely perceptible in its movement and gathering momentum

1959 Triumph factory brochure for the new Bonneville, showing Mike during his victorious ride (with Dan Shorey) in the Thruxton 500-mile race, on a Triumph Tiger 110, the previous year.

TRIUMPH

The Best Motorcycle in the World

The Triumph "Bonneville 120" offers the highest performance available today from a standard production motorcycle.
Developed from the famous Tiger 110, the 650 c.c. two-
carburetter engine is individually bench tested and produces
46 BHP at 6500 r.p.m. This is the motorcycle for the really

Bonneville 120

knowledgeable enthusiast who can appreciate and use the
power provided. At the same time it is tractable and quiet in
the Triumph tradition and is a worthy addition to the range.

TRIUMPH ENGINEERING CO. LTD., MERIDEN WORKS, ALLESLEY, COVENTRY, ENGLAND

Printed in England   Ref. 444/58

TRIUMPH

Bonneville 120

SPECIFICATION

Engine 650 c.c. o.h.v. vertical twin with two gear driven camshafts. Alloy splayed port cylinder head with two carburetters, cast iron barrel, high compression pistons. New one piece forged crankshaft with bolt on central flywheel, "H" section RR56 alloy connecting rods with plain big-ends. Dry sump lubrication with plunger type pump and pressure indicator. Gear driven dynamo and magneto with manual control. Polished aluminium oil bath primary chaincase.
Gearbox Triumph design and manu-facture. Shafts and gears of hardened nickel and nickel-chrome steel. Positive stop footchange. Multiplate clutch with indestructible Neolangite linings and rubber pad shock absorber.
Frame Brazed cradle type frame with swinging arm suspension,

hydraulically damped and adjustable. "Easylift" centre and prop stands (latter optional extra). Provision for anti-theft lock to steering head.
Forks Triumph design telescopic pattern with hydraulic damping and steering damper.
Fuel Tanks Handsome large capacity all-steel welded tanks. Quick release fillers. Oil tank in "one-piece" unit with battery and tool container. Froth tower on oil tank.
Nacelle (Patent No. 647670) Triumph design integral with top of forks enclosing headlamp instruments and switchgear. Instruments inter-ally illuminated.
Brakes Front: Full width hub, heavily finned, incorporating efficient 8 inch brake. Rear: 7 inch diameter with cast-iron drum integral with rear sprocket.

Wheels & Mudguards Triumph design wheels with plated spokes and rims. Fully valanced rear guard and side lifting handles.
Lighting Equipment Lucas 6 volt 60 watt dynamo with ball bearing armature. 12 a.h. battery, powerful headlamp with combined reflector/front lens assembly, "pre-focus" bulb and adjustable rim. Wide angle rear/stop light with reflector.
Speedometer Smiths 120 m.p.h. (220 Km.p.h.) chronometric type with r.p.m. scale, internal illumina-tion and trip recorder.
Handlebar Comfortable shape with quick action twistgrip and adjustable friction control. Integral horn push. Ball ended clutch and brake levers with cable adjusters.
Twinseat Triumph design, Latex foam cushion covered in black water-proof "Vynide".
Tools Kit of good quality tools and tyre inflator.

TECHNICAL DATA

Engine type	O.H.V.	Front chain size	½ x .305
No. of cylinders	2	Rear ,, ,,	⅝ x ⅜
Bore/Stroke mm.	71 x 82	Tyres, Dunlop—front ins.	3·25 x 19
ins.	2·79 x 3·23	rear	3·50 x 19
Capacity cms.	649	Brake dia.—ins (cms) front	8 (20·32)
ins.	40	rear	7 (17·78)
Compression Ratio	8·5 : 1	Finish	Pearl Grey/
B.H.P. and R.P.M.	46 at 6500		Tangerine/
Sprocket teeth—Engine	24		Black
Clutch	43	Seat height ins. (cms.)	30½ (77·5)
Gearbox	18	Wheelbase ,, ,,	55¾ (141·6)
Rear wheel	46	Length ,, ,,	85½ (217)
R.P.M. 10 m.p.h. top gear	594	Width ,, ,,	28¼ (72)
Gear ratios—Top	4·57	Clearance ,, ,,	5 (12·7)
Third	5·45	Weight—lbs. (kilos)	404 (181·8)
Second	7·75	Petrol—galls (litres)	4 (18)
First	11·2	Oil—pints ,,	5 (2·8)
Carburetters (2)	Amal 376/204		

*with each revolution until, at the end of the period, it is a blur of
frenzied motion.*

The Motor Cycle editorial leader in their first TT issue, dated 29 May 1958,
was headed 'Enduring mystique'. The article went on to paint a picture of

how things were almost half a century ago when the young Mike was about to experience the legendary TT (Tourist Trophy) for the very first time:

Members of the lay public, yes, and some motorcyclists too, find difficulty in understanding fully an enthusiast's passion for the Isle of Man races. Yet is it so difficult to appreciate? Visualise an island out in the Irish Sea, with Snaefell Mountain as its most prominent topographical feature and with roughly a half of the whole island's area embraced by a racing lap – a lap that begins at little above sea level, rises to 1,401 feet over the Snaefell climb and plummets back to sea level in a matter of six miles. The entire 37.73-mile classic Mountain lap consists, in fact, of the roads used by the Islanders and visitors in their normal everyday or holiday pursuits. No other road race circuit in the world – the German Nürburgring that was designed specifically for racing included – equals the Manx lap as a test both of rider and machine. To its problems and its intricacy Britain owes her age-long rider supremacy. The mystique of the Mountain course will endure as long as racing motorcycles are made.

Of course, the racing world has changed considerably since the above leader was written by *The Motor Cycle's* then editor Harry Louis – the TT has lost its World Championship status and Britain its grip on producing the best

A standard three-fifty Manx Norton of the type raced by Mike in 1958.

riders – but in Mike's formative years Louis's description was entirely true and sets the scene as it was perfectly.

With Mike racing at Brands Hatch on Monday 26 May, he missed the beginning of TT practice which began on the same day. So immediately after Brands, he left for the Island. Mike first got his name on the practice leader board in the evening session of Friday 31 May when he took his NSU round in 9 minutes 11.6 seconds, at a speed of 70.42mph; the shorter 10.79-mile Clypse course being used for the Lightweight races (and also the sidecars). In reality Mike set himself the task of attempting to learn the two circuits, and that he did so successfully is shown by the results he went on to achieve the following week.

Mike accelerates his three-fifty Norton out of the Governor's Bridge dip onto Glencrutchery Road, Douglas, during the 1958 Junior TT.

His first Isle of Man race was the Junior (350cc) TT, held over the 37.73-mile Mountain circuit on Monday 2 June 1958. The winner was MV star John Surtees, who led throughout and covered the 7 laps of the course (264.13 miles) in 2 hours 48 minutes 38.4 seconds, at an average speed of 93.97mph. Mike's friend Dave Chadwick (Norton) was runner-up in 2 hours 52 minutes and 50.6 seconds (91.68mph). And what of Mike? Well, considering this was his first Island race, he put in an outstanding performance to come home 12th in 2 hours 57 minutes 17 seconds, at an average speed of 89.39mph. In their race report *The Motor Cycle* said:

…young Mike Hailwood (Norton), racing in the Island for the first time, lay twelfth – a remarkable showing, but one that was hardly unexpected.

But the main point of the exercise, from Mike's point of view, was to have continued learning the fearsome Mountain course – and to have finished. To have come home in the first 12 was a bonus.

The Lightweight events

Two days later, on Wednesday 4 June, came the two Lightweight races over the shorter 10.79-mile Clypse circuit. Originally entered on an MV, Mike had changed to a Paton. The machine was the work of the former Benelli and Aermacchi designer Lino Tonti and Giuseppe Patoni, previously the head mechanic of FB Mondial Grand Prix team.

The double overhead camshaft single-cylinder engine, in fact, closely followed the FB Mondial layout. Bore and stroke were 53x56.4mm giving a displacement of 124cc. The machine had a dolphin fairing of light alloy, split on the centre line to ease maintenance. A further useful feature was that the aluminium cylinder head and barrel could be removed without disturbing cam gear adjustment.

Although still described as 'experimental', the machine was still a pretty well-developed piece of kit, benefiting from the combination of the two very talented individuals who had teamed up to produce it.

With the Paton, Mike had stiff opposition from strong factory entries in the shape of not only MV Agusta, but also Ducati and MZ. Even so, Mike brought the Paton home in seventh spot – the first non-factory-entered machine to finish.

Ultra-Lightweight (125cc) TT – 10 laps – 107.9 miles
1st   C. Ubbiali (MV Agusta)
2nd   R. Ferri (Ducati)
3rd   D. Chadwick (Ducati)
4th   S. Miller (Ducati)
5th   E. Degner (MZ)
6th   H. Fugner (MZ)
7th   M. Hailwood (Paton)
8th   F. Purslow (Ducati)

A rostrum finish
It was the Lightweight (250cc) event which was really to get everyone talking about that young man Hailwood. In absolutely perfect weather conditions, the race was run over the Clypse course. Perhaps it was no surprise that the winner, Tarquinio Provini, and his MV teammate, Carlo Ubbiali, should finish first and second. But, as *The Motor Cycle* said, the race was:

> *…overshadowed by the mesmerising performance of the Latin aces, the close-fought duel for third place between Mike Hailwood and Bob Brown, both on NSUs, was resolved in Hailwood's favour.*

Motor Cycle News described his success in slightly more enthusiastic prose:

> *…third place was taken by 'boy wonder' Mike Hailwood, riding the faithful ex-Surtees NSU on which he delighted the South African fans up to a few weeks ago.*

Lightweight (250cc) TT – 10 laps – 107.9 miles
1st   T. Provini (MV Agusta)
2nd   C. Ubbiali (MV Agusta)
3rd   M. Hailwood (NSU)
4th   B. Brown (NSU)
5th   D. Falk (Adler)
6th   S. Miller (CZ)
7th   E. Hinton (NSU)
8th   T. Robb (NSU)

Isle of Man TT

For many years, certainly during the Mike Hailwood era, the Isle of Man TT was the world's premier motorcycle racing event.

First employed in 1911 (though in slightly different guise), the legendary Mountain Course measured 37.73 miles in length and comprised roads which were the normal traffic arteries of the Isle of Man. To avoid too much interference with everyday trade on the island, therefore, the pre-race practice periods largely took place in the early hours of the morning. Closure of the roads for both practice and racing required a separate Act of the Isle of Man Parliament every year.

The start, grandstand, scoreboard and pits were situated in Glencrutchery Road high above the town of Douglas. Soon after leaving the slight rise of Brown's Hill, followed by the drop to Quarter Bridge, a slow right-hander necessitated hard braking, engagement of bottom gear and usually the use of the clutch.

Bradden Bridge was the next landmark, a spectacular S-bend over the railway and river, then on to Union Mills, three miles from the start, winding and undulating, the course dropped down to the Highlander and through the bends at Greeba to Ballacraine (7.25 miles); a sharp right-hander.

The course was now very much out in the country, with the road twisting and turning through the leafy tunnel of the Neb Valley, past Laurel Bank and Glen Helen, then up the 1-in-10 rise of Creg Willey's Hill on to the heights of Cronk-y-Voddee. The descent of Baaregarroo before the 13th milestone section was generally held as being the fastest part of the course. It was followed by a tricky section ending with Westwood's Corner, a relatively fast left-hander.

Soon riders reached Kirkmichael (14.5 miles) with its second gear right-hander followed by a trip through the narrow village street, after which there was a winding but fast stretch to Ballaugh – with the famous humpback bridge where both wheels left the ground. Left, right, left – the trio of Quarry Bends were taken in the region of 100mph or more, the bends leading out on to the start of the famous mile-long Sulby Straight, with, at its end, an extremely sharp right-hand corner at Sulby Bridge (20 miles). Then came hard acceleration up to and around the long, sweeping left-hander at Ginger Hall. Through wooded Kerromoar and the foot of Glen Auldyn, the circuit wound its way on to the town of Ramsey, where riders flicked right and left through Parliament Square in the very middle of the town. Then came the beginning of the long mountain climb, the road rising up May Hill to the testing Ramsey Hairpin (24.5 miles) and up again to Waterworks Corner and the Gooseneck.

Still climbing, riders passed Guthrie's Memorial and reached East Mountain Gate (28.5 miles) where the long gruelling ascent at last began to flatten out. A further mile on led to a quartet of gentle bends at the Verandah section, followed by the bumpy crossing of the mountain railway tracks at the Bungalow. The highest point on the course was at Brandywell, a left-hand sweep beyond the Bungalow, and from there the road began to fall gently, through the aptly named Windy Corner, a medium fast right-hander and the long 33rd milestone bend.

Kate's Cottage (300 yards past Keppal Gate) marked the beginning of the flat out, exhilarating sweep down to Creg-ny-Baa (34.5 miles). Still dropping, the course swept towards the left-hander at Brandish Corner and down yet more to the fast right-hander at Hilberry.

With less than two miles to the finish there followed the short climb of Cronk-ny-Mona and the sharp right-hand turn at Signpost Corner. Bedstead Corner and The Nook followed in swift succession and within a quarter of a mile it was a case of hard on the brakes for Governor's Bridge, an acute hairpin, which was the slowest corner on the course. The short detour through the hollow was a link to earlier days when it formed part of the main road. Once out of the hollow, riders accelerated into Glencrutchery Road less than half-a-mile from the grandstand and pit area.

In essence the course remains the same today, although at the beginning of the 21st century the TT has long since lost its World Championship status. However, it still remains one of the most famous venues in motorcycle racing, attracting huge crowds every June, and it was also the setting for some of Mike Hailwood's greatest-ever triumphs.

Reading the *Motor Cycle News* 'How they finished' section shows the excellent preparation put into Mike's machine:

> *Hailwood's third placed NSU – a perfectly standard single plug Sportmax model – was in showroom condition without a speck of oil on engine/gearbox unit. The engine stripped to show perfect carburation and no sign of any trouble. Brakes, clutch and tyres were in good order as was the rear chain. Only trouble appeared to be the rear mud guard which had split.*

Finally, on Friday 6 June 1958, came the blue riband event, the Senior TT. Again Mike showed his skill and endurance by finishing 13th (out of 48). His time of 2 hours 51 minutes 48.4 seconds at an average speed of 92.24mph compared well with that of winner John Surtees (MV) in 2 hours 40 minutes 39.8 seconds (98.63mph).

Mike the prankster

With results such as this, it's perhaps hard to realise that Mike was still only an 18-year-old teenager. One of his close friends at that time was Kathy Smith (daughter of Cyril Smith, the 1952 World Sidecar Driver). Kathy recalls a typical 'Mike the prankster' incident during TT practice week, when she and Mike looked into Florian Camathias's tent. The Swiss star was washing and had taken off his glasses. On seeing this Mike tiptoed up to the washstand

and removed Florian's specs! Without them Camathias was virtually blind and the result was akin to a bull in a china shop.

TT stars at Mallory

Only two days after the Senior TT, the TT stars were at the 1.35-mile Mallory Park circuit, where Mike immediately stamped his authority on the event, winning both the 250 and 350cc races after stiff challenges from Dickie Dale (NSU) and Bob Anderson (Norton). In addition, Mike and Dickie had the honour of sharing a new class lap record in the 250cc event. In the 50-lap 500cc, Mike's Norton suffered mechanical trouble and he was forced to retire.

More victories were chalked up the following weekend at Scarborough on Saturday 13 June and Snetterton the following day. First, at the famous Oliver's Mount circuit overlooking the North Yorkshire town of Scarborough, Mike took a win in the 250cc on his NSU. However, in the 150cc event he was eliminated in the heats when the carburettor stub on his Paton broke. Mike didn't ride his Norton at the event.

From there, it was a case of loading up and driving down to the Norfolk Snetterton airfield circuit for the next day. Mike had what the *Motor Cycle News* called 'a field day' and *The Motor Cycle* 'shattering', as he carried off the honours in the 125, 250 and 350cc races, as well as finishing runner-up to Derek Minter in the 500cc class. Not only this, but Mike set new class lap records in all four races. It was an incredible performance and it was now obvious that his skill in the larger classes was rapidly catching up with his existing mastery of the Lightweight categories.

Thruxton 500-mile race

Organised by the Southampton club and staged at Thruxton airfield, near Andover, Hampshire, the Thruxton 500-mile race was an event unique in British motorcycle sport. It was a race for standard production machines complete with lighting equipment, silencers and other road-legal components such as kick-starters, toolboxes and comprehensive mudguarding.

The 1958 event was held on Saturday 21 June and replaced the previous Nine Hours Race, which had been run in 1955, 1956 and 1957. In their preview to the event in their 19 June 1958 issue, *The Motor Cycle* said:

> *...given fair weather the race will be run at an average speed in the region of 70mph – equivalent to over 7 hours of racing. The sinuous 2.275-mile circuit puts a premium on riding ability but, in a race of this type, the wear and tear on machines may be such that success*

Another marque which Mike raced early in his career was the Italian Paton; a joint effort by engineers Pattoni and Tonti and based around previous experience gained at FB Mondial.

will lie as much in the hands of the pit crews as in those of the riders. Oil and fuel tanks will have to be replenished over and over again; tyre wear may reach the point where wheels have to be changed. But so long and arduous is the race that a man who is stuck at his pit for even as long as 15 minutes may still have a chance of winning.

The 1958 Thruxton 500-miler was a star-studded event. Within the 61 teams (26 in the multi-cylinder class, 20 single-cylindered and 15 three-fifties) were a number of well-known names. These included: Tony Godfrey, Howard German, John Lewis, Ray Cowles, Bob McIntyre, Derek Powell, Ken Buckmaster, Malcolm Uphill, Alan Pavey, Ed Minihen, George Catlin, Alan Trow, Percy Tait, Fred Launchbury, John Tickle, Peter Darvil, Ron Langston, Fron Purslow, Fred Wallis, Rex Avery, Horace Crowder, Tom Thorp and Louis Carr – plus Dan Shorey and Mike Hailwood.

The latter two riders were entered by Ecurie Sportive on a 649cc Triumph Tiger 110. Benefiting from the Hailwoods' close relationship with the Triumph works, their machine was fitted with the optional twin carburettor cylinder head, which would become a standard fitment on the new 1959 Bonneville sports model. As standard the 1958 Tiger 110 featured a single Amal Monobloc carburettor.

Beside the pairing of Mike and Dan, other fancied teams included Bob McIntyre/Derek Powell on Syd Lawton's 692cc Royal Enfield Super Meteor,

Factory brochure with successes and technical specifications of the 1958 Manx Norton racers.

Dan Shorey partnered Mike during the 1958 Thruxton 500 race on a 649cc Triumph Tiger 110.

Tony Godfrey

Tony Godfrey was a rider who was close to Mike Hailwood during the early part of the latter's racing career and shared Mike's love of jazz music. And, without doubt, had Tony not suffered a serious crash in June 1963 when making his factory Yamaha debut in the Isle of Man, he would have gone on to achieve much greater things.

In 1958 Tony, who hailed from Southampton, became the first winner of the 500cc ACU Road Racing Star. Mike Hailwood took the 125, 250 and 350cc titles.

During the winter of 1953, Tony Godfrey set about persuading Tommy Wood (a well-known rider of international standing during the late 1940s and early 1950s) to part with his KTT Velocette. Actually, Tommy actively encouraged the young enthusiast, and as Tony remarked later 'for ever I will be grateful for the invaluable assistance which Tommy provided in those early years'.

Tony's first outing on the Velocette was on Easter Monday 1954 at Thruxton, where he notched up sixth place in the Non-Experts final. But generally he simply couldn't get entries.

The following season entries were easier to come by. He managed 14 meetings and, among these, collected a second place in the 350cc class at the Thruxton Nine Hour race (on a BSA Gold Star).

There was little to encourage Tony during 1956 and the early part of 1957 proved even worse.

By this time many competitors were in possession of machinery far more potent than the reliable, but rather slow, Velocette – which that year earned the princely sum of £2 10s in prize money!

A spill at Scarborough resulted in a broken collarbone and necessitated a month away from Tony's employment as a design draughtsman at a local aircraft factory.

The decision was taken to find a replacement for the Velocette and once again, with help from Tommy Wood, plans were put in place for the Manx Grand Prix. The Norton arrived, but Tony's employer decided that it was time to put a brake on things and refused his request for leave.

Undismayed, Tony quit his job and with the Norton collected 14th place and a replica in the Senior Manx.

And so to 1958. Armed with two machines (a 350cc Manx having been added to the stable over the winter) and a van to provide transport, Tony set out to cover as many meetings as possible.

It proved a great season, with Tony scoring places at circuits all over Great Britain; culminating, as already stated, in the 'cherished Road Racing Star award'.

Tony Godfrey was a close friend of Mike's and also won the 500cc ACU Star in 1958, when Mike took the 125, 250 and 350cc titles.

The biggest disappointment of the following year, 1959, came when sharing one of the new Triumph Bonnevilles with John Holder. A pit stop at the 350-mile stage to fix a loose dynamo cost the pair victory in the Thruxton 500-mile race. However, all this was forgotten when the same two riders went on to win the event in 1961, entered by former TT winner Alec Bennett of Southampton.

Also in 1961, in February, Tony and Mike Hailwood had travelled from Southampton to New York by ocean liner to compete in the United States Grand Prix (an FIM-sanctioned event run by a small rival organisation to the American Motorcycle Association). Delayed by a day by rough seas they were forced to fly south, rather than take the train as originally planned. Riding a G50 Matchless borrowed from Geoff Monty, Tony went on to win the 500cc race. Mike retired with ignition trouble on his Norton. The full story of this adventure is contained in Chapter 5.

In June 1961 Tony finished sixth in the Senior TT on his own Norton, in the same race in which Mike Hailwood gave the British marque its final success during the classic era in this blue riband event. And in 1962 Tony placed fifth on his Norton in the 500cc Ulster GP, Mike winning on the four-cylinder MV.

Then came 1963. Armed with a pair of Nortons and a 125cc Tohatsu two-stroke twin Tony was always up among the leaders. These and his performances in earlier years led to the Yamaha ride in the Lightweight 250cc TT that June. Going flat out after being delayed with oiled plugs, Tony crashed at high speed and was critically injured. It was touch and go for several days, but the fighting spirit saw him through. Although he recovered – and even raced again – the previous spark which had provided so many excellent results was not quite there.

Tony (12) and Mike battle it out during 1962 with Manx Norton and AJS 7R bikes respectively.

The famous 37.73-mile Isle of Man Mountain Circuit.

John Lewis/Peter James (595cc BMW R69) and Percy Tait/Alan Trow on another Triumph Tiger 110.

With practice taking place between 10 and 11am, racing started at 11.25am. *The Motor Cycle's* race report began by saying:

...from just about every viewpoint the Southampton club's 500-mile

A youthful Mike, while testing a 7R-engined Manx Norton, was asked how light the machine was. 'This light' was his reply as he lifted the machine clear of the ground!

race at Thruxton on Saturday set new levels of vitality and interest in British marathon racing. Among the chaos of 7½ hours continuous lappery by 60 assorted roadsters of 348 – 692cc and the welter of feverish pit activity, were woven threads of tense excitement and high drama.

There was no doubt that the fastest motorcycle out on the circuit was the McIntyre/Powell Royal Enfield Super Meteor. However, as events were to prove, it wasn't the most reliable. Instead, as the report continued:

...after brilliantly consistent and trouble free riding, backed by the slickest pit work of the day, victory on overall classification and in the multi-cylinder class went to the 649cc Triumph Tiger 110 ridden by that fast-maturing young star, Mike Hailwood, and Dan Shorey.

The Ecurie Sportive entry covered 220 laps, completing the 500-mile distance in 7 hours 35 minutes at an average speed of 66mph, compared to the runner-up team of McIntyre and Powell who did 219 laps in 7 hours 35 minutes 32.4 seconds and averaged 65.62mph.

Thruxton 500 mile race – 220 laps – 500 miles
1st   M. Hailwood/D. Shorey (649cc Triumph Tiger 110)
2nd   B. McIntyre/D. Powell (692cc Royal Enfield Super Meteor)
3rd   K. James/B. Newman (692cc Royal Enfield Super Meteor)
4th   J. Lewis/P. James (595cc BMW R69)
5th   P. Tait/D. Peacock (649cc Triumph Tiger 110)
6th   H. German/C. Rowe (597cc Norton 99)

Only a week later, Mike had, in effect, moved up a gear when he competed in his first Continental race, no less an event than the Dutch TT at Assen. Not only that, but in doing so he also had his first race on a Ducati machine, a marque with which he was not only to garner his first Grand Prix success (1959 125cc Ulster), but also much, much later make his historic TT comeback in 1978 aboard one of the Bologna factory's 864cc V-twins.

However, all that was very much in the future. In June 1958, it could fairly be said that Mike Hailwood had 'moved up a gear'. Many were now tipping him for stardom, and they would not be disappointed.

Chapter 3

Doctor T and Ducati

A S THIS chapter will reveal, the Italian Ducati factory and its chief designer Ing. Fabio Taglioni (more commonly known simply as 'Doctor T') played a significant role in Mike's early career, providing the young Oxford star with many of his first major victories – including the first GP victory (the 1959 125cc Ulster). In addition, Stan Hailwood became the UK's first major importer of Ducati motorcycles.

First Ducati contact

The first Hailwood-Ducati contact came when, having witnessed the performance of the Desmo Ducati singles in the Ultra-Lightweight (125cc) TT in June 1958, and after consultation with old friend Dave Chadwick (who had ridden one of the works mounts in the race), Stan Hailwood purchased an ex-Fron Purslow valve-spring dohc Grand Prix model. Mike's first race on the Ducati came on 28 June at the Dutch TT – his European debut.

Mike finished 10th at Assen, albeit a lap down on the leaders. But when one considers that his was the first non-works bike home, this was an excellent performance. The full result was as follows:

125cc Dutch TT – 14 laps – 66.98 miles

1st	C. Ubbiali (MV Agusta)	
2nd	L. Taveri (Ducati)	
3rd	T. Provini (MV Agusta)	
4th	A. Gandossi (Ducati)	
5th	D. Chadwick (Ducati)	
6th	E. Degner (MZ)	
7th	S. Miller (Ducati)	
8th	H. Fugner (MZ)	
9th	R. Ferri (Ducati)	
10th	M. Hailwood (Ducati)	

Mike also finished fourth on the NSU Sportmax in the 250cc race and fifth on his three-fifty Manx Norton. This, combined with his Isle of Man TT successes outlined in the previous chapter, at last silenced the remaining critics who maintained his success was entirely due to the financial backing of his father.

Four victories at the Combe

The following weekend the *Motor Cycling* headline read: '*Four victories for Mike Hailwood*'. *Motor Cycle News*, dated Wednesday 16 July 1958, reported:

A Ducati 125 Grand Prix of the type raced by Mike during the latter half of 1958...

...heavy rain – that came too early for the good of weekend sport in general and the Wessex Centre's Avon Trophy meeting at Castle Combe in particular, that brought extremely unpleasant and tricky conditions throughout the practice period and kept the watching crowds around the 1.84-mile Wiltshire circuit to a bare minimum – failed to damp the irrepressible Mike Hailwood on Sunday.

The *MCN* report continued:

...adding to an already formidable list of successes, the Oxford rider claimed victories in the 125, 250 and 350cc scratch events, established a new record for the 125cc lap and, by winning the new 15-lap class handicap race, ensured that his will be the first name to appear upon the Avon Trophy (awarded by the local Melksham-based tyre company).

By the time the 125s came to the line, conditions were dry, if dull, and as the *MCN* reporter said, 'interest increased when it became known that Hailwood was to ride the Ducati in place of the MV stated in the programme'.

When the flag went down to herald the start of the race, the pack screamed their way into Paddock Corner. At the end of lap 1, Jim Baughn (EMC) – the reigning holder of the class lap record – led a bunch of riders which included Mike, Dave Moore and Dudley Edlin (the latter two both MV mounted). But before another lap had passed, Mike had taken the Ducati to the front. As *MCN* said: 'there was no holding the leader now and his scarlet Ducati drew farther ahead of the field with each lap'.

125cc Castle Combe – 5 laps – 9.2 miles
1st   M. Hailwood (Ducati)
2nd   D. Edlin (MV Agusta)
3rd   D. Moore (MV Agusta)
4th   J. Baughn (EMC)

...and without its fairing.

And so Mike's British Ducati debut had begun in winning style.

His other victories that day came on NSU and Norton machines; the latter bike being a three-fifty, his larger Norton having oiled a plug on the startline for the Senior (500cc) race.

In the main race of the day at Castle Combe, the Avon Trophy, Mike elected to ride his NSU and thus take full advantage of the handicap and, as *MCN* said: 'the result was perhaps a foregone conclusion'. As it was he led from the start and it was to be Tony Godfrey (499cc Norton) who eventually pulled himself into second spot in this 15-lap event, based on the handicap time for the first three riders in each of the 250, 350 and 500cc scratch races.

Avon Trophy (Handicap) Castle Combe – 15 laps – 27.6 miles
1st   M. Hailwood (247cc NSU)
2nd   T. Godfrey (499cc) Norton)
3rd   P. Chatterton (348cc Norton)
4th   L. Rutherford (348cc AJS)
5th   P. Read (348cc Norton)
6th   B. Setchell (348cc Norton)

Off to Germany

Then came the next round in the World Championship – the German GP at the Nürburgring.

Laid out in 1927, the Nürburgring was not only the pride of German motorsport, but also the most famous and demanding of circuits. In many ways it was an even more difficult course than the 37.73-mile long Isle of Man TT.

The magnificence of the setting and the concentration of its hazards were a truly awe-inspiring sight for the young Hailwood. Having an average width of 27 feet, the tarmac-surfaced road wound and dipped, in a

Desmodromics and Ducati have a link stretching back to the mid-1950s. The system is still employed on the Bologna company's motorcycles at the beginning of the 21st century.

Desmodromics

The word 'Desmo' has long been associated with both Ducati and Ing. Fabio Taglioni. In fact, many incorrectly assume that Taglioni actually invented it. However, the theoretical advantages have been known since the dawn of the combustion engine itself. What Taglioni did was to make it actually work – both on the track and later in series production.

Desmodromic, as the word is in full, is coined from two Greek words meaning 'controlled run'. The idea was intended as a way of eliminating one of the chief problems of valve operation at high engine revolutions – the phenomenon of valve float, or 'bounce'. This was a particular problem for designers in the days before 4-valves-per-cylinder technology and the advent of rev limiters found on many modern car and motorcycle power units.

'Bounce' occurs when the valve springs are unable to respond fast enough to close the valves back on to their seats. The Desmodromic principle involved replacing the troublesome springs with a mechanical closing system much like that employed to open them, so providing a positive action. The idea was that by eliminating the springs, you also eliminate the bounce and get a higher-revving engine.

The Desmo system uses either a separate camshaft (as on Taglioni's Desmo 125cc single of the late 1950s) or a cam lobe to close the valve, thus dispensing with conventional valve springs.

Much of this had been known since the earliest days of the internal combustion engine, but no motorcycle designer had managed to harness it.

Norton and others had tried, but all had been largely unsuccessful. Even the mighty automobile industry had done little better, the one exception being Mercedes Benz with its magnificent and highly specialised W196 racing car. But Taglioni and Ducati were to buck the trend. At first, the Desmo system was used purely on the factory's racers, but the Bologna company adopted the system for series production with its new widecase Mark3D (Desmo) single-cylinder range from 1968.

Then came the new V-twin family, which from the Imola racers of 1972 increasingly made use of the principle. By 1980 all Ducati models – both racing and production – were thus equipped. And it should be pointed out that Mike Hailwood's finest achievements on Ducatis during the late 1950s and early 1960s, plus his comeback on the big V-twin in 1978, all used the technology.

The top end of the 124cc Ducati Grand Prix dohc single-cylinder engine, showing the bevel drive and the gear train for the camshaft.

confusing sequence of blind bends and undulations, over the beautifully wooded slopes of the Eifel mountains. In its 14.165-mile lap, the road fell and climbed nearly 1,000 feet.

The task of riders in attempting to memorise the circuit's 174 bends was made difficult by the similarity in appearance of the majority of its curves. There were precious few identification markers to distinguish one bend from another. Nor was that the only difficulty, for even after the circuit had been memorised, actual racing experience was indispensable if a rider was to perfect his technique in blending the exit from one curve into the entry of its successor and thus achieve a smooth, flowing style.

None of the bends were very slow; few of them really fast. Nevertheless, the Nürburgring ranked with the Isle of Man Mountain course as the ultimate test of real riding ability for, with the exception of a 1½-mile straight, there was no respite for the memory or concentration.

Of course, here we are talking about the original Nürburgring, not the much shorter and far less difficult South Circuit that was used from the 1960s onwards.

As at certain times during his early career, Mike had the more experienced and older Dave Chadwick on hand. And although he didn't have an entry in the 125cc race, he took a fourth in the 350cc event behind Chadwick, who was also Norton-mounted. In front of these two were the race winner John Surtees and John Hartle, both on four-cylinder MVs.

350cc German GP – 7 laps – 99.15 miles

1st	J. Surtees (MV Agusta)
2nd	J. Hartle (MV Agusta)
3rd	D. Chadwick (Norton)
4th	M. Hailwood (Norton)
5th	B. Anderson (Norton)
6th	D. Dale (Norton)
7th	G. Hocking (Norton)
8th	L. Taveri (Norton)

After starting on the front row of the grid in the 250cc class at the Nürburgring on his NSU, Mike was forced to retire early in the race when the machine's front brake locked up, bending the wheel spindle in the process.

First world championship rostrum

Six days later, on Saturday 26 July 1958, Mike and Dave Chadwick were in Hedemora for the Swedish Grand Prix. The 125 and 350cc races were held that day, while the 250 and 500cc races were the following day, Sunday 27 June.

Mike was entered only in the 350 and 250cc events. In the former he gained his first world championship rostrum finish, with an excellent third place. Unfortunately, his friend Dave Chadwick crashed heavily and was taken to hospital with suspected back injuries.

350cc Swedish GP – 25 laps – 113.02 miles

1st	G. Duke (Norton)
2nd	B. Anderson (Norton)
3rd	M. Hailwood (Norton)
4th	A. Trow (Norton)
5th	G. Monty (Norton)
6th	M. O'Rourke (Norton)

Mike had an even better result in the 250cc race that followed the next day. The fastest men in practice had been Tarquinio Provini and Carlo Ubbiali (MVs) and the East German pair Horst Fugner and Ernst Degner on the new twin-cylinder MZ two-stroke machine. However, all but race winner Fugner were forced to retire with assorted trouble in the race, leaving Mike as runner-up on his trusty NSU Sportmax. Mike's race average was 91.60mph, compared to winner Fugner's 94.08mph.

The 175 Ducati dohc twin that Stan Hailwood brought to England for Mike to ride on Good Friday 1959 at Brands Hatch. Mike never raced the bike.

250cc Swedish GP – 18 laps – 81.35 miles

1st   H. Fugner (MZ)

2nd   M. Hailwood (NSU)

3rd   G. Monty (GMS)

4th   G. Beer (Adler)

5th   J. Autengruber (NSU)

6th   W. Lecke (DKW)

It should be noted that Autengruber and Lecke only completed 17 laps.

Considering that Mike had only begun his racing career some 14 months previously, his performances in Germany and Sweden (to add to his third place in the Lightweight (250cc) TT in the Isle of Man in June that year) were simply outstanding, particularly when one considers that he had only just turned 18 years of age.

Back home

On August Bank Holiday Monday 4 August 1958, almost 28,000 spectators flooded into the famous Crystal Palace circuit in south-east London to see some excellent racing over a period of four hours. Although local rider Bruce Daniels (Norton) won the two main solo races, as *Motor Cycle News* reported:

...the star of the meeting was undoubtedly 18 year old Mike Hailwood from Oxford. He broke the lap and race records in the 125cc event and also won the 250cc race. In both his 350 and 1000cc events Hailwood was way off to an exceptionally bad start, but provided an added interest to the jockeying for positions further down the field.

Ing. Fabio Taglioni

There is no doubt that before his days as World Champion aboard Honda and MV Agusta machines, Mike Hailwood's first really big successes were achieved aboard Ducati motorcycles, including his first Grand Prix victory. In fact, in his 1963 book *The Art of Motorcycle Racing* (co-written with Murray Walker), Mike says: 'it is fair to say that this Ducati really started me on my climb to the top'.

The man behind the Ducati motorcycles that Mike rode during the late 1950s and early 1960s, and again when he made his historic comeback in the 1978 TT, was their chief designer, Ing. Fabio Taglioni.

Fabio Taglioni was born on 20 September 1920, in the small country town of Lugo in north-east Italy, an area known as Emilia-Romagna, covering the fertile plains of the Po river valley.

After his primary education, the young Taglioni progressed first to Imola and later Bologna University. However, his studies were interrupted by World War Two, which Italy joined in June 1940. Then aged 21, Taglioni was called up for military service in February 1941. After serving in the tank corps, he transferred in May 1942 to Mechanical Transport.

The young mechanic soon found himself in charge of a workshop in Sicily, repairing military vehicles. The work involved not just ordinary items such as trucks and field equipment, but also aircraft that had been damaged in combat or on the ground during the fierce fighting which took place in both the North African campaign and later in Sicily itself. It was during this period that Taglioni first began his practical work with the very latest technology, particularly the special materials used within the aircraft industry.

His association with aero-engines was to have a profound effect on Taglioni's future thinking.

It was also during his war service in Sicily that he was able to renew his pre-war interest in motorcycles, coming into contact with military models – mainly Gilera and Moto Guzzi 500cc singles – which he spent much of his spare time tuning.

During the Allied landings in Sicily during July 1943, Taglioni was wounded. After a stay in hospital he spent two years instructing recruits on engines and the like, before finally being discharged from military service in 1945.

Then it was back to his studies at Bologna University, gaining an industrial engineering degree in 1948. In 1950 he joined the Ceccato motorcycle firm as a design consultant. Then, in 1951, he transferred to the much larger and more well-known FB Mondial marque, gaining much first-hand experience working alongside the development team, including the famous designer Ing. Alfonso Druiani.

In April 1954, Taglioni resigned from Mondial and joined Ducati on 1 May, as head of the Technical, Planning and Experiment Departments at the Bologna works. His first all-new design for Ducati was the 98cc Gran Sport (known as the Marianna), which debuted in the spring of 1955, just in time for the *Gira d'Italia* at Milano-Taranto road events. Soon a 125cc model followed. Both featured a single-cylinder engine with a bevel driven camshaft. From this series was to come not only a family

MIKE HAILWOOD IN THE SENIOR T.T.

of roadster models culminating in the 450 in 1969, but also, more importantly for this book, the dohc Grand Prix and Desmo 125cc racers, the first of which arrived in 1956. In July of that year, Taglioni's 125 Desmo single made a stunning debut in the Swedish Grand Prix, with rider Gianni Degli Antoni not only winning the race, but lapping the entire field in the process at least once. Unfortunately, Degli Antoni then suffered a fatal accident the following month while practicing at Monza prior to the Italian GP.

In November 1956, a fully enclosed 98cc Gran Sport broke no fewer than 44 world speed records. Also in 1956, Taglioni designed his first twin-cylinder model. With the cylinders set vertically across the frame, the engine displaced 175cc.

Then came a 175cc version of the Gran Sport and later 125 and 175cc Formula 3 models (essentially similar to the GS, but with enclosed valve gear).

In April 1958, Ducati announced that they would be fielding a full Grand Prix effort. The squad appeared at that year's TT, headed by Romolo Ferri and Luigi Taveri, but also with the British riders Dave Chadwick and Sammy Miller. Ferri finished runner-up to Carlo Ubbiali (MV), while over the season Alberto Gandossi was runner-up in the World Championships, again to Ubbiali.

Mike Hailwood had his Ducati debut aboard a dohc GP production model in the 1958 Dutch TT, his first-ever continental outing, finishing 10th.

For 1959 Mike became a full-blown Ducati works rider with his own 125 Desmo single and factory mechanic, scoring his first Grand Prix victory, the Ulster, with the bike in August that year.

Next Taglioni designed new 250 and 350cc Desmo twins, which despite class-leading power figures were hampered by poor handling. But Mike won several races on the 250 twin in 1960 – and continued his run of success on the 125 Desmo single. There is no doubt that these rides had a major bearing on his future progress with first Honda (via the British importer) and later MV Agusta.

As for Taglioni, he stayed with Ducati for the remainder of his working life. During the 1960s and 1970s Ing. Taglioni designed a succession of overhead camshaft street bikes. These included the legendary Mach 1, the world's first 100mph production 250cc roadster, and the groundbreaking Desmodromic roadsters, beginning with the 3D single of 1968. Then in 1970 came the most famous of all Taglioni's Ducati designs, the V-twin. The first production version was the 750GT, which was followed by the Sport in 1972 and the Super Sport in 1974. The latter, which had debuted in 1972 as the racing-only Imola 1-2 winning bikes of Paul Smart and Bruno Spaggiari, featured Desmo heads.

Next, for the 1975 model year, came the 860GT tourer and 900 Super Sport, with square outer engine casings replacing the round type found on the 750s. The 860 and 900 models actually displaced 864cc and the 900 Super Sport formed the basis of the NCR racer, which Mike Hailwood took to victory in his famous Isle of Man TT comeback in June 1978. From 1979 Ducati cashed in on Mike's success with the Hailwood Replica.

In 1979 the Pantah, the first of a new series of Taglioni-designed Ducati V-twins, made its appearance. This featured belt instead of bevel drive camshafts. Produced in 350, 500, 600 and finally 650cc guises, the Pantah

Ing. Fabio Taglioni (right) and his assistant Franco Farné, pictured in 1979. Both men played a key role in Ducati's racing successes over almost 40 years.

led to the 750F1 of 1985; effectively Taglioni's last design to reach production. By now he was in semi-retirement; his final day at the Ducati works coming on 30 May 1989 – just over 34 years since he first joined the Bologna factory.

During that time he had designed more than 1,000 different engines in either outline or detail. These had included various ohc and ohv singles, V-twins and V4s, ohv and ohc parallel twins, two-strokes for mopeds, scooters and Ultra-lightweight motorcycles. And of course an equally bewildering array of racing designs ridden to major victories by the likes of Paul Smart, Bruno Spaggiari, Tony Rutter and Mike Hailwood himself.

As *MCN* also reveals, there was 'some doubt as to whether he would ride the Paton (the bike he had ridden in the TT) or a Ducati – but finally he decided to use an MV'. And of course, with such a selection of machinery to choose from, it is easy to see why, at the time, there were many envious eyes on the Hailwood camp.

It is also interesting to consider the *Motor Cycle News* race report that said:

> *Hailwood's half-lap lead on his NSU at the finish proved his superiority. Despite his clear run, though he was nearly 2½mph behind John Surtees' record for this class.*

Mike was certainly leading an active racing life. During August he was riding non-stop. On Saturday 9 he was in Ulster for the Grand Prix, where he came eighth on the 350cc Norton, and had a fall on the NSU in the 250cc; on Saturday 23 he was at Aberdare Park and took first place in the 125cc (MV) and in the 250cc (NSU) and came third in the 350cc (Norton). At Brands Hatch on Sunday 24 he was second in the 200cc (125 Ducati), 1st 250cc (NSU) and 2nd 500cc (Norton). Finally, on Sunday 31 August 1958 he was at Zandvoort in Holland, finishing runner-up on his valve-spring Ducati in the 125cc, but failed to finish in the 350cc race on his Norton.

September was just as hectic for young Mike with a string of meetings: Mallory Park (7 September); Silverstone (13 September); Cadwell Park (14 September); Scarborough (19–20 September) and Aintree (27 September). In all Mike had 19 races, of which no fewer than 14 resulted in victories. Three of these came on his Ducati 125cc Grand Prix model (a double overhead camshaft single-cylinder with a five-speed gearbox). In fact, every time he rode the Ducati that month there were victories, with wins at Silverstone, Snetterton and Aintree.

First Mondial ride

Then came Mike's first race on an FB Mondial. His father Stan had purchased a pair of the Italian machines from Arthur Wheeler. Strangely, although this first Mondial victory came on the 125cc model (at Crystal Palace on 4 October 1958), Mike never rode this bike again, probably as a result of Stan Hailwood's tie-up with the Ducati factory, which saw him become the company's British importer in January 1959 via a new company, Ducati Concessionaires, based in Stretford, Manchester. Instead, it was the larger of the two ex-Wheeler bikes (plus another two-fifty Mondial purchased later) upon which Mike was to achieve his run of successes on the marque, even after the arrival of the brand new Ducati two-fifty Desmo twin, which Mike raced in 1960.

The 1958 British season ended with varying degrees of success at Brands Hatch on 12 October. Mike won on the 250cc FB Mondial (his first race on this bike); scored a runner-up spot on the 125cc Paton in the 200cc event (which was won by Dave Chadwick on a 175cc MV) and finished seventh in the 500cc race on his larger Norton, although he crashed in the 350cc event and suffered electrical problems in the Invitation race. And so another British racing season came to a close.

The accolades arrive

As the UK season ended, so the accolades for Mike's performances came in.

Mike leading a field of 125s at
Silverstone in spring 1959. This is
one of the very few times he used a
'space' type helmet on two wheels.

Although it was his second year of racing 1957 had been very much a learning year; one in which he had begun his career, but not been in the public eye to any degree. In 1958 all this changed. In 1957 he had scored just five victories, but in 1958 this had risen to a whopping 58 – plus many more in heats. He had also won three of the four ACU Road Racing Stars (which were awarded to the rider who had amassed the most points at selected meetings by the Auto Cycle Union, the body in charge of motorcycle sport in Great Britain). Mike had won the 125, 250 and 350cc classes; the other, the 500cc, went to another of Mike's racing friends, Tony Godfrey. Mike himself was placed fifth in this division, but it is fair to point out that at the beginning of the year he didn't take part on his larger Norton.

Next Mike was awarded the annual Pinhard Prize, which was given to the most outstanding under-21 motorcyclist of the year; scrambler Dave Bickers was runner-up.

Real proof of the public appreciation for Mike's performances in 1958 came via the *Motor Cycle News* Man of the Year poll, when readers' votes counted. Double 1958 world champion John Surtees was the first holder of the *MCN* award (which has been awarded annually ever since), then came Mike, Bob McIntyre, Derek Minter, Geoff Duke and Brian Stonebridge.

Both the Pinhard Prize and the *MCN* presentations came during the London Motorcycle Show week.

Off to South Africa

Then it was off to South Africa for a second winter's racing. As *Motor Cycle News* reported in their 12 November 1958 issue: 'Hailwood is taking two Nortons and his faithful 250 NSU to South Africa for the winter. They go by sea tomorrow, with mechanic Jim Adams'. With several show week commitments, Mike had to delay his departure until Friday of the following week. He was then scheduled to fly out and 'was hoping that the machines will arrive safely on 27 November, in time to re-jet and tune them for the new climate conditions before the races at Cape Town on the 29th'.

Mike didn't take his newly acquired 250cc FB Mondial to South Africa, preferring the 'reliable NSU'.

It is interesting that Mike was actually offered a works 125cc Desmo single by Ducati for use during his trip to South Africa, but he had to decline as there were no races for this class in that country. This also proved that even as early as October 1958 (when this offer was made) Mike was being lined up to race for the Italian factory in 1959.

Mike's southern visit got off to a cracking start as the 3 December 1958 issue of *MCN* was able to report:

Mike Hailwood gave an enthusiastic South African crowd their biggest thrill of the year when he won all three races and broke 250 and 500cc records on his first appearance at Killarney, the Cape Town racing circuit, on Saturday.

Riding a 500cc Manx Norton, Mike clipped a second off the existing lap record set by none other than Geoff Duke in 1956 on a four-cylinder Gilera. He also equalled the 350cc lap record.

Yet Mike nearly did not ride at all. Having unpacked his machine only the day before, with Jim Adams re-jetting to suit the 90 degree heat of winter in the province, he came off during a practice try-out when another rider came out of the paddock and sent him off line. After hastily patching up the streamlining and straightening his handlebars, Mike limped to the start of the 250cc race with, as *MCN* reported: 'his NSU looking very second-hand'. For three laps he was headed by Roger MacCleery (Triumph) but thereafter he surged ahead to win comfortably, including breaking the existing class lap record by no less than five seconds. Actually, these victories were to prove the only ones for Mike during his South African visit. He had a DNF (rag in carburettor) at Port Elizabeth on 1 January 1959, while at Pietermaritzburg on 18 January he had a trio of runner-up positions.

Progress in Italy

Meanwhile, back in Europe, Bill Webster and Bill Lacey, two trusted lieutenants of Stan Hailwood, had toured Italy in December 1958, to visit the Ducati, FB Mondial, Moto Morini and MV Agusta factories. Also on this visit was Bert North, the man in charge of King's northern headquarters in Manchester and soon to be promoted to boss of the new British importers, Ducati Concessionaires. *Motor Cycle News* reported:

Tuner Bill Lacey was taking the engine that Mike Hailwood used to win the 125cc ACU Road Racing Star back to the factory for a winter check and for a rebuild to 1959 specification. The engine is, in fact, two years old and during the complete season the only attention it received was to have the valves ground-in once.

One also has to remember that in its first full year of Grand Prix racing, the Ducati factory had achieved considerable success, scoring three victories in the seven Grand Prix they contested and making fastest lap in five. All this was against the established might of MV Agusta and their star riders Carlo Ubbiali and Tarquinio Provini.

Behind the scene moves

After Webster, Lacey and North returned to England, Stan Hailwood made his moves – carried out very much behind closed doors. As already noted, this led to the establishment of a brand new company, Ducati Concessionaires Ltd, of 80 Burleigh Road, Stretford, Manchester. While it was run by Bert North, its sales director was Alan Mullee. The enterprise opened for business in January 1959.

Those who knew Stan Hailwood's tactics saw this move very much as a bargaining chip to help Mike's racing career – and they were to be proved correct, although the general public had to wait some time for the official announcement. This was released to the press at the beginning of March 1959, and the report that appeared in the issue of *The Motor Cycle* dated 5 March was typical:

Ducati for Hailwood

Final arrangements for Mike Hailwood to ride a 125cc desmodromic Ducati were made in Italy last week by Hailwood père. Ducati are providing two models which may, indeed, be in this country by the time you read these words. A third Ducati is being flown over – for Arthur Wheeler who, as reported last week, was also in Italy on a machine-hunting safari. The power unit is a 175cc twin and the machine will be loaned to Mike for the Good Friday meeting at Brands Hatch. Stan Hailwood describes the twin as being 'right out of this world'. Only two have been made – the other has gone to Venezuela. News from Morini is that Dr Morini has still not decided whether he will provide machines for world championship events. If he does, however, Mike will have a two-fifty.

The two works 125cc Desmo singles also came with the services of a full-time factory mechanic, Oscar Folesani. The Italian joined the existing engineering staff of Ecurie Sportive, which by now comprised not only Bill Lacey, but mechanics Jim Adams and John Dadley.

The 175cc valve-spring twin

Mention of the 175cc Ducati twin should be explained in more detail. Essentially, this design had been made by Ing. Taglioni in 1956, with the long distance events such as the Milano-Taranto and *Giro d'Italia* (Tour of Italy) very much in mind. However, from 1957 these two events had been banned following the Mille Miglia car tragedy (in which a car left the road, killing several spectators).

Although a truly beautiful-looking motorcycle, the 175cc ohc valve-spring twin, which attracted considerable attention in the British press during the spring of 1959, was both old and uncompetitive for British short circuit events. Frankly, it proved a total flop. And although *The Motor Cycle* story had said that Mike was to ride it at Brands Hatch on Good Friday, this didn't happen, because when he tested it earlier that week at the Kent circuit, he wasn't impressed.

The man most affected by the bike's failure was Arthur Wheeler. Arthur, who had also purchased a 125cc Grand Prix production racer (similar to the one ridden by Mike the previous year), was none too pleased with the 175cc twin and subsequently forced Stan Hailwood to buy it back. Stan then did the same thing in turn to the factory!

As recounted in my 1985 book *Ducati Twins* (Osprey), the bike then sat around the factory gathering dust for many months before eventually being converted into a full two-fifty.

The curtain raiser

The curtain raiser for what promised to be an exciting season for the Hailwood camp kicked off at Mallory Park on 22 March, with a win on the 350cc Norton, a fifth place in the 500cc race and a retirement (with ignition gremlins) on the 250cc FB Mondial. (Mike now had two of these bikes, including a 1957 ex-factory model purchased over the winter). There was no 125cc class at Mallory, so it was left to the Easter weekend which followed to begin the Ducati programme. This saw Mike competing at Brands Hatch (Friday), Snetterton (Sunday) and Thruxton (Monday).

At Brands Hatch, a three-lap opening 50cc race was followed by one for up to 200cc machines. Here Mike had his first-ever race on one of the new works 125cc Desmo singles. He was pitted against his old travelling companion Dave Chadwick on a 175cc MV. A closely-fought duel ensued, but eventually Mike had to concede on a very wet track. In the 250cc race which followed, Mike gave the ex-works FB Mondial a victory. He also rode his Nortons in the bigger classes, but not with the same level of success.

Two days later, at Snetterton, the *Motor Cycling* race report headline shouted: 'Two Men Share Five Wins – Mike Hailwood and Pip Harris dominate'. *Motor Cycling* went on to say:

Three solo races in a row fell to young Mike Hailwood at Norfolk's Snetterton last Sunday. Only a brilliant ride by Bob Anderson in the Senior event robbed him of a clean sweep of the solo part of the programme.

Besides his 125 and 250 rides, Mike also rode British singles in the larger classes. He is seen here in the summer of 1959 on one of his 499cc Nortons.

The first of the day's races was the 125cc four-lap event. Astride his works Desmo single, Mike was away like a rocket at the drop of the flag. By the end of the first lap of the 2.71-mile airfield circuit, he had built up a fantastic lead of over half a mile. By the finish Mike had shattered the class lap record by over 5mph, with a new speed of 77.73mph. His other wins that day came on the FB Mondial and 350cc Norton.

'A Hailwood Benefit'

The following day, at Thruxton, the press was able to proclaim 'A Hailwood Benefit'. Mike totally dominated the national, solo-only meeting. Torrential showers made the broken surface of the 2.275-mile Hampshire course hazardous, but Mike piloted his Ducati, FB Mondial and pair of Nortons with a skill which belied his lack of years.

And this, at least in the smaller classes, was a taste of what was to be repeated time and time again on the British short circuits that summer.

The 1959 Isle of Man TT

In the classics, the Isle of Man was the first round counting towards championship points that year for all four solo classes (the French GP at Clermont-Ferrand had taken place in May, but only for the 350 and 500cc solos, plus sidecars).

In the TT series that year, Mike had the distinction of being the first man away at the start of the practice week, when he pushed his 499cc Manx Norton into action on Saturday evening, 23 May 1959.

But it was not until Monday evening, 25 May, that the opening 125cc session got under way. Press interest centred on the debut of the Japanese Honda team, which although appearing a menace, nonetheless failed to achieve leader-board places in qualifying.

Two works Ducatis

There were two riders on works 125cc Ducatis, Mike himself and Bruno Spaggiari, the latter making his TT debut. In practice, Mike rode one of the new Ducati twin-cylinder models (the first time he had used it in anger), while his Italian teammate was on a single. Spaggiari was third fastest at 71.25mph, while Mike was fifth at 69.54mph. Remember, this race was run on the shorter, slower, Clypse circuit.

In the race itself Mike rode the single, coming home third at an average speed of 72.15mph, while on the twin Spaggiari retired on lap three of the

Mike (right) with his 125 Ducati at the Isle of Man TT in June 1959.

During 1959 Mike rode an FB Mondial two-fifty. He is seen here during that year's Lightweight TT in the Isle of Man, but he was destined to retire with engine trouble.

10-lap race. The winner was Tarquinio Provini (averaging 74.06mph), with MZ-mounted Luigi Taveri runner-up at 73.95mph.

Ultra-Lightweight (125cc) TT – 10 laps – 107.9 miles

1st	T. Provini (MV Agusta)
2nd	L. Taveri (MZ)
3rd	M. Hailwood (Ducati)
4th	H. Fugner (MZ)
5th	C. Ubbiali (MV Agusta)
6th	N. Tanaguchi (Honda)

Although Honda hadn't set the world alight, they had at least proved the reliability of their product by taking the team prize, with riders Tanaguchi (sixth), G. Suzuki (seventh) and J. Suzuki (11th). And of course, this was Honda's first ever European effort… a clear warning to the opposition, which back in 1959 simply wasn't heeded.

In three of his other four races, Mike failed to finish, while he came third in the Formula 1 event on his 350cc Norton.

Hockenheim

The next classic was the German Grand Prix at Hockenheim. Here Ducati fielded a team of three works bikes, ridden by Mike, Spaggiari and Francesco Villa. A fourth rider, Alberto Gandossi (who finished runner-up in the 1958 125cc championship table), was absent, having been seriously

The Barcone story

Barcone is the Italian word for barge. So what, you might ask, has this got to do with the Hailwood history? Well, the answer comes via Ing. Fabio Taglioni, who gave this name to what was the final development of the Ducati engineer's legendary 125cc Desmo single-cylinder racing model – because of the size and length of the engine crankcase structure. The Barcone differed from the versions that had come before it due to a six-speed gearbox and a new frame. The latter assembly was unique in the series, having the combination of a single front downtube with a pair of tubes which then splayed out and ran underneath the main crankcase structure.

There has previously been some uncertainty over whether just one or two Barcones were actually constructed, although research by the author has established that two bikes were in fact built. Today, one of these machines resides in North America, while the other is in Great Britain.

Mike's mechanic, Jim Adams, works on Hailwood's Barcone at Brands Hatch, 18 September 1960. The Ducati rider finished runner-up to Tom Phillis (Honda) in the 200cc event; both were riding 125s.

The American-based Barcone still has the original 1960-type Amadoro brakes, while the British bike had an Oldlani rear stopper. It seems certain that one, if not both, was raced by Mike and Ken Kavanagh in the 1960 Ultra-Lightweight TT. Then the story gets less clear. Stan Hailwood sold one of the machines to Shrewsbury rider/dealer Fron Purslow when Mike quit Ducati to race Hondas at the end of 1960. Purslow entered both Luigi Taveri and Percy Tait on the bike several times in 1961. It was then sold to the Dugdale family in 1962, before being finally sold and exported to the US. It has been owned by the same person in the States for three decades.

It would seem that Kavanagh's machine was loaned to him by the factory and was subsequently returned when he fell out with Ducati's management following the purchase of a 350cc Desmo twin, which he raced for the final time at the Italian GP at Monza in September 1960. Subsequently this machine was sold to Arthur Wheeler by the factory, in 1961. Before being sold to its present owner, the bike was part of a large collection in England.

injured while practicing at Modena during early May. And it was Mike's spirited attempt, when piloting his Desmo single in the 125cc race, to break up the MV pairing of Ubbiali and Provini, which was the undoubted highlight of the German round. In the race, the leadership changed hands no fewer than 10 times.

Although Mike had never ridden at Hockenheim previously, he gave the two highly experienced MV stars something to think about, and at the end was not far adrift of the Italian duo. Mike's average race speed of 97.62mph (against Ubbiali's winning 97.74mph) shows just how close the top three were at the end.

125cc German GP – 10 laps – 100 miles
1st   C. Ubbiali (MV Agusta)
2nd   T. Provini (MV Agusta)
3rd   M. Hailwood (Ducati)
4th   F. Villa (Ducati)
5th   B. Spaggiari (Ducati)
6th   E. Degner (MZ)

Next came the Dutch TT at Assen in northern Holland on Saturday 27 June. Mike again finished third, but this time teammate Spaggiari was runner-up behind MV world champion Carlo Ubbiali. Eight days later, on Sunday 5 July 1959, at the Belgian Grand Prix at Spa Francorchamps in the Ardennes, Ducati fortunes were at a low ebb, with Mike retiring and Spaggiari finishing a lowly eighth. Luigi Taveri helped raise spirits, finishing third behind an MV 1-2 of Ubbiali and Provini on another Bologna machine. Mike's retirement had been due to a failed piston. Other results in the GPs at the time were:

Germany	250cc	5th (FB Mondial)
Holland	250cc	4th (FB Mondial)
Belgium	F1 350cc	retired (AJS)
Belgium	500cc	retired (Norton)

Besides the classics, Mike was also taking in a vast programme of the British short circuits as time allowed. From the beginning of the season in March to the end of July he racked up no fewer than 25 victories, including his AJS debut at Scarborough on the weekend of 19–20 June. On home soil he won virtually every time he ventured out on the 125cc Desmo Ducati machines.

More GP action

Then came the Swedish GP, which had moved from Hedemora to Kristianstad. Here Mike took in all four solo classes:

125cc	4th	Ducati twin-cylinder Desmo
250cc	5th	FB Mondial
350cc	5th	AJS (lost time in pits)
500cc	4th	Matchless (F1 race)

At Oulton Park on Monday 3 August 1959, Mike was in breathtaking form to grab the British Championship titles in the 500, 250 and 350cc classes – breaking Cecil Sandford's lap records in the two smaller events. *The Motor Cycle* reported: 'As usual Hailwood rode a one-two-five desmodromic Ducati single, a two-fifty FB Mondial and a five-hundred Norton'. The British title was awarded annually for several years at the August Oulton Park meeting and was an entirely different award to the ACU Star, which was over a season-long championship series.

Mike's pal Paddy Driver (Manx Norton) in another photograph from the 1959 Ulster GP, where Hailwood scored his first GP victory (in the 125cc race on a Ducati).

A first Grand Prix victory

After Oulton Park, the top riders – including the Grand Prix circus – crossed the Irish Sea for the Ulster round of the World Championship, held on Saturday 8 August 1959. It was destined to be a day which two future world champions would never forget – it would bring their first GP victories.

In both the 125 and 250cc classes champion elect Carlo Ubbiali's lead

was not entirely safe from attack from teammate Tarquinio Provini. But the smaller factory MVs failed to show up, so Carlo was the 1959 125 and 250cc world champion anyway.

This meant that Gary Hocking, with a pair of works MZs, and Mike, with his Desmo Ducati single and 250cc FB Mondial, were ready to do battle. Each was to taste victory and wear a laurel wreath before the day was out.

Dundrod; length 7.42 miles.

The Ulster GP, 8 August 1959. Mike (centre) chats to Dr Joe Ehrlich (left) and Gary Hocking before the start of the 250cc race, in which he took his works MZ twin to victory, with Mike coming second on his Mondial.

On the hilltops above Belfast, the 7.42-mile Dundrod circuit could be an unpleasant place on a rainy day (as seen at the 1958 event). But for once the sun shone, and a large crowd gathered to watch some exciting racing. As the 125cc race got under way to start the programme, Hocking hurtled into the lead, with our hero finding a niche just ahead of Ernst Degner (MZ). That order was not to change throughout the opening lap.

By lap two things were really hotting up, for Mike was hard on Hocking's tail. Degner held the second MZ in a solitary third position, in front of several private Ducatis and MVs, headed by ex-Moto Guzzi and Norton teamster Ken Kavanagh and young Alberto Pagani, son of MV Agusta team manager and former world champion Nello Pagani.

At Cochranstown Mike slipped past Gary, but at the pits they were almost side by side, and Hocking passed Mike again on the long straight towards Leathemstown. But with one lap remaining, Mike began to pull away from the Rhodesian as the MZ's engine lost its edge. Hocking got home in a safe second place but in the end it was an easy victory for Mike – his first classic.

125cc Ulster GP – 12 laps – 74.16 miles

1st   M. Hailwood (Ducati)
2nd   G. Hocking (MZ)
3rd   E. Degner (MZ)
4th   K. Kavanagh (Ducati)
5th   A. Pagani (Ducati)
6th   A. Wheeler (Ducati)

In the 250cc event Hocking turned the tables, with the MZ rider finishing ahead of Mike, who was now mounted on the FB Mondial. When interviewed after the end of the 1959 season, Mike picked out his first-ever Grand Prix win in Ulster as the highlight of his career up to that time.

Exactly seven days after this memorable milestone in the Hailwood story, Mike was back in short circuit action. The location was the 1,320-yard Aberdare Parkland circuit. Located in South Wales, enthusiasts were treated to a feast of 'outstanding racing' as *Motor Cycling* described it. As the crowd left the Welsh venue, the name on everyone's lips was that of the Oxford wonderboy 'Mike-the-Bike' Hailwood, who had won every race he started, which of course included the 125cc on his factory Ducati. It was a nickname which was to stick for the remainder of Mike's racing career and beyond.

In quick succession there followed a whole host of Hailwood–Ducati triumphs, as race and lap records fell at the British short circuit venues.

'Mike's Mellano'

'Mike's Mellano' shouted the press headlines following a record breaking session aboard his 125cc Desmo single at Silverstone on Saturday 22 August 1959, the meeting being the international Hutchinson 100 organised by the BMCRC (or Bemsee as it was more commonly known). By leading the 125cc championship race at 84.54mph – a **race** average of 2.2mph faster than the previous **lap** record, Mike won the coveted Mellano Trophy for the first time in his career. It was not to be the last!

The award went to the rider whose average race speed exceeded the existing lap record by the greatest margin, or approached it most closely if no lap record was broken. Held over the full 2.92-mile circuit, the organisers had attracted a truly star-studded line-up.

When the 125s came to the line it was no secret that Mike, and his machine, would set a sizzling pace in a bid to take the Mellano Trophy. Even so, few were prepared for the state of affairs at the end of the first lap, when his lead extended from Copse Corner to Woodcote – more than a quarter of a mile.

Mike in action on the 250 Desmo twin in spring 1960. Although it won the first race the machine was dogged by excess weight and poor handling.

By the end of the six-lap, 17.52-mile race, not only had Mike smashed the old lap record, upping it from 82.14mph to 86.60mph, but he was half a lap in front of second-placed Dan Shorey on an ex-Hailwood 125cc valve-spring Grand Prix model, with Irishman Tommy Robb on another GP Ducati in third spot.

Off-colour in Italy

As if to prove that no racing motorcycle performs perfectly all of the time, Mike's Desmo single was decidedly off-colour at Monza Autodrome, the setting for the Italian Grand Prix on Sunday 10 September. He could only finish a lowly eighth, narrowly avoiding being lapped by race-winner Ernst Degner's MZ two-stroke. Even this, however, was better than his 250cc race result, when, on a borrowed factory MZ twin, he could only finish 10th.

The Australian Ken Kavanagh with his 350 Desmo twin. He, like Mike, had a catalogue of problems.

Despite this set-back, in his first full Grand Prix season Mike had finished third in the 125cc rankings on his Ducati and fifth in the 250cc class on the FB Mondial.

A week later, on Sunday 13 September, Mike was back in Britain, winning the 250 and 350cc (FB Mondial and Norton respectively) at Cadwell Park's annual international meeting. Then it was on to Scarborough where he won the 350cc (AJS) on 19 September, before journeying to

Snetterton the following day, Sunday 20. The 2.71-mile East Anglian airfield course was blessed with brilliant sunshine and windless conditions for its final meeting of 1959, and Mike had an outstanding day.

Not only did Mike win all his four main races (plus heats in two larger classes, where he rode a 7R AJS and Manx Norton in the 350 and 500cc respectively), but he also set new class lap records in the 124, 250 and 500cc events.

From the start of the 125cc event Mike and his Ducati 'just disappeared' *(The Motor Cycle)*, leaving Dave Moore (Paton) and Arthur Wheeler (Ducati) to fight it out for second place. After a neck-and-neck struggle, Moore pulled away from Wheeler on the last lap.

The first two laps of the 250cc race saw a Hailwood Mondial in the lead – Mike's spare machine, being ridden by mechanic Jim Adams – and, as *The Motor Cycle* described, 'he was riding like fury'. But the wily Mike was tucked in behind. On the third lap, Adams came a cropper, his actions being described as 'a shade over enthusiastic', and he dug in a footrest on the fast Coram Curve, and that was his race over. He was 'ruffled but unhurt' said *The Motor Cycle* report of the incident.

While Mike was in the process of avoiding his fallen comrade, NSU-mounted Jack Murgatroyd, who had been lying third, seized his chance, nipping ahead and staying there until just before the end, when Mike tore into the lead with another record lap.

In the 350cc final Mike won from Phil Read, but in the 500cc Read was third with Lewis Young second and Mike, yet again, took the win.

More victories came at Aintree (350cc Handicap) and Mallory Park (250cc) over the weekend of 26 and 27 September, followed by a clean sweep at Biggin Hill on 4 October (200cc, 250cc, 350cc and 1000cc classes). Finally came yet more success at the final British meeting of the year, at Brands Hatch on 11 October, the score being wins in the 250 and 500cc class (FB Mondial and Norton), plus runner-up places in the 350cc (AJS) and Invitation (Norton).

And so Mike's 1959 season came to an end. Besides his world championship placings he had also won 57 races (plus many more heat wins). He had made a clean sweep of all four solo classes (125, 250, 350 and 500cc) of the ACU Star titles. What a season!

A new two-fifty model
Hardly had the dust settled on the racing season when the first official news came through of a 250cc twin-cylinder Ducati Desmo model which was being specially constructed in the Bologna race shop.

As with Mike's Desmo single, the new twin was the work of Ing. Fabio Taglioni (see box section within this chapter). Though the engine was essentially a scaled up 125cc twin (which had debuted at the Italian Grand Prix in September 1958 and been raced at times by both Mike and other members of the Ducati factory squad in 1959), the new bike was said to have a frame based on drawings supplied by Stan Hailwood. If this is true, it was something which would haunt Hailwood senior in the coming months.

There is no doubt that everyone associated with the new project was genuinely excited, particularly the Hailwood family, and this can be understood when one looks at the achievements gained during the previous months with the 125cc Desmo single.

Mike had also been offered works MZs, but was reported to favour the new Ducati instead, such was his and his father's confidence in the factory's abilities. Various stories also circulated at the time linking Mike with other marques. Ducati's chief designer Fabio Taglioni was even rumoured to be leaving the Bologna company, which was also reported to be in financial trouble. Only the financial stories actually had any foundation, and Ing. Taglioni was in fact to stay in his post until his ultimate retirement in the mid-1980s.

In November 1959 Taglioni himself said there was every possibility that valve-spring versions of the 250 Desmo twin engine would be made available to top privateers (although nothing was ever to come of this). A new type of German-made Mahle piston for the 125cc single was reckoned to provide an additional 2bhp. Finally, he repeated his denial of the rumour that he would be joining MV Agusta and added that if the Ducati racing department was made semi-independent he would take charge of it.

That machine

By now the UK press was in something of a frenzy and when the new machine, which *Motor Cycle News* referred to as 'that 250', finally arrived in England at the end of March 1960, just in time for the forthcoming racing season, there was almost mass hysteria. Taglioni had spent the entire winter working flat out, not only designing and constructing the 250 for Mike, but also working on a couple of other designs (including a 350 version of the twin) for the Australian Ken Kavanagh. When he heard about Kavanagh's 350, Stan Hailwood demanded that he receive the first bike made. This did nothing to help Hailwood (senior) and Kavanagh's relations.

When it arrived, Mike took the new 250 straight to Silverstone for tests. It was his first real chance to try the machine. He had ridden it at Modena but the track was, in his opinion, 'far too bumpy and too slow to genuinely assess its capabilities'.

From Silverstone Mike reported that the new Desmo twin 'had really got something and is capable of at least 130mph'. Timed by the press on varied laps it was found that as the day progressed times came down from around 2 minutes 10 seconds to just over 2 minutes, representing a speed of between 86 and 87mph.

The bore and stroke dimensions of the engine were 55.25x52mm – identical to the 125cc single, giving a displacement of 249.7cc. Power output was officially given as 37bhp at the rear wheel, or 43.3bhp at the crankshaft at 11,600rpm – with maximum torque at 11,200rpm. Transmission was via a six-speed gearbox built-in unit with the engine following the practice of earlier Taglioni Ducati designs. Of particular note was the engine porting arrangement: the carburetion induction tracks were divergent while the exhaust ports were convergent. Float chambers of the twin 30mm Dell'Orto SS racing carburettors were of the flat type (as employed on the period four-cylinder MVs) – due to the limitation of space. These were similar to those fitted on the 125cc twin – which on the smaller engine gave nothing but trouble, being prone to flooding the engine once the machine left the vertical position.

There is no doubt that it was the cycle parts and the frame and forks which were to cause the most problems – and controversy. The front forks were actually Manx Norton components, suitably shortened (also used on the works MZs), while the frame was a twin duplex affair. The design incorporated an effective, but simple, arrangement for rear chain adjustment. The wheel spindle was mounted eccentrically within two circles of metal, which in turn rotated with two clamps located at the extreme ends of the swinging arm. Years later a similar, although technically different, system was to be employed on some Ducati production models from the mid-1970s onwards. A pair of six-volt seven-amp hour batteries were used in series together with twin coils for the ignition.

Twin generously proportioned megaphones extended almost to the rear

The 249.77cc (55.25x52mm) Desmo twin-cylinder engine, with a power output of 37bhp at the rear wheel and 43.3bhp at the crankshaft, was, at the time, the most powerful in its class.

Mike (37) keeps his AJS 7R in front of Norton-mounted Tom Thorp at Silverstone, spring 1960.

tyre and were swept upwards in a peculiar bend. This was not so much for engine efficiency, but for ground clearance reasons.

When it made its entrance in the spring of 1960, the Ducati 250 Desmo twin was without doubt the most highly powered four-stroke motorcycle racing engine of its size in the world. Unfortunately, it also had three major drawbacks. Firstly, it needed at least a season's development under racing conditions with the full support of the factory, secondly it was at least 50 pounds overweight, and finally, to quote Mike, 'it was the fastest five-bar gate in the world'. Which didn't say much for the handling!

Retaining the Mellano Trophy

These major failings with the bike were largely hidden from the assorted members of the world's press when the bike made a victorious debut at the international Silverstone BMCRC championship meeting on Saturday 9 April 1960. Following his Mellano Trophy ride of the previous year, Mike was able to retain the coveted award with the brand-new twin when he won the 250cc race, and in the process set a new lap record of 91.43mph. For anyone who was there the deep note of the Ducati engine could be heard all the way round the Northamptonshire circuit.

Silverstone BMCRC Championship – 10 laps – 27.1 miles
1st   M. Hailwood (Ducati)
2nd   J. Murgatroyd (NSU)
3rd   A. Wheeler (Moto Guzzi)

4th   D. Moore (NSU)

5th   D. Shorey (NSU)

6th   T. Robb (GMS)

To conclude a successful day, Mike also won the 125cc race on his latest Desmo single, and took runner-up places in both the 350 and 500cc (AJS and Norton respectively) to Bob McIntyre.

A 350 twin

The 14 April 1960 issue of *The Motor Cycle* reported 'that Ken Kavanagh will ride a 350 Ducati desmodromic twin in the Junior TT'. The journal went on to say that Kavanagh had been so pleased with the 125 and 220 dohc Ducati singles, on which he had scored seven wins on his winter tour of his native Australia, that he had 'persuaded' Ing. Taglioni to increase the bore and stroke of the 250 Desmo twin. Ken was also reported as having given the 350cc model its baptism at Imola on Sunday 24 April, while Taglioni was striving to get a sister model ready for Mike Hailwood to ride in the Isle of Man.

The new engine had a bore and stroke of 64x54mm (against 55.25x52mm for the 250) and maximum power, measured at the rear wheel, was claimed to be 48bhp at 11,000rpm. As the machine was in all other respects identical to the existing 250, it was expected that its performance would be 'impressive', thanks to a much superior power-to-weight ratio.

Mike's double Desmo act continued on Good Friday 15 April 1960, when he took his 125cc single and 250cc twin to easy victories at Brands Hatch. But, two days later, Mike's Easter racing, which had begun so well at Brands Hatch, ended abruptly at Snetterton. Shortly after notching up a new 250cc lap record, the Oxfordshire ace swung his Ducati into the second bend of the esses (nicknamed the 'Bomb Hole' because during World War Two a bomb had exploded there), when a Velocette rider, whom Mike was lapping, dropped his machine almost under the twin's front wheel and Mike had to lie the model down and slide to a halt to avoid collision.

The unfortunate Velocette rider was taken to hospital with concussion and suspected head injuries, but Mike escaped with a severe shaking and a badly gashed heel, although this was enough to put him out of action for the remainder of the weekend.

Although the new Ducati twin had not been beaten, some questioned even at this early stage just how successful it would ultimately prove. Typical of these comments were those of journalist Mick Woollet who, writing in

THE LOOK OF A WINNER

Motor Cycle News's weekly 'Paddock Gossip' column dated 4 May 1960, said:

> *...although Mike Hailwood's 250cc 'desmo' Ducati proved fast enough to win the class quite easily in our races, I wasn't very impressed by the speeds put up – to stand a chance in the world championship series these days you have to have a '250' considerably faster than standard production 350cc Manx Nortons and 7R AJSs.*

With this in mind, Woollet called round to see Mike and his mechanic Jim Adams at their Nettlebed workshop. When questioned about the 250's maximum speed (claimed by the factory to be 135mph), Mike replied, 'I don't know. The road holding and general handling were so bad that I never had it flat out'.

As they talked the machine was actually back in Italy to have a new frame fitted (having been damaged in the Snetterton crash). However, there is uncertainty about whether this was the same design or a freshly laid out one. By the end of May, Stan Hailwood was able to announce that he'd purchased all three works 125cc Desmo twins complete with spares. However, the fact that Bruno Spaggiari raced one in Spain during 1963 calls this claim into question. But there is little doubt that Stan had realised that the 125 twin's road-holding was not in the same league as the 125 Desmo singles and they were still plagued with carburation problems. At that time he was not quite sure what to do. He might keep all three and 'run a team', or he might 'sell two and keep one for Mike'. In the event, the two examples known to have reached the UK were sold on to Southampton dealer/entrant Syd Lawton for his son Barry to race.

The new 350 arrives

The new 350cc Desmo twin for Mike (as opposed to the one for Kavanagh) arrived in England by air on the morning of Thursday 26 May 1960. Mike tried it at Silverstone that afternoon but in his opinion 'the road holding just wasn't good enough for this weekend's big Silverstone meeting', so in the event he opted to race his trusty 7R AJS.

But perhaps the most serious problem was the fact that the 250cc model didn't seem to have benefited from its trip back to Italy – in fact Mike couldn't match his lap times made only a few weeks before, even though he still won the 250 event.

Once again, the faithful Desmo single proved the best bet when Mike not

An Oulton Park shot of Mike with the 250 Desmo twin, now equipped with a new frame, August 1960.

only won the 125cc race, but broke his own lap record with a speed of 87.22mph.

The Isle of Man TT

Then came the annual visit to the Isle of Man for the TT. Unlike some riders, Mike always said he 'thoroughly enjoyed racing over natural road courses like those found on the Island'. He entered three classes on Ducati machines in 1960. His 125 now sported a single downtube frame and revised engine, the latter referred to as the 'Barcone' (see separate boxed section). Strangely, it had been discovered that the old single downtube design of 1956–7 was superior to the double downtube type used in 1958–9. Both front and rear surfaces of the front member were reinforced by a welded-on strip. And all acute angles were gusseted for extra strength.

On his 250 twin, Mike's fastest practice lap was 82.04mph, while he got his 125 round at 78.47mph. The races, however, turned out to be a nightmare. In the first event of the 1960 TT series, the three-lap Ultra-Lightweight (125cc), held over the 37.73-mile Mountain circuit for the first time since 1953, Mike and Gary Hocking (MV) got the racing under way. But Mike's ride ended less than a third of the way round the first lap, when at Glen Helen he fell off and toured in to retire. Things were no better in the Lightweight (250cc) TT, as Mike was forced to retire with a broken throttle cable on the Desmo twin.

In the Junior (350cc), he chose to play safe and rode his 7R AJS, only to notch up yet another retirement. Only in the Senior (500cc) TT did things go according to plan, when he not only became the second man in history to lap the Island at over 100mph on a single (Derek Minter having achieved the feat a few moments earlier), but also went on to finish third on his Norton behind the four-cylinder MVs of John Surtees and John Hartle.

Dutch TT

The next round in the world championship series was the Dutch TT at Assen on Saturday 25 June 1960. Here Mike rode his 125 single to eighth place – for by now there were not only the MVs, but also the emerging MZ and Honda twins to contend with. Added to this Ducati themselves had all but stopped direct involvement in the development of the machine. In the 250 race Mike chose his FB Mondial, even though it was patently slower than the Ducati, finishing a fine fifth in front of Jan Huberts and Jim Redman on Honda fours (the latter having his first ride for the Japanese factory).

The following week in Belgium, on a much faster circuit, Mike opted to use the Ducati twin and came seventh. His average speed was 108.16mph, against 113.46mph for winner Carlo Ubbiali's MV twin (which put out 5bhp less). In the 125cc race, on the Ducati single, Mike was sixth.

Back in Britain

A week later and the Hailwood équipe were back on British short circuit duty to score an array of wins at the first meeting on the extended 2.65-mile Brands Hatch GP circuit. *The Motor Cycle* headline said it all: 'Master

Oulton Park again, this time with Mike taking his works 125 Desmo single to yet another victory.

Mariner Hailwood'. Wet roads for his inaugural international status meeting proved that by now Mike was not only skilled, but also shrewd into the bargain. In scooping all four solo races he blended dash with restraint so wisely that he stayed afloat while rasher men slid off, yet went so fast that no one who slithered round behind him had a ghost of a chance.

He won the 125cc race and *The Motor Cycle* commented: 'the superiority of Hailwood and his desmodromic Ducati single was so overwhelming that he lapped the third finisher'.

The German Grand Prix was given a miss as there was no 125cc race and the 250cc twin was having more attention in the navigation department. Fast as it may have proved, the machine's handling had simply not been in the same league as its power output. Birmingham engineer Ernie Earles was commissioned by Stan Hailwood to build a new frame, which if successful would be fitted to Mike's other 250cc twin, as well as the 350.

The main aim was to lengthen the wheelbase from the original 51½ inches to 54 inches (similar to a Manx Norton), and the opportunity was also taken to lower the engine by 1½ inches in the frame and move it forward to improve weight distribution. Earles estimated that, as originally constructed, the original design carried 75 percent of the engine weight above wheel spindle height.

Tubes of the new frame were in Reynolds 531, 1½ in by 16 gauge. A layout was adopted, with the top and engine loop tubes crossed at the steering head. From the base of the head, the twin top tubes ran horizontally rearward at a diverging angle to afford a triangular structure resistant to whip. Cross-members braced the triangle and from the forward cross-tube there was a bracing strut to the top of the steering head. A loop to support the rear mudguard engaged with the top tube open ends.

Mike in determined mood aboard the Ecurie Sportive 7R at Silverstone in 1960. Note the Italian Oldani front brake.

The engine-loop tube descended from the top of the steering head and these, too, were at first at a diverging angle, with a cross-member ahead of the engine so that the construction was triangulated. They then ran parallel, sweeping beneath the power unit and rising to meet the top tubes under the seat. Rear suspension was by an orthodox pivoted fork fabricated from tubing. The frame was of welded construction throughout. Finally, a notable feature of the new design meant that the megaphones were now straight and not kinked as on the original.

The Earles frame debut
The race debut for the Earles frame came at the Ulster GP in early August.

Mike (2, Ducati) and Gary Hocking (1, MV) await the start of the 1960 Ultra-lightweight TT. Mike was destined to retire after a crash early in the race.

Even though he came home fourth – in front of Takahashi's Honda 4 and Taveri's MV Agusta twin, Mike was still not happy with the handling, in spite of the frame change. John Surtees, reflecting on the Ulster GP, commented in *The Motor Cycle*:

> *Mike Hailwood's Ducati twin was a bit disappointing. As with the MZs I think it is wrong to hang a Manx Norton front fork to a lightweight frame, it doesn't help the power-to-weight ratio even if it is a good stop-gap where handling is concerned. The Ducati has stacks of power but the machine as a whole is too bulky, it needs paring down to make better use of the power.*

After a trio of successful British short circuit meetings at Aberdare Park (13 August), Brands Hatch (21 August) and Snetterton (4 September) Mike was off to Monza for the Italian Grand Prix. Although he came third in the 500cc race, his two Ducati outings were less successful. An ignition fault put him out on the two-fifty Desmo twin, while in the 350cc race the rear wheel of his larger Ducati twin collapsed. As Mike had tested a works dohc Moto Morini at Monza before the GP, he no doubt wished he had taken up the offer of this machine instead of his own Ducati for the 250cc event.

Mike raced his 125 Desmo single for the final time at the Senora de Pilar

Mike rode his privately-entered Manx Norton to third in the 500cc Italian GP at Monza on 11 September 1960 behind the four-cylinder MVs of John Surtees and Emilio Mendogni.

road races near Barcelona, Spain (his first appearance in that country) on Sunday 16 October 1960. Unlike many of his British victories on the machine, this one was hard-earned. For the first 15 laps of the mile-long Zaragosa circuit, Jorge Sirera (Montessa) led, pursued by Marcello Cama (Bultaco), with Mike third. For the next 18 laps Cama was in front, Sirera second. Then Mike slipped past and four laps from the end Johnny Grace (Bultaco) took third place from Cama who had been replaced by Sirera.

And so with this final victory in Spain came Mike's last race of the 1960 season. It was one in which he had again won all four ACU solo stars, won 60 major races (plus many more in heats) and become as proficient on big bikes as he already was in the Lightweight classes. He had also done enough to push himself into the public limelight. In the *BP Book of Motor Cycle Racing*, published in late 1960, he was described thus:

> *...although only just out of his teens, Mike Hailwood already numbers his success in hundreds, whilst before him lies the prospect of becoming the most successful rider in the history of motor cycle racing!*

Chapter 4

Stan the wallet

MIKE, JOKINGLY, used to refer to his father Stan as 'the Wallet'. This simple statement says much about Stan and how he went about setting Mike on his road to stardom. But it doesn't tell the full story of either father or son.

Mike could never have become a world champion on money alone, without the required natural talent, and Stan's role in Mike's racing is a complicated affair that certainly cannot be explained in a few sentences. So I decided to attempt to give a true picture of the man who played such a significant role in shaping Mike's life and racing career by dedicating an entire chapter to Stanley William Bailey Hailwood.

Stan was a self-made man. Born during 1903 in the north-west of England, his father George Arthur Hailwood and mother Elisabeth had three other children, the oldest, George Junior, Maude and younger son Douglas.

Stan left school at 13 years of age to join the local Foden wagon factory. He left there at 16 to begin work with a local motorcycle dealership and as an 'out-of-work' hobby began buying and selling motorcycles. Then, at 17 years of age, Stan competed in motorsport for the first time on a single-speed Norton at Axe Edge, Buxton, Derbyshire.

In 1924, at the age of 21, young Stan read an advertisement that said that Howard King of Egrove Farm, Kennington, Oxford, required a mechanic. Upon answering the said advertisement, he received an invitation to visit the King emporium in New Road, Oxford. Howard King was engaged in buying and selling motorcycles. King had the finance, but knew little about motorcycles, whereas Stan had no money, but the expertise to repair and sell the product. And thus a highly unlikely partnership was formed based on mutual need. Stan joined Howard King and his father in the business but they were originally concerned about Stan's leg (he always limped) so they took him on a commission basis: he got paid if he repaired and actually sold a motorcycle. He was to stay for the next 38 years. In those years Stan built up the original Oxford King's dealership into an enterprise with some 50 sites in 21 towns and cities across the United Kingdom, selling some 12,000

S.W.B. (Stanley William Bailey) Hailwood was very much a self-made man. Leaving school at 13 years of age, Stan joined King's of Oxford in 1924 at 21, arriving from the north-west of England with 'not a penny to his name'. He stayed for the next four decades, creating the largest chain of dealerships in the land and becoming a multi-millionaire.

motorcycles a year. With the arrival of the affordable small car during the late 1950s, King's also began selling vehicles with four wheels.

One of the secrets of King's success was that they were pioneers in offering potential customers credit. Unlike today, where offers of extended credit arrive in every form from television advertising to junk mail, in the 1920s and 1930s it was almost unheard of – unless you were a King's customer.

Another advantage was that Stan had the ability to buy cheap and sell high. In the early days this involved rebuilding wrecks and moving them through the Oxford site. Later Stan traded in more expensive, better quality machines.

He also had the knack of getting the best out of his workforce. Christopher Hilton, in his 1992 book *A Man Called Mike*, described Stan Hailwood's employment methods in the following terms:

> *...here in essence is a Victorian concept, the commercial baron wielding power, but do not judge Stan by that alone. He inspired affection, loyalty and respect in equal measure.*

Stan was very much a commander-in-chief figure, whose employees jumped when he said 'jump'. To his close office staff at King's national head-quarters in Oxford he was known simply as 'SW'. But all this was very much in the future when he first joined King's.

The first Hailwood équipe

After settling into his new life in Oxford, Stan, with funds generated by his high work rate and success, was able to pursue his interest in racing. His efforts – like most motorcycle race meetings at the time – were on grass rather than tarmac. Because of his leg, Stan mainly raced sidecars. A feature of this, the first Hailwood équipe, was the pristine appearance of both the machinery and the competitors. When reviewing his own racing achieve-ments many years later Stan recalled:

> *...when I was riding I always wore white overalls, as did my sidecar passenger. Leathers were not necessary in those days. We had to put up with a few sarcastic remarks, but this, plus immaculate machines, paid off in goodwill and reputation.*

It was something that Stan demanded of Mike when father and son sallied forth under the Ecurie Sportive banner during Mike's formative racing days.

In 1930, Stan switched to four wheels, purchasing an MG from the local Abingdon factory. With the MG he competed three times in the annual Brooklands 500-mile race, at the Weybridge, Surrey, speed bowl circuit.

It was during his MG racing days that he came into contact with the famous Brooklands racer and record breaker Bill Lacey. Later, Stan was to enlist the services of Lacey as the tuner of Mike's racing bikes.

Besides actually racing, which included events of up to 1,000 miles in length, Stan attempted the world one-hour speed record (again at Brooklands) but was forced to abort the attempt due to bad weather. He also did trials and hillclimbs with some measure of success, but finally in 1933 he quit 'to concentrate on business', even though, as he freely admitted: 'racing is a disease. Once it is in your blood you can never get rid of it'. As Christopher Hilton was to remark, these were 'interesting words, very interesting words...'

After Stan had retired from competition, he got married. The couple's first child died soon after birth. Then came Christine (Chris) and finally, on 2 April 1940, Stanley Michael Bailey Hailwood – or more simply to family and friends and fans alike, Mike.

As already chronicled in Chapter 1, the Hailwood family homes were usually impressive buildings, including those at Goring-on-Thames and Highmore Hall, Nettlebed, on the Oxfordshire/Berkshire border.

One of the very few things in his life that was not a success was Stan's first marriage – and this was to remain a dark secret, as Chris Buckler (Mike's sister) recalled in Christopher Hilton's *A Man Called Mike*: 'I remember her, but I don't talk about her very much'. Well, her mother had

Stan, Pat and Mike in South Africa during the winter, 1957–8.

left her children when they were very young. But to give credit to Stan he brought up both Chris and Mike himself, albeit with the help of various staff including nannies and butlers – and later boarding schools.

Although Stan was driven by the need to be successful in everything he did, in his own way he still found time for and took an interest in his children. Even the subsequent divorce was not made public, even though later, after the war, Stan married a lady called Pat – who proved a much more stable and suitable mother than the original had ever been.

Creating a business empire

In many ways Stan's life was built around creating a business empire, because that is exactly what he did at King's. Although his name was not on the shop door, it was very much a Hailwood enterprise. Stan not only did the wheeling and dealing, but he also drove the business ever forward to become the success it was. And once he retired during the early 1960s, the King's dealership chain ceased to expand.

Stan was a shrewd man and not used to coming off second best. This in itself was both a help and a hindrance in Mike's early racing career. The positive side was that Stan's ability to fund, organise and advise was of tremendous benefit to Mike and it can't be underestimated. However, Mike was also placed under a type of pressure that his rivals would never experience. This for someone who was as naturally shy as Mike was not easy to cope with. Stan planned Mike's career as a general would execute a major battle campaign. Also, Stan was someone who was used to getting his own way. And he certainly was not averse to buying success – whether it was obtaining the best bicycles or even occasionally trying to bribe the opposition! Yes, that's how far Stan would go in his drive to make his son into a champion. The author is certain that Stan could see that Mike had some natural ability from the way he had handled the 197cc James, but not as Stan himself was to say in the booklet *My Son Mike*, published in the mid-1960s:

> *Yes, just a good rider. The thought that one day he would be a world champion never entered my head. If anyone had suggested it I should have said 'Nuts!'.*

A sensible approach

Stan also had a sensible approach to just how one should start racing. This was: 'To start at the bottom in the smallest class and work upwards is the finest experience and to my mind breeds the "best-in-the-end" rider'. He went on to say: 'I know so many good riders who started on big bikes, but with no prize money and many disappointments, gave up'.

Also, at Mike's very first meeting at Oulton Park in the spring of 1957 aboard a 125cc MV Agusta loaned by Stan's friend Bill Webster, Stan was to say that he went there with an open mind – if Mike had not shaped up, nothing more would have been heard of him. But Stan recalled in *My Son Mike* that Bill Webster remarked after his debut outing: 'Stan, you have a future world champion there. You can buy a machine for him'. And from that moment, Stan went about achieving this prophecy. Then came the difficult bit and because leading players such as Stan, Mike, Bill Webster and Bill Lacey are no longer with us, it is hard to get at the truth of the matter. This was what Stan himself referred to as 'The Money Myth'.

In *My Son Mike*, Stan commented:

> *...whatever Mike has got, he has earned by his own natural ability as a rider. The only thing I gave him was my enthusiasm, encouragement, advice and a temporary loan towards that first 125 MV.*

However, in the author's opinion as someone who not only raced in the period, but has also subsequently been a sponsor and later still a team manager and coach, the figures alone simply do not add up. But in any case, there did come a time when Mike was able to repay at least a proportion of the investment that Stan put into the Ecurie Sportive enterprise. And an enterprise was precisely what it was. Probably no one else in the world could have done what Stan did during Mike's early racing days, until he became a works rider and able to stand entirely alone. Stan was also a great showman, and he had the vision to see beyond what he called the 'dirt and grease' with which motorcycles had previously been associated.

There is no doubt that for the first few months of his racing, Mike was entirely dependent upon his father in every way. John Surtees described it another way:

> *I remember feeling rather sorry for Mike, because if ever anybody set out to manufacture a world champion, Stan set out to make Mike one, and fed him relentlessly into a starmaking machine fuelled by his money and his overwhelming personality.*

I came across this state of affairs when, as the British Cagiva importer in 1980, my company was selling the WMX 125 motocrosser. As the world's first 'production' liquid-cooled dirt racer, the little Italian bike attracted considerable publicity, appearing as it did bang in the middle of the motocross season. Ranged against the air-cooled Japanese machines it was a race winner in the highly competitive schoolboy motocross events. A feature of the schoolboy dirtbike racing scene was the Stan Hailwood type character, men who had made their own way and had succeeded in the dog-eat-dog world of commercial life. These men were in a position to provide the very best equipment for their sons. Unfortunately, quite often these youngsters were just not talented enough to take advantage or simply had no interest in racing. More often than not, the father just couldn't see this, or accept it. The result was that the son could be seen in tears, sometimes even before the race started.

   In Stan and Mike's case things were slightly different, in that Stan was sensible enough to see whether Mike really wanted to go racing and whether he was likely to be any good, before splashing out on a bike. But once this had been decided, Stan drove Mike on. This could, potentially, have been extremely difficult for Mike. And that he came out the other end of this sharp learning curve was in itself a fantastic achievement. It's one thing to do it entirely off your own bat, with no parental pressure. But just stop and

Mallory Park, spring 1959. Left to right: Bill Lacey, Mike, mechanic Jim Adams and Stan.

consider whether *you* would have been able to race – and win – with a millionaire father breathing down your neck!

So from the very beginning – once Stan had decided Mike had potential – the Hailwood équipe had nothing but the best. John Surtees again:

> *That was typical of Stan, and certainly in those days when you thought of Hailwood, you thought of Stan first and Mike second, trailing along behind Dad, dominated.*

The press

The press soon began (largely at Stan's behest) to run stories with titles such as 'The Golden Boy'; 'The Fastest Teenager on Earth'; 'The Lad born with the Silver Clutch Lever in his Hand' and many others.

But strangely, this father-son relationship seems to be a genuine reason why Mike made the grade – and certainly contributed to him being able to fast-forward this process. The only place where Mike was truly able to be in charge of himself, without his father there, was when he was alone on the race circuit. And perhaps, even without realising it, this spurred on his natural motivation to win.

Certainly in that first season (1957) the big, brash arrival on the scene by the Hailwood équipe created as many enemies as it did friends. Many objected to what, as they saw it, was a 'money talks' operation. This was another problem which the young Mike had to deal with, and something Stan was immune to. Many disliked the name Hailwood, not because of the son who was doing the riding out on the track, but because of the team's creator, father Stan.

Dan Shorey (Mike's teammate in the 1958 Thruxton 500-mile race victory on a Triumph Tiger 110) recalls Stan as someone who was 'not afraid to call a spade a spade – and a shrewd businessman'. Dan also says he could get on with Stan, although he accepted that 'many couldn't'.

Stan was also someone who was not averse to using his position as head of the King's empire to further Mike's racing career. Examples of this are the fact that King's became the British Ducati importers in January 1959; buying a batch of NSUs to retain the ex-John Surtees machine and spare engine; and advising journalists that they should tell the public about Mike's performance or risk having advertising withdrawn from the journals. Even Derek Minter was to recall Stan offering Derek money to 'leave your bikes in the van today'.

At the time Mike knew nothing of these behind the scenes goings-on. In fact, Mike was not someone who enjoyed wheeling and dealing anyway, and as his career blossomed, so it was the racing performances rather than Stan's bargaining skills and money which propelled Mike's career onwards.

The truth is, that unlike many of the schoolboy motocrossers mentioned earlier, the father and son team of Stan and Mike survived all the early antics. And together they progressed, becoming friends rather than purely father and son.

It should also be taken into account that through Stan, Mike was introduced to many useful contacts, some, like Dave Chadwick, Percy Tait and Geoff Duke, helping him hone his riding skills, while others were the trade barons and manufacturers who supported racing. Again, without Stan it would have taken Mike much longer to benefit from these people.

Stan fully endorsed a statement once made by Manchester-based entrant Reg Dearden on how he saw the manager/rider relationship: 'It's your job to ride the machine, leave the work and worry to me'. Stan said:

> *I adopted the same attitude and I believe Jack Surtees did the same to John when he started, except that John was very mechanically minded and eventually did most of his own work.*

Hutchinson 100, Silverstone, 22 August 1959. Stan and Mike flank Ducati factory mechanic Oscar Folesani. Folesani was loaned to the Hailwoods by the Italian factory during 1959 and 1960.

Problem solver

Another feature of the Stan and Mike relationship was that Stan had the ability to smooth over potential problems. For example, on one occasion at the Belgian Grand Prix, the Hailwoods had applied, as allowed for in the regulations, to bring their own petrol. Stan was quoted as saying:

> An hour before the race we had to fill up and what a dispute blew up. I knew we were right and stuck it out until I proved my case. If Mike had argued the case, I dread to think what would have happened with his quick temper.

Patience was not one of Mike's strong points.

On the other hand, the Ecurie Sportive's chief technical wizard, Bill Lacey, once had an almighty bust-up with Stan – and only stayed with the team because of his respect for Mike. The father and the son clearly had complimentary qualities. In the final analysis, Stan really did play a pivotal role in Mike Hailwood's success. Of that there can be absolutely no doubt.

Whatever anyone's personal opinion is of Stan, the bottom line has to be that he supported his son's racing 100 percent. And he could certainly never be accused of spoiling Mike – if anything Stan was a hard taskmaster, always looking for Mike to improve. A little known fact is that Mike actually repaid Stan considerable sums of money during the 1960s – proof, if ever it was needed, of the respect and appreciation he had for his father, even after the latter had bulldozed Mike so often during his early racing days.

For tax reasons, Stan Hailwood left Britain during the 1960s and set up two homes, one in Barbados and the other in Cannes in the south of France. He was by then a truly wealthy man, one of the super rich indeed. There were rumours that he had successfully played the stock market to add to his fortune.

Stan then spent a lot of time on cruises and in fact had just completed a round-the-world trip when he collapsed in Miami during December 1977.

Sadly, Stan, the man who had been so instrumental in furthering his son's career, died in Barbados on 4 March 1978, aged 75, a few weeks short of Mike's sensational Isle of Man TT comeback.

Stan, Mike and Oscar Folesani with the new works Ducati 250 Desmo after winning the prestigious Mellano Trophy at Silverstone in April 1960.

Chapter 5

World Champion

ALTHOUGH MIKE had won many races, been holder of every one of the four ACU Stars and a Grand Prix winner, so far a TT victory and a World Championship title had eluded him. But 1961 was to be the year when he achieved both, marking his transition to being a truly world-class star.

Stan was still very much in charge of Mike's racing career, ensuring that everything ran like clockwork and that Mike had the very best machinery.

As Mike's friend Ted Macaulay once said:

> ...if Mike's skill was in getting results from whatever machine was put underneath him, his father's was in persuading people to part with the equipment.

There is absolutely no doubt that Stan employed the very same tactics which had helped him to build up his business empire when it came to racing. Left alone Mike would still probably have got there in the end, but Stan most definitely made things happen more quickly.

During the closed season, various rumours had flooded the motorcycle press about just what Mike would be riding in 1961. Some of these stories were pure fiction, but others, for example Mick Woollet's concerning a possible Honda ride, turned out to be correct. In early January, Mike was quoted as saying: 'I haven't got fixed up yet; at the moment it looks like I'll be riding, same as last year'.

Meanwhile, in typical fashion, Mike and fellow racer Tony Godfrey left for the United States of America, having both been invited, at short

Mike and Tony Godfrey (right) shake hands with Tom Galen of the USMC after arriving in New York in early February 1961 aboard the SS *America*.

notice, to race in the US Grand Prix at Daytona in February. This invitation had come via the British ACU from Major Goode, the Secretary-General of the FIM in Geneva. As the letter only arrived four days before the ship was due to leave, speed was of the essence. However, before Mike left he had been able to test the newly purchased FB two-fifty – a 1957 ex-works bike, which Stan had 'acquired' direct from the Italian factory – at Brands Hatch on Saturday 14 January. Unlike the earlier models raced by Mike, this had bevel-driven double overhead camshafts, whereas the other models employed a gear-driven mechanism.

After what *Motor Cycle News* described as 'a frantic battle of activity', Mike and Tony Godfrey left Southampton on Monday morning, 30 January 1961. They sailed aboard the SS *America* (first class) bound for New York. As for machinery, Mike took a 250cc FB Mondial and a 500cc Manx Norton, while Tony's mount was a Matchless G50 loaned by Geoff Monty.

The purpose of their trip was to compete in the FIM-sanctioned road races being organised by the United States Motorcycle Club at the new Daytona Speedway circuit on Sunday 12 February.

From New York, the original idea was to make their way down the eastern seaboard by train, arriving in sufficient time to be at Daytona a day before the actual races. However, in practice this plan didn't work out, because of rough weather while at sea, which delayed the ship's arrival time by over a day.

As Tony Godfrey was later to describe:

...we arrived in New York a day late and there to meet us was Tom Galen of the USMC. He'd hired a Rolls Royce for the occasion and we drove off of the docks in real style – like visiting royalty! That afternoon we did the sights, visiting the Empire State Building and the United Nations.

The next day, Mike, Tony and Tom Galen flew from New York to Daytona. The bikes were supposed to follow on a freight plane, but they got lost somewhere along the route and it wasn't until Friday morning that they were finally located 200 miles away in Miami. As Tony said:

...an obliging enthusiast nipped them up by trailer and with only one day's practice left – the track having been open all week – we started to get things sorted out.

During the Saturday qualifying period, Mike's Norton struck trouble and he actually had to ride Tony's Matchless. But as the qualifying times provided the grid positions for the race, the official said that Mike's time wouldn't count, as he hadn't ridden his Norton.

The race day dawned sunny and warm, with the 250cc race the first in the programme. Mike, on the FB Mondial, made a superb start, but the four-cylinder Honda of Moto Kitano was flying. The Japanese rider passed Mike on the first lap and won – even though he had crashed and remounted on a slow corner. Mike finished runner-up, less than 20 seconds adrift, both men having lapped the third man – Louis Giran of Guatemala riding an NSU – three times!

Between the motorcycle events came a couple of stock car races. And as Tony said:

> ...it's not our type of stock car racing in old jalopies – they use souped up versions of brand new saloons – and when I tell you that a gent named 'Fireball' Roberts driving a Pontiac won a race on the speed bowl at an average of 155.4mph, you'll realise they don't hang about.

Tony Godfrey after winning the 1961 500cc United States Grand Prix at Daytona aboard a Matchless G50. Mike Hailwood's race came to an abrupt halt when the magneto on his Manx Norton failed.

500cc US Grand Prix

The bike races were over a part speed bowl/part infield circuit, measuring 3.1 miles in length. The main event, the 500cc, began at 4pm in the afternoon and had a race distance of 124 miles.

Kitano, on the two-fifty Honda four, leapt ahead at the start, but Tony Godfrey soon passed him. Mike, who as he had not qualified on his own machine had to start from the back of the grid, moved up to join his fellow Englishman at the front. Later, they eased the pace and were joined by Californian Norton rider Buddy Parrott. So then Tony and Mike pressed on ahead of the American. But Mike's Norton magneto started to play up, and he was forced to drop back and later retired. In the end, Tony Godfrey won by half a mile from Parrott and a lap from Bob Burnett (Matchless) and Ed La Belle (BMW).

So it was Tony, not Mike, who got the spoils of victory on this occasion. In this case, it meant being mobbed by reporters and photographers, a parade of honour in an open car with cups and a local beauty queen, and being interviewed on the NBC network.

After all the hectic rush and bustle, Mike and Tony spent the remainder

The 1961 Honda RC 162 four. The power output was a claimed 40bhp at 14,000rpm, giving a top speed of around 140mph.

of the week lying on the sunny Florida beaches and sightseeing. Stan had also flown out there for the races and had been: 'very impressed by the enthusiasm of the Americans' (something with which the author would concur).

Back in Britain

Meanwhile, back in Britain, Mike's mechanic Jim Adams had been testing the Ducati Desmo twins, which were now fitted with Reynolds leading link front forks, having been pioneered by Geoff Duke during the late 1950s on his Lightweight 350cc Norton. The three-fifty Ducati showed up a tendency to lift the front wheel out of slow corners when accelerating hard. He thought this could be cured by lengthening the wheelbase from 50 to 52 inches.

While on a car racing tour of New Zealand, John Surtees had been the guest of the Onehunga motorcycle club. Asked which were the best of the following four riders, Bob McIntyre, Mike Hailwood, Derek Minter and John Hartle, John diplomatically replied that he: 'would not like to place them in any order of merit for on their day all could be outstandingly brilliant'. However, he considered it 'amazing that Hailwood managed to keep on at times, racing so many classes'.

Testing MZs

In mid-March, Mike flew to East Germany (landing in Berlin) in company

Jim Redman

Jim Redman was a rider who never seemed to hit the headlines in quite the same way as other world champions and, in truth, never had the fan base of men such as Giacomo Agostini or Mike Hailwood. However, in terms of results and power he was a huge success. And in any case, with six world titles (two 250 and four 350cc) he was certainly no dummy on the track.

As journalist Gerard Periam wrote in 1964:

> ...the reason probably is that Jim Redman's approach to motor-cycle racing is purely professional. No more and no less than is required to win. No unnecessary records, no unnecessary fastest laps.

Jim was born in Hampstead on 8 November 1931, and attended primary school in Greenford, Middlesex. He passed his eleven-plus and went to grammar school. But he had to leave at 15 'because the family needed the money'.

He found a job as a motor mechanic, but was 'disappointed, as I wanted to stay on at school to take exams'. And his garage job was 'a bit of a comedown'.

When he was just over 16, Jim's father died – and to make matters even worse, his mother passed away within a month. There was a sister, Jacqueline, a year older than Jim, and twins Peter and Wendy, 10 years old. Before she died, their mother had urged them to 'stick together as a family'. Aunts and uncles offered to take the children. Welfare authorities wanted to put them in homes. This was one of Jim's first brushes with authority. However, the family stood firm, 'determined to stick together'. Money was obviously tight. Jim wanted a bike and took on additional work in the evenings to pay for an ex-WD Matchless G3/L single, later swapped for a Triumph twin.

1961 Mallory Park Race of the Year. Jim Redman (5) leads Tom Phillis (4) out of the hairpin. Both are mounted on four-cylinder Honda two-fifties.

National service was still in place and Jim faced an exemption tribunal. But the crisis was solved in two ways. Sister Jackie married and she and her husband took on responsibility for the twins. And Jim had a friend in Bulawayo, so off to Southern Rhodesia (now Zimbabwe) he went as going there meant he did not have to do his national service.

Jim got a job as a mechanic and later moved into a government transport department. At first, Jim sent money home for the family, and later he paid for them to come over to Rhodesia.

At this stage the reader should be aware of the considerable responsibilities *and* sacrifices for a teenager. And also the reason for Jim's 'professional' way of doing things in his racing career.

Jim's first race came via a friend, John Love, who loaned him a Triumph Grand Prix. This was followed by an International Norton. Then in 1955 he purchased a 1951 AJS 7R and it was on this bike that Jim scored his first big victory. Meanwhile, a sign was going up over a new business in Bulawayo – Love and Redman Motor Cycles.

Jim then set his sights on winning the South African 500cc championship, but in 1957 he was just pipped by the highly experienced Borro Castellani. The championship was important to Jim, who was keen to go to Europe along with his pal Paddy Driver. Actually Jim hadn't realised that in fact he had won a championship title – the 350cc on the faithful 7R!

Then came 1958, and it was Jim who stunned everyone, when that Easter weekend he created headlines in the British press by finishing runner-up to Derek Minter at Brands Hatch. Behind him were the likes of Bob McIntyre, Alastair King... and Mike Hailwood. Other similar results followed, riding a brace of Nortons and a 125cc Ducati.

Jim's first ride for Honda came in the 1960 Dutch TT, when Tom Phillis was unfit. At that time the Hondas were 'not terrifically quick and not many of the top runners wanted to know them'. When Hondas really began to perform and the company wanted to plan their full-scale assault in the GPs, Tom Phillis and Jim were summoned to Tokyo.

On Honda's desk the pair saw 'letters from some of the biggest names in motorcycling wanting to ride Hondas'. But Honda's view was 'Tom and Jim rode when they were slow. Tom and Jim will ride them now they are quick'. And there is no doubt whatsoever that Jim Redman was Honda's most loyal servant – and this is why he was subsequently made captain of the Honda works team.

The closeness of the team is clear from the following words, uttered after Jim got to the top and won several world titles:

> I'll always remember 1962 as a hard year. I lost my best friends, Tom Phillis, Bob McIntyre and Gary Hocking. Bob hadn't been in the Honda team long, but we had taken a liking to each other and he fitted in well.

As for his Honda performance, Jim's first Grand Prix victory came aboard one of the revised fours in the 250cc Belgian event. Then, in 1962, he won six of the 10 rounds counting towards the 250cc championship, winning the title. He also finished runner-up (behind Luigi Taveri) in the 125cc class. But the big surprise was winning the 350cc crown – a feat he was to repeat in 1963, 1964 and 1965.

Oulton Park; length 2.7 miles.

The 1962 Spanish GP and 250cc race winner Jim Redman. To Jim's right is team manager and ex-Grand Prix star Reg Armstrong.

He also won the 250cc title again in 1963, after a season-long battle with Italian challenger Tarquinio Provini on the Moto Morini. In 1964, he was runner-up to Phil Read (Yamaha) in the 250cc stakes.

Then came 1965 and the arrival of new boy Giacomo Agostini at MV. But even Ago and teammate Mike Hailwood couldn't stop Jim taking his sixth world title.

At the beginning of 1966, with Mike Hailwood now in the Honda team, Jim took the new four-cylinder Honda to victory in the first round of the 500cc championship at Hockenheim, with Agostini runner-up. In the Isle of Man it was Hailwood first, Agostini second. The third round at Assen saw Redman victorious with the Italian again runner-up.

Then came that fateful day in Belgium, when, during torrential driving rain, Jim crashed at Spa Francorchamps, breaking his arm. He subsequently returned to his home in Bulawayo and announced his retirement from the sport to become Yamaha importer for Rhodesia. In recent years Jim has become a familiar figure, like many other stars of yesteryear, at historic events around the world.

with new MZ rider Alan Shepherd, to test the latest 125 and 250cc two-stroke racers from the Saxony-based firm.

The tests were held on an airfield near Berlin and although Mike was impressed by the performance of the MZ machine (particularly the 125), he later told *Motor Cycle News* that he: 'had reached no decision as to whether he would race them in the GPs that year'. Actually, the stumbling block was money. Quite simply, MZ had no hard currency (i.e. dollars, pounds or lire) and although Mike genuinely liked race boss Walter Kaaden, he ultimately declined the MZ offer of machinery. Another problem would have been maintenance, because although Alan Shepherd was a first-class mechanic who could look after his own bikes, all Mike's tuners/mechanics were skilled in the traditional four-stroke, and not the black art of the two-stroke.

The official line from Stan Hailwood, as published in the 22 March issue of *MCN* was: 'still no decision from the Hailwood équipe regarding the invitation from MZ for Mike to ride their works machine this year'.

But behind the scenes Stan had already made contact with Honda regarding the possibility of the Japanese company supplying bikes – again a carrot was left hanging that Stan controlled the largest dealer network in the UK and King's would stock Hondas if Honda played ball…

There was, however, a problem to be overcome. Honda was contracted to Castrol, whereas Mike was a BP-backed rider. Back in 1961 the oil companies very much controlled the racing purse strings – something even Stan Hailwood realised and accepted.

A factory drawing of the RC 162. The engine formed a stressed member as part of the frame, as there were no front downtubes. The front brake was a double-sided SLS drum.

A way was found round this dilemma. Instead of Honda directly supplying bikes, the new British importer Hondis Ltd would field a team of three British riders: John Hartle, Bob McIntyre and Mike Hailwood. So Mike made a decision to race as a Honda privateer, rather than as an official MZ teamster.

While all this was going on, Mike was out testing at Silverstone in mid-March. He was there with a two-fifty Ducati Desmo twin, a three-fifty AJS 7R, a rather special 500 Norton, plus an equally special AJS model. This latter machine, again powered by a 7R engine, featured a 'one-off' frame built by Reynolds – similar to the Geoff Duke Lightweight Norton three-fifty referred to earlier. But instead of the massive single oil-containing tube on Duke's machine, Mike's AJS featured twin down tubes. In addition, it was fitted with an experimental double disc front brake. The Hailwood équipe actually had two of these brakes. Manufactured in Italy, they had arrived at great cost by air.

The British season gets under way
The 1961 British racing season got under way at Brands Hatch on Good Friday 31 March, with the first in a series of meetings at the popular Kentish circuit to decide just who was 'King of Brands'. As *Motor Cycle News* said, this honour 'went to Mike Hailwood, who was in scintillating form at the national road race meeting'.

Racing over the full 2.65-mile circuit in ideal conditions before a near record crowd, Mike (AJS) first won the 350cc Invitation event by a comfortable margin from Phil Read and John Hartle (both Norton mounted). Then, riding his FB Mondial, Mike easily took the 250cc honours.

350cc Invitation Brands Hatch – 10 laps – 26.5 miles
1st   M. Hailwood (AJS)
2nd   P. Read (Norton)
3rd   J. Hartle (Norton)
4th   D. Minter (Norton)
5th   P. Driver (Norton)
6th   D. Dale (Norton)

The first 1000cc Invitation race saw a fantastic dice between Mike, Minter and Hartle. Then came disaster – Minter was baulked by a lapped rider at Druids, and as he braked sharply, Hartle's front wheel broke away, sending him sprawling across the track. Mike had no chance to avoid the mêlée, and he too slid off. After that, Minter won easily from Phil Read.

Mike (7) and Luigi Taveri (5) during the Ultra-lightweight (125cc) TT in June 1961. Only Stan Hailwood's persistence ensured that Mike was able to take part on a works Honda, and Mike went on to win the race.

The second unlimited race, which ended the day's racing, saw Mike shoot ahead from the start, and although Minter tried hard, he couldn't close the gap, with Mike taking another victory.

On Sunday 2 April 1961, Mike celebrated his 21st birthday with a double victory at the Snetterton Combine's national road races at the 2.71-mile Norfolk airfield circuit. Mike's successes came in the 250cc and 350cc events, on Ducati and AJS machines respectively.

But Derek Minter (who had been runner-up in the 350cc) spoilt the chance of a trio of wins by coming out on top in the 500cc race, with Mike runner-up this time. But Mike was unlucky. As *Motor Cycle News* reported:

> *...restlessly and with a demonstration of 'ear'oling' that was positively frightening to watch, Mike cut Minter's lead ten yards a lap, but then on the fifth lap, just as he was on Derek's rear wheel, the experimental Norton with a one-piece crank that Mike was racing for the first time, slowed and from there on Minter rocketed away to win as he pleased, setting up a new lap record in the process.*

Finally, on Easter Monday, 3 April, and in what *MCN* described as 'the vilest of conditions', Mike made a clean sweep of the Commonwealth meeting at Thruxton. He won all seven races (including heats) of a slick, 16-race, part-televised (BBC) programme organised by the Southampton club, and sponsored by the *Daily Telegraph* newspaper. Mike rode FB Mondial, AJS and Norton machines.

Then came the annual *Motor Cycling* Silverstone Mellano Trophy meeting on Saturday 8 April. Here, after winning the trophy for the third time in three years, Mike was excluded. Why? Well, instead of the FB Mondial upon which he had originally entered, he rode one of his Ducati Desmo twins. Before being black-flagged, he had pushed the 250cc lap record up from 91.63mph to well over 93mph. Then, to cap a thoroughly miserable day, Mike suffered engine problems with his AJS and Norton machines and retired in both races.

After his unlucky day at Silverstone, Mike returned to winning form at Mallory Park the following day, taking both the 250cc (FB Mondial) and 500cc (Norton) finals. In the latter, he pushed his absolute lap record for the 1.35-mile Leicestershire circuit up to 89.33mph. In the 350cc race he was third on his AJS, behind the winner Phil Read and Bob McIntyre.

Ducati and FB Mondial sold

The Hailwood équipe had been selling off a few of its surplus machines now that Mike would be riding a Honda in the 250cc class, and the latest news was that he was to pilot Dr Joe Ehrlich's 125cc EMC in the Spanish GP. The older (1956) FB Mondial had been bought (via Bill Webster) by Manchester dealer/entrant Reg Dearden, while one of the two Ducati Desmo singles had been purchased direct from Stan Hailwood by Welshman Ivor Watton.

Sunday 23 April 1961 saw Mike make his debut on the EMC at Montjuich Park, Barcelona. The combination were also the sensation of the Spanish GP – the first round in the 1961 World Championship series. A split exhaust slowed Mike down in the closing stages of a race he had seemed destined to win. *Motor Cycle News* said:

> For British enthusiasts it was a dream come true – at last a British built machine to lick the pants off the best that the foreigners could produce, and make no doubt about it, Mike and the EMC simply wiped the floor with the rest of them, gaining over 100 yards a lap until he eased up.

Mike also set a new class record of 67.62mph, eventually finishing fourth behind Tom Phillis (Honda), Ernst Degner (MZ) and Jim Redman (Honda).

Soichiro Honda

Soichiro Honda was born on 15 November 1906, the eldest son of the village blacksmith in Komyo, long since swallowed up by the urban sprawl of modern-day Hamamatsu. From an early age, the young Honda displayed an interest in mechanical things, and at school showed a distinct leaning towards the practical approach.

Honda left school in 1922, at the age of 16, and took up an apprenticeship in Tokyo, as a car mechanic. Later he returned to Hamamatsu and opened his own garage business. This proved a great success in the early 1930s, and, with his new-found wealth, he took up car racing. This came to an abrupt halt after a serious accident at the Tama River circuit, near Tokyo, in July 1936.

Then, at the age of 30, he began a new enterprise, selling his dealership and entering the world of manufacturing with a piston-ring factory. After some extremely difficult times, Soichiro Honda eventually made a success of his venture. With the outbreak of war, he developed a special machine, which meant that the piston rings could be produced by unskilled women. Later, Honda's company was also involved in the manufacture of wooden aircraft propellers for the Japanese Army Air Force.

Towards the end of hostilities, the Honda facilities were bombed by the Americans, and then in early 1945 it was completely destroyed by an earthquake. Japan's final surrender in August 1945 came as Honda and his employees were attempting to repair a section of the shattered plant.

With war finally at an end, Soichiro Honda sold the remains of his factory to Toyota, and effectively took a year off. But such an active mind couldn't rest for long, and in October 1946 he set up the impressive sounding Honda Technical Research Institute. Unfortunately, this grand title hid the fact that the new venture was located in a tiny wooden hut, little bigger than a garden shed, on a levelled bombsite on the outskirts of Hamamatsu.

With post-war Japan hungry for personal transport – provided it was cheap – Honda was extremely fortunate to uncover a cache of 500 war surplus petrol engines, which had been employed by the military authorities to power small generators. Soichiro Honda then took the first step to his ultimate emergence as the largest motorcycle manufacturer in the world by adapting these tiny engines to power conventional pedal cycles. Within a short time he was offering the first of these for sale.

Soon Honda was overwhelmed with orders for his new creation and the stock of engines was soon exhausted. So what was he to do? The answer was simple – he set to and designed a petrol engine of his own. And with ready supplies of this new engine expansion was rapid! However, the financial base was not there to cope and, in 1953, Honda was almost forced out of business when he hit serious cash-flow problems, only to be bailed out by his bank. Honda was a fighter, and by early 1954 he was sufficiently far along the road to recovery to plan an export drive. He reasoned that to enable a full-scale effort it was necessary to publicise the Honda name overseas, and what better way than by going racing?

His first effort came in February 1954, when a works-prepared Dream, ridden by Mikio Omura, finished last in the internationally-supported 125cc race at Sâo Paulo in Brazil. The event was won by an Italian FB Mondial, ridden by Nello Pagani, but even so Honda gained considerable publicity as it was the first time a Japanese rider on a Japanese motorcycle had appeared at a major event outside the homeland. In addition, the poor showing did not restrict Honda's enthusiasm. Subsequently, he announced a plan of action which, over the next five years, would see the company actively strive to field a world-class racer by the 1959 season.

In June 1954 Soichiro Honda toured Europe, visiting, among other places, West Germany, England and the Isle of Man. At the last location his enduring impression was of the display put on by the German NSU team. He made no secret of his admiration for the whole set-up. Not just the speed and reliability of the machines, but the slick organisation of the team as a whole.

There is no doubt that although NSU effectively quit the Grand Prix arena at the end of 1954 (although a production-based Sportmax retained their 250cc crown in 1955), the first Honda Grand Prix bikes, which appeared in 1959, were strongly influenced by the German models.

Two decisive factors helped Honda. The first came in the mid-1950s when the Japanese government put into place certain banking restric-

tions, which made importing motorcycles into that country impossible. This created a situation where the home producers could not fail to prosper. The second was the advent, in 1958, of the best-selling C100 Super Cub, which sold in truly vast numbers and effectively bankrolled Honda's entry into the arena of European Grand Prix racing.

Honda first sent bikes to the Isle of Man TT in 1959 – where although not the quickest they were extremely reliable – winning the manufacturers' team prize.

Then in 1960 they signed up their first big foreign stars and added the 250cc class to the 125cc. In 1961 – as this book charts in detail – Mike Hailwood not only won two TTs (125 and 250cc) but also the 250cc World Championship, while Australian rider Tom Phillis won the 125cc title.

Honda had arrived! From then on no one could stop Honda on either the track or in the number of bikes sold.

By the late 1960s Honda was talking millions rather than thousands, by the 1970s Honda was into cars and so the story has continued. Today, Honda has plants all over the world and is still expanding its sales and manufacturing base.

Soichiro Honda in 1968 with the 10-millionth motorcycle produced by his company, a CB450 twin.

Mike sent this signed photograph of himself winning the 1961 Ultra-lightweight TT to Japan. It reads 'Thank You Mr Honda, Mike Hailwood, 125cc 1961 TT.'

Next came another debut, this time on Mike's recently received Honda four, at Brands Hatch on Sunday 30 April. This was actually a 1960 model, with 1961 modifications, and he won first time out – breaking the lap record in the process! At Brands Mike also had his second ride on the EMC, but in practice the primary drive gears stripped so he was a non-starter.

In the 350cc race Mike crashed, then in the 500cc he crashed again! Mike once said that if you didn't crash occasionally you were not trying hard enough.

On Monday 8 May, Mike left England for Hockenheim, where he was due to contest the second round of the World Championship series the following Sunday, 14 May. In the 125cc class he was down to ride the EMC, in the 250cc class the Honda, and in the 500cc division his own Norton.

This latter bike was fitted with a conventional AMC four-speed gearbox, but an Italian five-speed transmission (race-tested at Brands Hatch) was to be fitted, together with another engine, to the Norton for the French GP at Clermont-Ferrand a week after Hockenheim.

Mike had two of these Italian five-speeders. They were built for him to special order. The second of these 'boxes was fitted to an AJS 7R that Mike was taking with him to the German and French GPs 'as a reserve machine in case any of my other rides fell through!'

Mike was largely out of luck over the ultra-fast 4.99-mile Hockenheim circuit. First he retired in the 125cc when his EMC had piston trouble. Then his year-old Honda proved no match for the latest bikes ridden by the official team members and he could only it coax it into eighth, a lap behind the winner. Finally, in the 500cc race, Mike was placed fourth behind the winner Gary Hocking (MV), Frank Perris (Norton) and Hans-Gunter Jaeger (BMW). Particularly disappointing was the EMC effort, after the promise shown in Spain. Besides pistons, the British two-stroke also suffered battery failure. To stop the expansion boxes breaking new ones fabricated from Nimonic steel had been made up and these were used in Germany. The same material was employed in jet engines manufactured by de Havilland, who sponsored the EMC effort.

French GP

All who have raced at the Montagne d'Auvergne circuit where the third round of the 1961 road racing World Championship series was held agree that the venue was one of the finest and most beautiful in the world. Built during the late 1950s, it was situated high above the large industrial city of Clermont-Ferrand, in the mountains of the Auvergne from which it took its name.

Clermont-Ferrand. Length 5 miles.

The 125cc race came first. Mike (EMC) and Ernst Degner (MZ) had set the fastest practice times – a fraction of a second apart. Also the Yamaha team – new arrivals in Europe – were making their first appearance in a World Championship event. At the start Mike's EMC fired up, but refused to pick up, and consequently he was well down the field as they disappeared out of sight. By the end of the 13-lap, 65.03-mile race Mike had worked his way through to fourth, but could get no further.

Next came the 250cc race as *Motor Cycle News* reported:

> *Mike Hailwood has put the cat among the pigeons in the Honda camp for he's got round faster on his 1960 model Honda 4 than the official works team of Tom Phillis, Jim Redman and Takahashi, all of whom are riding the improved 1961 models.*

Other riders to watch out for included Morini's Tarquinio Provini and MV's Gary Hocking. Then came the race. At the end of the first lap it was

Hocking, Phillis and Hailwood. In fact, Gary was lapping faster on his 250cc twin than John Surtees did the previous year on his 500 four! But Hocking was eventually to retire, leaving Mike to finish the race runner-up to Tom Phillis.

250cc French GP – 15 laps – 70.03 miles
1st T. Phillis (Honda)
2nd M. Hailwood (Honda)
3rd K. Takahashi (Honda)
4th T. Provini (Morini)
5th S. Grassetti (Benelli)
6th J. Redman (Honda)

In contrast the 500cc race was 'pathetic' *(MCN)*. This was because, with no start money being paid, all the top-class riders had preferred to go to Chimay in Belgium instead. The result was that only four riders of international standard had entered – Mike (Norton) plus Gary Hocking on the MV4 and Hans Pesl (Norton) of Germany and Jacques Insermini (Norton) of France. So perhaps it was a foregone conclusion that Gary Hocking would win, with Mike runner-up.

'Hailwood – King of the Castle'

So said *Motor Cycle News* in their 31 May 1961 issue, with Mike winning the 250cc (Honda) and 500cc (Norton) races. The latter machine was fitted with a Peel Mountain Mile fairing, five-speed gearbox and Oldani front brake.

In the 350cc class, Mike appeared on the new Ducati Desmo twin. He was beaten by inches in his heat by Tony Godfrey (Norton) but then mechanic Jim Adams discovered that the vicious bumps of the 1.8-mile Wiltshire circuit had fractured one arm of the pivoted rear fork, and he was unable to race in the final.

In the same issue came news that John Surtees had swapped his own very special 500cc Norton for two of Mike's twin-cylinder Desmo Ducatis, (both 250s and to be ridden by John's brother Norman). Mike had the Surtees Norton at Castle Combe, but didn't ride it. This featured one of the massive MV dual front brakes, MV-type clip-ons, a special frame built for John by Reynolds and a 1961-type oil tank. The original engine had been replaced by the Lacey-tuned unit which had carried Mike to second spot in the French GP a week earlier. Mike rode another Lacey-prepared mount in the 500cc race at Castle Combe: 'running it in for TT practice', he said. He intended taking the two five-hundreds to the Isle of Man, where he would be able to compare them before deciding which one to ride in the Senior race.

In addition, following the frame breakage incident and although 'the 350 Ducati twin is now handling and going extremely well', Mike had more or less decided to 'probably stick with my AJS for the Junior'.

What would he ride?
Much controversy surrounded just what Mike would ride in the Ultra-Lightweight TT. *Motor Cycle News* again:

> *...actually, his position in the smallest class is rather obscure – he entered on a Ducati, expected to ride an EMC and may well end up by racing a Honda, although he's also been made a very definite offer of a works MZ!*

The truth was that Stan was pursuing the Honda camp in his own unique way. As Mike once described:

> *...if you short-changed him a penny he'd be down on you like a ton of bricks. If something is set in his mind it's a devil of a job to shake him off it, Honda had a taste of this at the 1961 TT.*

The Japanese factory had promised Stan 125cc and 250cc models, but found themselves short of the smaller bikes. Mike continued:

> *...it looked as if I wasn't going to get one after all, I was quite resigned to it, but Stan wouldn't give up. He almost lived at the Honda camp. They couldn't get rid of him.*

In the end, Honda caved in and gave the Hailwoods Luigi Taveri's practice machine. This story again illustrates just how important Stan was in Mike's

The runner-up in the 1961 125cc TT was the Swiss Honda works rider Luigi Taveri.

Taveri with his works Honda approaching Ramsey Hairpin during the 1961 TT.

career. Quite simply, without his father Mike would not have had that 125 Honda.

The machine turned out to provide one of three TT victories for Mike in 1961. The other two came from the 250cc four-cylinder Honda and Mike's own 500 Manx Norton. It could so easily have been four TT wins, as he was leading the Junior on his AJS when the gudgeon pin broke with only a few miles of the race left.

Mike's trio of victories was a record, while his success on the 125cc Honda was his first TT win. Mike also had a special 6.8-gallon (30-litre) fuel tank for his 250cc Honda model. These were fitted to the full factory entries plus the McIntyre and Hailwood bikes to allow them to do the race non-stop. But Bob's effort came to an end when his engine expired after setting a new class lap record. There were in fact no less than seven Honda fours in the 1961 Lightweight TT – as *MCN* said: 'a line up to make any opposition tremble!' – and with the Yamaha and Suzuki entries one newspaper said 'Japs everywhere – that's the outstanding impression on all visitors to the TT this year'.

Ultra-Lightweight (125cc) TT – 3 laps
1st	M. Hailwood (Honda)
2nd	L. Taveri (Honda)
3rd	T. Phillis (Honda)
4th	J. Redman (Honda)
5th	S. Shimazaki (Honda)
6th	R. Rensen (Bultaco)

Lightweight (250cc) – 5 laps
1st	M. Hailwood (Honda)
2nd	T. Phillis (Honda)
3rd	J. Redman (Honda)
4th	K. Takahashi (Honda)
5th	N. Taniguchi (Honda)
6th	F. Ito (Yamaha)

The Senior race

In winning the 1961 Senior TT, Mike made history by recording the first victory for a British machine in the event for seven years, the first race average on a British machine at over 100mph (100.60mph to be exact) and the first-ever three TT victories in one week.

On Friday 16 June, he covered the six laps of the 37.73-mile course (226.4 miles) in 2 hours 15 minutes 2 seconds, to cap what *MCN* described as 'magnificent riding'. After the finish of the Senior, Mike was congratulated by Rem Fowler, the winner of the very first multi-cylinder TT back in 1907 (who also shared Mike's birthday, 2 April).

The final stages of this historic race were described in *Motor Cycle News*, dated 21 June 1961:

Mike Hailwood – one of the very few men ever to win four TT replicas in one week – is getting closer and closer to the hat trick, three victories in one week. We watch his progress through the signalling points. He successfully negotiates the last climb of the Mountain, and a few minutes later he sweeps round Kate's Cottage, with the crowds waving and cheering.

...he is home! The 21-year-old ace from Oxford is home to record the first British Senior TT victory on a British machine since Ray Amm's success in 1954, the first over-100mph race average on a Norton. What a celebration there'll be tonight at Geoff Duke's Arragon Hotel, where Mike and his Ecurie Sportive team have their headquarters.

Just some of the competition Mike faced on his way to winning his first World Championship (the 250cc) in 1961. This May 1961 Hockenheim shot shows Tarquinio Provini (Moto Morini, 143); Jim Redman (Honda, 107); Kunimitsu Takahashi (Honda, 100) and Gary Hocking (MV 111).

Senior TT – 6 laps – 226.4 miles

1st	M. Hailwood (Norton)
2nd	B. McIntyre (Norton)
3rd	T. Phillis (Norton twin)
4th	A. King (Norton)
5th	R. Langston (Matchless)
6th	T. Godfrey (Norton)

Tommy Robb aboard a production Honda CR93 at Oulton Park in 1963. Tommy raced against Mike for many years aboard a variety of bikes including NSU, Honda, Bultaco and Yamaha, plus Geoff Monty's famous GMS (Geoff Monty Special).

Tommy Robb

One of Mike Hailwood's closest racing buddies was Ulsterman Tommy Robb, who is also unique in being the only rider during the 1960s to have ridden factory bikes for both Honda and Yamaha.

Tommy was born in Belfast, Northern Ireland, on 14 October 1934. His father, Tommy senior, was a well-known motorcycle sport official and was at one stage MCUI (Ulster Centre) President.

The Robb family lived on the south side of Belfast and, together with life-long friend Sammy Miller (who hailed from the opposite side of the Ulster capital), Tommy junior and Sammy rode pedal cycles prior to their motorcycle days.

Tommy's baptism in motorcycle sport came in 1951 when he competed on a 197cc Villiers-engined James Captain in a local trial.

Subsequently, the same bike was used for grass track racing, where the young Tommy won a handicap award in April 1952.

Then, in 1955, he entered his first road race, at Kirkistown Airfield on a 197cc Sun. Soon he was spotted by Belfast racing sponsor Terry Hill, which led to Tommy riding one of Hill's rapid NSU Sportmax machines – leading to a third place finish in the 1957 Ulster Grand Prix, and runner-up behind MV's Tarquinio Provini in the same event the following year.

Next, in 1959, the English dealer/entrant Geoff Monty not only provided Tommy with the famous GMS (Geoff Monty Special), but also a couple of Manx Nortons and later still a twin-cam Ducati 125cc single.

However, Tommy remained in Ulster, travelling to all the British mainland and continental European events from his Belfast home. The Monty connection spanned 1951–61, though the 1960 season had a section missing due to Tommy breaking his neck in the fog at Windy Corner on Geoff's G50 Matchless on the first morning of TT practice.

In 1961 came a works 125cc Bultaco, Tommy having tested one of these bikes in Spain the previous year. Then came the really big one – the offer of a Honda contract. Tommy signed for the Japanese company during the winter of 1961. His first race for Honda came in the Spanish GP in May 1962 (he finished fifth on the new, but outclassed, 50cc single). He was much more successful in the 125cc and above classes, finishing the season third in the 125cc championship table behind teammates Luigi Taveri and Jim Redman. But the undoubted highlight of the 1962 season was victory on home ground in the 250cc Ulster Grand Prix – he was also runner-up in the 350cc event on one of the new 285cc fours.

A little known fact is that Tommy finished in the first six placings in the 50, 125, 250 and 350cc World Championship tables that year, a performance not matched by any other rider.

But he feels that his best result in 1962 was winning the 350cc Finnish GP. He recalls this meeting: 'as one of the slipperiest events in which I have ever ridden, Mike Hailwood crashing his MZ in a big way, but luckily getting away with it'.

1963 was also spent as a factory Honda rider, but then in the spring of 1964, with no warning, both Tommy and teammate Kunimitsu Takahashi had their contracts terminated. Tommy recalls:

I never found out the real reason, but I enjoyed my period with Honda and I feel that my world championship placings do not belittle either the Honda name or my own.

Next came what Tommy says was 'a wonderful experience riding works Yamahas RD56s in 1964'. But Tommy suffered plug oiling problems, which rather stunted his spell with the company. Then it was back to the ranks of the privateers with a pair of new Bultacos, a marque he was to campaign for several years before switching to a Seeley G50. The high point of this latter machine was finishing fourth in the 1970 500cc World Championship.

The final race in Tommy's long career came aboard a 500 Yamaha in September 1973, which appropriately he won and in the process was crowned 'King of Kirkistown'. So he both began and ended his racing days at the same venue.

McIntyre's Mallory

After a disappointing week in the Isle of Man, Bob McIntyre's luck turned at Mallory Park a couple of days after the Senior TT, on Sunday 18 June, where in what were described as 'perfect conditions of summer sunshine', he well and truly beat TT winners Phil Read and Mike to win both the 350 and 500cc finals. In fact, Mike didn't win a single race that day, finishing third in the 250cc event on his FB Mondial (behind the Hondas of Phillis and Redman).

In the early stages of the 500cc race, Mike was well down the field, but pulled through to take third place behind Bob and Alastair King. But just

Mike with his privately-entered 499cc Norton at Quarry Corner, Castle Combe, on the way to winning the 500cc final at the Wessex Centre National Road Races.

when he looked set for second spot, his Norton's engine tightened up at the Hairpin and he crashed at low speed.

Dutch and Belgian rounds

It was then off to continental Europe to dispute the Dutch and Belgian rounds of the World Championship series. Traditionally the Dutch round had fine weather, and so it proved in 1961, the meeting, held at Assen, being a favourite for riders and spectators alike. The circuit, constructed purely for racing and first used in 1956, was unique in as much as it was built for motorcycling and not cars. The lap measured 4.64 miles and was situated among the flat sandy heathland so typical of northern Holland.

One newspaper of the period described the setting for the 1961 races:

The sun's shining brilliantly from an almost cloudless sky and there's a stiff breeze to keep the crowd cool and to flutter the long line of flags that top the pits. And what a crowd! The multitude here makes the spectators that flock to the Isle of Man look like a mere trickle. The magnificent vantage points that surround this circuit are absolutely packed and an hour ago the traffic jams leading to the course were over four miles long... well over 150,000 will have paid to see the racing today.

It was very much a case of high temperatures and high speeds. The first race of the day was the 250cc event. Here Mike and Bob McIntyre stamped their authority on a race which saw all the official Honda riders except Redman fall by the wayside. In a blistering display of sheer speed Mike won, in the process hoisting the lap record (previously held by Provini on the Morini) to 87.70mph.

250cc Dutch TT – 17 laps – 81.33 miles
1st   M. Hailwood (Honda)
2nd   B. McIntyre (Honda)
3rd   J. Redman (Honda)
4th   S. Grassetti (Benelli)
5th   F. Stastny (Jawa)
6th   F. Ito (Yamaha)

Although there was a 350cc race, Mike didn't ride, due to a mileage limit imposed by the FIM. So the races he chose to ride were the 125cc and 500cc events. In the 125 event a race-long duel transpired, with Tom Phillis and Mike trading places all the way around the circuit. But when the pair were lapping a rider, he fell in front of them. Phillis took to the grass and managed to avoid the fallen machine, whereas Mike cranked his Honda twin over at too acute an angle and slid off. He was uninjured, but unable to continue.

In the 500cc race on his Norton Mike didn't win, but came home runner-up behind the man who did, MV's Gary Hocking.

Spa Francorchamps

In Belgium, eight days later, the 500cc story was much the same, with Mike again finishing runner-up to Hocking and the MV four.

The Spa Francorchamps circuit, 8.76 miles in length, was situated in the forests and hills of the beautiful Ardennes region in eastern Belgium near the German border, and was one of the most famous and spectacular racing venues in the world. It was also a very fast course and this proved a problem for Mike Hailwood's 1960 four-cylinder 250 Honda, which had 'played up' during the practice sessions – a problem which continued into the race. The best Mike could do in the race was finish third, headed by the official Honda team duo of Jim Redman and Tom Phillis. In the 125cc race, after a good start, Mike soon dropped out with engine trouble. There was no 350cc event in Belgium.

Although Hondas completely dominated the 250cc World Championship hunt, there was certainly no lack of interest in the class, as after the Belgian

GP Mike, Tom Phillis and Jim Redman all topped the table with 26 points apiece.

Both Mike and John Hartle's two-fifty fours were then sent to Honda's European headquarters in Rotterdam for 'tuning' after both experienced troubles in Belgium. This meant that Mike had to revert to his single-cylinder FB Mondial for Brands Hatch on 9 July and Castle Combe on 15 July – but he won both 250cc races anyway! At Brands he wasn't so fortunate on his larger mounts, finishing fourth in the 350cc (AJS) and then crashing his 500 Norton in the 1000cc race.

Although he managed to win on the Norton at Castle Combe, in the 350cc event, his Ducati again gave trouble and, as the *MCN* report said: 'the Ducati twin slowed until he (Mike) toured in to retire'.

East Germany

The next event was the East German GP at the Sachsenring. The 5.2-mile road circuit had been completely resurfaced and modified to bring it up to the World Championship standard demanded by the FIM. Situated in the industrial province of Saxony, near the ancient twin towns of Hohenstein-Ernstthal, the Sachsenring was the scene of many pre-war German Grand Prix and in 1961 was making history, because it was to be used for a World Championship road race meeting, the first time such an event had been held behind the Iron Curtain since the series had been launched for the 1949 season.

In the 125cc race Mike again experienced troubles, this time concerning the ignition on his twin-cylinder Honda.

In the 250cc event Mike set the fastest practice lap at 3 minutes 35.7 seconds, followed by the MZ twin of Walter Brehme with 3 minutes 36.3 seconds. In the race the Englishman was never headed. In fact, in Mike's pit Bill Webster, at the end of the ninth lap, gave him a signal which told Mike that he was easily in control of the situation. He had such a lead that he was able to sit up and shrug his shoulders, much to the amusement of the crowd. And by the end his victory was complete – and with it he had taken a firm lead in the championship.

250cc East German GP – 15 laps – 81.33 miles

1st	M. Hailwood (Honda)
2nd	J. Redman (Honda)
3rd	K. Takahashi (Honda)
4th	T. Phillis (Honda)
5th	A. Shepherd (MZ)
6th	W. Musiol (MZ)

The 500cc race was the last of the day, held over 20 laps (108.44 miles). Mike yet again finished runner-up to the lone MV Agusta of Gary Hocking.

In early August, it was announced that Mike's 350 Ducati Desmo twin had been added to the two 250cc models already acquired by John Surtees.

At the British Championship meeting at Oulton Park on Monday 7 August 1961, Mike won on his 1960 Honda four, sharing a new class lap record with John Hartle at 86.43mph (the old record had been held by Mike on his FB Mondial at 83.53mph – which gives an idea of just how much more competitive the Japanese machine was).

250cc British Championship Oulton Park – 20 laps – 55.22 miles

1st	M. Hailwood (Honda)
2nd	J. Hartle (Honda)
3rd	J. Dixon (Adler)
4th	G. Smith (FB Mondial)
5th	T. Robb (GMS)
6th	A. Shepherd (Aermacchi)

In the 350cc race, Mike suffered carburettor trouble and retired, whereas in the 500cc class Mike was third behind Derek Minter (Norton) and Fred Neville (Matchless).

British Championships, Oulton Park, Monday 7 August 1961. John Hartle (5) and Mike (1) battle for the lead on their 250cc four-cylinder Hondas. Mike won, John finished second.

Ulster GP

For the Ulster GP on Saturday 12 August, Mike had both his Hondas back in action (the 125 twin having been away in Rotterdam for remedial work). And at least Mike was able to post a finish on the smallest Honda, albeit a fifth, in a race won by Takahashi. Again the 350cc event was not contested. So with the lunch break over, the 250s came out to play. Yet again Honda dominated. Bob McIntyre was in top form and for once his Honda four held together and the Scot ran out the winner, also setting a new class record of 96.94mph. Mike was second, Redman third, Phillis fourth and MZ-mounted Shepherd fifth. In the 500cc race Mike scored yet another runner-up position behind Hocking to consolidate second spot in the championship table.

In the 23 August issue of *Motor Cycle News*, a front page headline asked the question: 'MV for Mike?', the article going on to say:

> *Strong rumours from Italy and England indicate that Mike Hailwood may be mounted on works MV Agusta fours for both the 350 and 500cc classes of the Italian Grand Prix at Monza on Sunday September 3rd.*

But before September came a couple of British short circuit meetings: Brands Hatch on 20 August, which saw Mike win the 350cc race on his AJS and retire when leading in the 500cc on his Norton, after suffering a broken exhaust; and Aberdare Park, where Mike won both the 350 and 500cc races on 26 August – breaking both lap records for the tiny Welsh parkland circuit in the process.

Traditionally, Monza in Italy held the honour of being the final meeting in the World Championship season, but not so in 1961, when the Swedish and Argentinian events were to be held later in the year.

The circuit was the traditional 3.57-mile ultra-fast course. This was very flat and called for sheer speed rather than road holding but, as with all fast circuits, close and fast racing was possible, with slipstreaming being very important.

And, yes, the rumours had been true – Mike was to ride four-cylinder MV Agustas in both the 350 and 500cc races. He therefore decided to miss the 125cc event – which in any case he had openly said he disliked – due to his increasing weight.

During the 250cc race, Mike showed why he was favourite to win the championship that year, not only finishing runner-up (behind Redman), but also setting a new lap record at 114.06mph.

But of course it was the bigger classes that everyone had their eyes on. How would Mike fare on the MV? Would he be able to match Gary Hocking, who had already clinched the 500cc title and was a whisker away from taking the 350cc too?

The 350cc race came first. Mike had been fastest in practice, having, as *MCN* reported: 'taken to the scarlet "fire engine" like a duck to water'. He had lapped at 1 minute 54.4 seconds – faster than the old 'dolphin' record set by Hocking a year earlier but not so good as Libero Liberati's 'dustbin' record put up in 1956 on a Gilera. In the race the two MVs simply cleared off from the opposition, which included works entries from Benelli (1), Jawa (2) and Bianchi (5). In this first encounter Hocking came out on top, but Mike still put in an excellent showing.

350cc Italian GP – 27 laps – 96.41 miles
1st   G. Hocking (MV Agusta)
2nd   M. Hailwood (MV Agusta)
3rd   G. Havel (Jawa)
4th   A. Shepherd (Bianchi)
5th   S. Grassetti (Benelli)
6th   H. Anderson (Norton)

OFFICIAL PROGRAMME 2s.

CADWELL PARK
INTERNATIONAL ROAD RACES
10 September 1961

MOTOR CYCLE
YOUR FASTEST WAY TO THE FACTS · THURSDAY 9d

In the 500cc race it was Hocking v Hailwood again. In training Gary had lapped in 1 minute 46.6 seconds, beating all previous motorcycle records for Monza. Mike was two seconds slower, but a full five seconds from the fastest single-cylinder rider.

Right from the start it was a tremendous duel between the two MV riders, the lead swapping places several times. Then, on the 31st lap, Hocking slid off his MV and Mike was left to canter home the winner after what *MCN* said was 'a fine ride'. It was remarkable, I would say, for his first race on the big MV, as in effect he had outfoxed the existing champion.

250cc World Champion
In a sun-drenched Swedish Grand Prix on 17 September, held over the four-mile Kristianstad circuit, Mike won the 250cc race on his four-cylinder Honda to clinch his and Honda's first World Championship title. But this came only after a titanic struggle with his nearest challenger, Jim Redman, which ended when Redman overdid things and crashed his Honda while leading. Jim remounted to finish fourth.

Surprisingly, the Czech veteran Franta Stastny (Jawa) won the 350cc race, after both Mike and Gary Hocking had struck problems with their MVs.

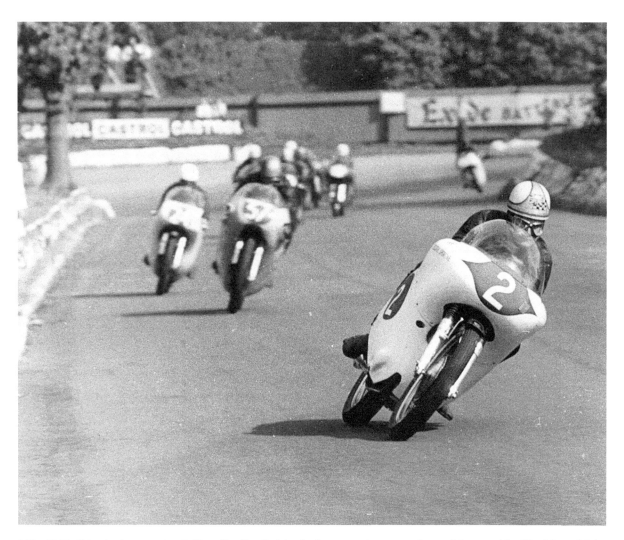

Mike (AJS, 2) leads the field in the 350cc event at the Mallory Park Race of the Year meeting on Sunday 24 September 1961. Over 60,000 spectators crammed into the small Leicestershire circuit to see Mike win from similarly-mounted Alan Shepherd and Phil Read (Norton).

Mike finally finished the race in seventh position, with Hocking 13th. Mike's troubles stemmed from a missed gear change when he had bent valves in the MV's engine. Hocking's problem was magneto.

Over 60,000 spectators, a record, crammed into the compact Mallory Park circuit on Sunday 24 September 1961 to see that circuit's first-ever international meeting. There was no doubt many had come to see double World Champion Gary Hocking. In fact, as the *MCN* race report stated: 'the only time his rivals were on level terms was when the riders formed up on the grid for when the flag dropped, Gary went'.

Mike rode – *MCN* said 'toiled' – hard in both the 500cc and the main Race of the Year, but he couldn't match the MV's speed (Mike was back on his Bill Lacey-tuned Norton) and had to be content with two second places, well ahead of his Norton and Matchless rivals.

However, in the 350cc class Mike gained some consolation by winning on his 7R AJS machine. Even though the MV had been the big attraction, informed observers could see that, except for this, Mike was the top man at Mallory, outdistancing men who only a few months before had been his equal in the bigger classes.

350cc Mallory Park – 25 laps – 33.75 miles
1st   M. Hailwood (AJS)
2nd   A. Shepherd (AJS)
3rd   P. Read (Norton)
4th   R. Mayhew (AJS)
5th   D. Shorey (Norton)
6th   D. Degens (Norton)

Another 1961 Race of the Year meeting shot, this time with Mike aboard his 499cc Norton. (Note the MV front brake.)

In the same week as Mallory Park, Mike had been presented with a superbly accurate miniature Manx Norton, made from odd bits of brass, copper, dural and wood, and complete with tiny chains and fully-spoked racing rims. It was presented on Thursday 21 September 1961 by Norton managing director Alec Skinner, as a memento of his 100.60mph Senior TT win on a similar machine earlier that year.

A quartet at Aintree

'A day to remember' was how *Motor Cycle News* reporter Brian Caldecott described the Aintree international meeting held on Saturday 30 September 1961. The reason? Mike's 'magnificent display' in winning all four major races on his FB Mondial, AJS and Norton machinery. And with stars such as Derek Minter, Phil Read, Tony Godfrey and Lewis Young around it wasn't simply a case of sitting astride the machinery and twisting the throttle. That day no-one could touch Mike. He was in a class of his own.

At Oulton Park a week later, Mike also won the 250 and 500cc races (FB Mondial and Norton respectively). But in the 350cc class after winning his heat, he and his AJS missed the final due to a 'frightful mix-up' which resulted in several top riders, including Phil Read and Jack Brett, missing the start. This state of affairs was caused by the organisers not following their own 'Final Instructions', which clearly stated that the 350cc final would be run after the heats for the Dave Chadwick Trophy event. Instead, it was run before – over half an hour before its scheduled time.

The British racing season ended with a meeting at Brands Hatch on Sunday 8 October 1961. In this Mike again had mixed fortunes, winning the 250cc (FB Mondial) while coming third (behind Derek Minter and Phil Read) in the 500cc final. Mike's AJS went sick even before he reached the start line in the 350cc final and then refused to start when he elected to ride it in the last race of the day (1000cc event).

After Brands Hatch, Mike flew out to Milan in Italy on Monday 9 October and from there on to the MV factory at Cascina Costa, Gallerate. The purpose of this visit was that Mike had been asked to ride works MVs in both the 125 and 500cc classes at Zaragosa in Spain – the last international road race of the 1961 season – on Sunday 15 October. It also became evident that Mike's old supporter, Bill Webster, was still doing his best to promote Mike's interests. It was Bill, in fact, who had been instrumental in getting Count Agusta to let Mike ride the 125cc MV in Spain; the bike being one raced by world champion Carlo Ubbiali the year before.

After Spain, Mike 'hoped' to be racing at an international meeting scheduled to take place in California on Sunday 5 November. The organisers had written to Mike and he was then in the process of finalising details. If he was to go, it was thought his most likely mount was a Norton for the 500cc class.

Zaragosa

The first race of the day over the short, tree-lined park circuit at Zaragosa was for 125cc machines over 40 laps. From the start Mike went into the lead, heading a pack comprising Francesco Villa (Ducati), Luigi Taveri (Honda), Ricardo Quintanilla, Paco Gonzalez and Johnny Grace (all three on factory Bultacos). Unfortunately an oil pipe on the engine split, and Mike slid off with an oil-saturated rear tyre. The race victory eventually went to Villa.

In the 500cc race, Mike was in a class of his own, and, going faster and faster, he shattered Carlo Bandirola's MV lap record time and time again.

So why had the Count wanted Mike to race in Spain?

The answer is to be found in the sales of MV's standard production motorcycles, which were built in that country under licence for the lucrative Spanish market. It should be remembered that Ducati and Moto Guzzi also had similar plants; even the British engine specialists Villiers and the Amal carburettor concern had Spanish production facilities during the 1950s and 1960s, as under Franco's rule, motorcycle imports were forbidden; hence the healthy Spanish motorcycle industry.

After Spain Mike travelled to the United States for the USMC (United

The early 1961 version of the factory Honda RC143 125cc twin which was presented by Honda to the Murray's Motorcycle Museum in the Isle of Man in tribute to Mike Hailwood's victory in the TT that year.

States Motorcycling Club) FIM-sanctioned international road race meeting, held at the Willow Springs circuit, Rosamund, California, in early November.

Riding his own Norton (shipped out from England), Mike completely outclassed the opposition, winning at record speed and setting a new lap record for the 2.5-mile circuit situated in the Antelope Valley some 2,000 feet above sea level in a near-desert region.

Paddy Driver, who travelled out with Mike and rode his spare Norton, was not so fortunate. After experiencing engine problems in practice, Paddy was taken ill during the race and had to retire.

Mike and Paddy had both hoped to borrow Hondas for the 250cc race but, in spite of the fact that Mike had just won the 250cc world title for the Japanese company, their American distributors refused to provide any assistance, even though several fours were ridden in the race by American riders.

And so 1961 came to an end, but not before, on his return to Great Britain, Mike won the *Motor Cycle News* 'Man of the Year' award, beating motocross star Dave Bickers (who had won the previous year) and sidecar racing star Chris Vincent, who was third in this popular readers' poll.

Hopes that Mike would also pull off the BBC Television 'Sportsman of the Year' award were dashed when he could only finish fourth. Even so, it had been an absolutely fantastic year, with not only a host of victories and new records, but also that TT triple and a first world title. Also, for 1962, there was the prospect of racing four-cylinder MV Agustas, with every hope of being in serious contention for the blue riband 500cc world title.

Chapter 6

The MV years

NOW A FULL member of the Italian MV Agusta team, Mike could look forward to 1962 with confidence, at least as far as the World Championship series was concerned. Things were less clear as regards non-championship racing. In the past, he had the use of a wide variety of bikes. But with the MV contract, father Stan had sold many of these former mounts. Even so, it was still possible for Mike to call upon his AJS and Norton machinery. And as events were to unfold both Dr Joe Ehrlich and Fron Purslow were to provide EMC and Benelli bikes for the 125 and 250cc class respectively. But Mike's previous stock of Ducati and FB Mondial motorcycles had gone.

For some time, Mike's racing had been run very much on the basis that he, rather than Stan, paid the bills – paying his way was now the order of things in Hailwood équipe. But, of course, as related in Chapter 4, Stan was still very much involved, not only as Mike's biggest fan, but also providing useful advice and guidance.

In many ways Mike now viewed Stan more as a 'friend rather than a father'.

Mike had hoped that MV, or even Honda, would provide him with a bike for the United States GP (still a non-championship event) to be held at Daytona on 4 February 1962. However, as early as 17 January *Motor Cycle News* was able to report: 'Hailwood won't have MV's at Daytona'.

So what was he to do?

Disappointment at Daytona
A year earlier, Mike had been a non-finisher at Daytona. And,

Mike piloting the Fron Purslow-sponsored Benelli 250 dohc single to victory in the opening day of the British road racing season at Mallory Park, 1 April 1962. Later, on the same machine, Mike was destined for fourth in the 250cc TT behind a trio of works Hondas, only to retire on the last lap with engine trouble.

again Norton mounted, he hoped for better things in the 1962 event. Hopes were high when Mike streaked into the lead of the Senior event over the 3.1-mile circuit. With Tony Godfrey second and Ron Grant third, a British rider/British bike victory seemed on the cards: the trio were well in front of Honda riders Kunimitsu Takahashi and Gichi Suzuki. For 18 laps the British trio (all riding Nortons) were the undisputed masters, but then Godfrey had to pull into the pits with a slipping clutch. Mike was riding with all his usual verve and ferocity and the 95mph plus lap speed had really staggered the Honda camp.

The heat and unrelenting pace were taking their toll, however, and a seized big-end put Mike out with a mere four laps left. Now British hopes rested on Grant, only to be dashed again when his engine went sour on the last lap. This left victory to Takahashi and Honda, who previously had seemed totally out of the picture.

When Mike returned to the UK in mid-February, he travelled aboard the new liner SS *France*. His well-known fully-equipped transporter (originally purchased by Stan), with fitted bunks, a washbasin, work drawers and space enough for some eight motorcycles, was put on sale for the princely sum of £100. Prospective buyers were advised to write to Mike c/o King's of Oxford. In addition, the services of mechanics Jim Adams and John Dadley had been dispensed with now that Mike would mainly be riding other people's bikes.

At the end of February, with the British racing season only weeks away, rumour had it that Mike would be racing an Aermacchi at Mallory Park on Sunday 1 April.

On Monday 19 March 1962, Mike, described by *Motor Cycle News* as 'Britain's roving motorcycle ambassador-at-large' raced his 500cc four-cylinder MV Agusta to victory at Modena in Italy, ahead of teammate Remo Venturi on a sister machine. Mike finished half-a-mile ahead of the Italian, who in turn was well ahead of Silvio Grassetti riding a 350cc Bianchi twin; Phil Read was fourth on a Norton.

Mike completed the 68.5-mile race in 54 minutes 42.5 seconds, at a race average of 75mph. He set the fastest lap of 76.1mph. He also rode a works MV 250cc twin, but was forced to retire with ignition troubles.

With only four days to go before the British season kicked off at Mallory Park, everyone woke up on Wednesday morning 28 March 1962 to read the *Motor Cycle News* headline: 'Hailwood rides Benelli!'. The 250cc world champion had been entered at Mallory on Bill Webster's Aermacchi (Bill being the British importer at the time), but the story told readers that in fact Mike would be racing Fron Purslow's recently acquired 1961 ex-works dohc

OFFICIAL PROGRAMME 2s. 6d.

DAILY MAIL

International Motor Cycle
Race of the Year

MALLORY **PARK**

26 Sept. 1965

Motor
Cycle THE COMPLETE
MAGAZINE
THURSDAY 1s. 3d.

Benelli single. Originally John Hartle was to have ridden the bike, but unhealed injuries ruled him out. Derek Minter then took over, but he stepped aside (due to the imminent arrival of a Honda-sponsored four cylinder machine), allowing Mike to take up the offer the day before his 22nd birthday. It was also reported that Mike was 'almost certain to be riding the Benelli at Silverstone on Saturday week – and for the remainder of the season'.

The Mallory opener

And so to Mallory itself on Sunday 1 April 1962. Even before racing began, Bob McIntyre had crashed his works 285cc Honda four, putting himself out of the meeting.

After two exciting 250cc heats, won by Mike on the Benelli and Percy Tait (Aermacchi), the final was expected to see Jim Redman (Honda four) make a challenge, but a broken rev counter drive meant that he had to ride by ear – not good on such a high-revving engine. The result was that Mike rocketed away into an unchallenged lead from the start of the 15-lap final, setting the fastest lap in 59.2 seconds, a speed of 82.09mph.

In his heat, Mike's AJS was forced out with ignition trouble. The 500cc race saw Mike and his Norton clear off at high speed with Alan Shepherd (Matchless), Derek Minter (Norton) and Phil Read (Norton) making up the top four places.

Six days after Mallory Park came Silverstone on Saturday 7 April. Except in the 500cc race, which he won, Mike had to accept second best to Minter (EMC) in the 125cc class, Minter again (Norton) in the 350cc and Jim Redman (Honda four) in the 250cc race. Mike rode EMC, AJS and Benelli respectively.

After that Mike left for Italy, where at Imola on 15 April he retired on the Benelli with ignition trouble, while on the larger four-cylinder MV in the main 30-lap 93.5-mile Shell Gold Cup 500cc race he put in the fastest lap at 85.72mph, but suffered from blocked carburettor jets, which eventually meant he finished fifth, a lap behind the winner, MV teammate Gary Hocking. There was no 350cc event.

Easter weekend

Then came the Easter weekend, with Mike taking in Brands Hatch on Friday 20 April, Snetterton on Sunday 22 April and Thruxton on the following day. The first meeting, watch by an estimated 45,000 spectators, was dominated by Derek Minter, who scored a hat-trick of wins compared to just one for Mike (on his AJS in the 350cc race).

Count Domenico Agusta

Count Domenico Agusta was a legend in his own lifetime, but in truth very few people *really knew* the man. Like Stan Hailwood, he was a man driven by the need to succeed in whatever he did. He ruled a business empire with a rod of iron. And until his death in early 1971, there were no conventional commercial directors at MV, only the remainder of the family. And certainly the Count was autocratic in the extreme. There was no doubt in anybody's mind – rider, employee, journalist or rival manufacturer – that what the Count said, went at MV Agusta.

As Mike was once to recall:

> *...it would be difficult to get five shillings out of the factory without his personal endorsement, he has his finger firmly on the pulse; nothing happens there that he doesn't know about. Every action, every move through the works has to have his personal signature before it is approved and accepted. Nobody dares make a decision without consulting him.*

This unwillingness to delegate any responsibility was the reason why he – and the organisation he controlled – often fell behind the clock. John Surtees confirms this view:

> *...often when I would visit the factory, probably after coming especially from England, I would be kept waiting, sometimes for hours on end. ...once it was three days before I got to meet him. I'm convinced that he was showing me who was the boss. Every move he made – everything concerning MV Agusta – seemed designed to give him psychological advantage.*

Once described as a cross between actor Humphrey Bogart and a Mafia godfather, the Count was a short, stocky man, but, because of his manner, he always gave the impression of being bigger than he actually was. He even had a special desk in his office, which was raised from the ground so that he could look down at those he was receiving. Because of his immense workload – he would usually arrive at 10.30am and not depart until the early hours of the next morning (except for a couple of hours at lunchtime) – he ensured that everything was designed to help smooth the running of the business. His home was a villa within the factory grounds, only a couple of minutes walk from his office. Mike once said:

> *...he has a swivel chair at his desk so that he can spin round to get at the radio-telephone link that he has with his helicopters, or to slide over to the battery of telephones that never seem to stop ringing.*

A little-known fact is that the Count hated flying – even though Agusta was primarily an aviation concern both before and after World War Two. Instead, he preferred to travel on his big yacht, his private train, or by any of his dozen or so chauffeur-driven limousines. Because of this and his workaholic lifestyle, he rarely watched his motorcycles in action, except at the local Monza circuit. He never visited the Isle of Man, even though he rated the event so highly that he commissioned full-size replicas of the silver trophies won by his riders over the world's longest and most demanding circuit.

Domenico, the eldest of four sons born to Giovanni and Giuseppina Agusta, was born in Palermo, Sicily, in 1907. He was a mere 21 years of age when his father died prematurely, aged 48. The young Domenico was thrown headlong into running the company his father had built up to become one of Italy's leading aviation concerns. When one also realises that his father's untimely death coincided with the most fearful industrial depression of the 20th century, the fact that the Agusta empire survived the storm suggests a natural flair for the rigours of commercial life on the part of Domenico.

During the 1930s, with the rise of Fascism in Italy under its leader Benito Mussolini, Agusta, like many other industrial companies, decided to take military contracts rather than risk going out of business. When Italy finally joined the war on 10 June 1940, the Gallerate-based company was swept into the war effort and grew rapidly – massive production requiring a much larger workforce. But when the Allies landed in Sicily, before moving on to the southern tip of the Italian mainland during the autumn of 1943, the shrewd Count could clearly see the writing on the wall and began to prepare business plans for the coming peace. He chose to develop powered two-wheelers – not just motorcycles, but scooters and mopeds too. At first the new company, MV (Meccanica Verghera), used two-stroke engines, but they soon made the switch to the more sophisticated four-stroke, both for its series production roadsters and its competition machines, the latter including both road racers and off-road bikes at first.

Many commentators have said that the original reason why Count Domenico Agusta went racing was his love of the sport. This is incorrect, as during the late 1940s and early 1950s he went racing purely for publicity purposes, to promote his fledgling motorcycle marque. However, later, with more wealth at his disposal thanks to the rebirth of the aviation sector of the Agusta empire, he saw racing as a way of expressing his own power. He ran his race team largely from his business offices, directing the proceedings as a general would do, many miles away from the scene of the battle. His loyal lieutenants, men like Nello Pagani and Arturo Magni, would be at the circuit with the riders and other team personnel. From the mid-1950s, thanks to a lucrative licence agreement from the American Bell helicopter firm, Agusta's business expanded greatly. However, the motorcycle arm (both racing and series production street bikes) was not neglected and for many years provided a significant part of the group's annual turnover. By the end of the 1960s the Count was presiding over an industrial empire employing in excess of 5,000 workers. Then, on 2 February 1971, while visiting Milan on business, and shortly before his 64th birthday, Count Domenico Agusta suffered a fatal heart attack. And while it was announced that Corrado Agusta, the 47-year-old survivor of the family of four brothers, was to take over the reins of what was by then the world's second-largest helicopter manufacturer and the most famous name in post-war motorcycle racing, things would never be the same again. The real powerhouse and driving force of the Agusta brand had passed on.

350cc Brands Hatch – 10 laps –
27.91 miles

1st	M. Hailwood (AJS)
2nd	D. Minter (Norton)
3rd	P. Read (Norton)
4th	A. Shepherd (AJS)
5th	H. Anderson (AJS)
6th	R. Mayhew (AJS)

The 1962 350 and 500 MV fours (one of the larger-engined models is shown) as raced by Mike that year.

Mike was third on an EMC in the 125cc race, fifth on the Norton in the 500cc class (after encountering gearbox problems) and runner-up behind Minter (650 Norton twin) on his five-hundred Manx Norton in the 1000cc race.

Mike made his British MV debut at Snetterton on Easter Sunday 1962, winning both the 350 and 500cc on his Italian factory bikes. It was a feat he repeated the following day at Thruxton. *Motor Cycle News*, dated 25 April 1962, carried the headline: 'Happy Hailwood Tops Easter Parade on the MVs'. The article went on to say:

> *It's been a sport-dominated motorcycling Easter for thousands, with crowds at Snetterton and Thruxton enjoying a real holiday surprise package – the sight of the irrepressible Mike Hailwood rocketing round both courses on a brace of MV Agusta machines flown especially from Italy and shattering the existing records for the circuits in both Senior and Junior classes.*

At Snetterton, Mike raised his own 350cc lap record figure from 90.16mph to 92.55mph and then raised the 500cc record held by Derek Minter from 94.35mph to 96.21mph.

At Thruxton, in front of some 36,000 spectators, Mike swept to victory on his MV in the Commonwealth race at a new record speed of 82.23mph.

Writing in *Motor Cycle News* dated 2 May 1962 Mike said:

> *...after a very enjoyable Easter with the MVs, I'm off to the Continent for a few weeks and by the time you read this I shall have competed in the Austrian Grand Prix at Salzburg yesterday, and be on my way to Barcelona to compete in the Spanish Grand Prix – the first of the World Championship series this year – on Sunday. I'll be riding the two MV4s I used at Snetterton and Thruxton. From*

Two of Mike's strongest challenges in the 500cc class came from Phil Read (seen here winning the Senior Manx GP on a Norton in September 1960...

Spain I go to the French GP, compete at a meeting at Saar on May 20th, then come home for the TT practice in the Isle of Man. So I'll be missing the home meetings at Mallory Park, Brands Hatch, Aberdare and the North West 200. I must say I enjoy these meetings on the Continent. They always seem so much more carefree and happy-go-lucky than many of our sometimes over-organised meetings in England.

In the Austrian GP on 1 May (amid snow showers), Mike won the 500cc race on his bigger MV four, while on the 350cc version he came home second to Franta Stastny (Jawa) in the other race.

Then in Spain Mike finished fourth on his EMC (a 1961 model because he preferred the handling), but rued not having a 250cc model (there were no 350 or 500cc events) saying:

...out on the circuit in Montjuich Park (Barcelona) the 250 boys are busy practicing. I ought to be out there with them but I've no

machine in that class. I don't mind admitting that I should kick myself. Earlier in the season Honda made me an offer, but I turned it down.

After driving 1,000 miles in two days from Salzburg to Barcelona, Mike found all the hotels full. So as he said:

Joe (Dr Ehrlich) offered me a bed here (in his tent!). Tommy Robb lent me a duffle coat and for the first night I had that on plus a rain coat, three pullovers and an Anorak jacket and I could hardly move, but I'm enjoying it so much that I think I shall start camping myself. There's no worry about hotel accommodation and I can eat what I like.

...and Derek Minter, photographed after winning the 1962 250cc TT on a 1961 Honda four loaned by the British importers, Hondis Ltd.

At the French Grand Prix at Clermont-Ferrand, Mike was disputing the lead in the 125cc event on the EMC and putting up a tremendous performance against the might of the Honda team. But then it began to rain and in attempting to take the lead Mike crashed out, *Motor Cycle News* reporting that he went: 'sailing through the air to land in a swamp, from which he crawled out wet but unhurt!'

Unfazed by this, Mike journeyed to St Wendel for the Saar GP (not part of the championship calendar, but still a popular meeting) where he at last got an EMC victory. In his own words:

I must say I was very happy with the way the EMC buzzed around at St Wendel last Sunday. With Rex Avery and my old mate Paddy Driver following me home, it was a grand 1–2–3 for Dr Joe, and gave us all more confidence than ever in the de Havilland two-stroke.

The Isle of Man TT

The 1962 TT got under way with the news that Mike's MV teammate Gary Hocking had crashed early on in the practice week, badly damaging his machine (a 500cc), which then burst into flames and was completely destroyed. Fortunately, Gary's injuries were slight and he was soon back in action. Meanwhile, Mike was happier after his two MVs arrived, together with a spare engine, on Monday 28 May, the same day as Hocking's crash.

Early the next day Mike was out for practice on the 500 MV and then during the same session pulled into the pits to change his mount for the 125 EMC – proving yet again his ability to switch capacities and engine types with ease (the MV being a 499cc dohc four, the EMC a 124cc disc-valve two-stroke single).

Compared to the fabulous TT Mike had experienced the year previously, 1962 was to be very much an anti-climax.

Firstly, on Monday 4 June, Mike rode Fron Purslow's ageing two-fifty Benelli single. Riding like a man possessed, he managed to keep the Benelli up on the leaderboard. Then, when the fairing came loose, it was ripped off at his pit, enabling him to continue before suffering engine trouble, forcing his retirement.

Next, two days later, on Wednesday 6 June, he experienced more problems, this time aboard the EMC in the Ultra-Lightweight event – a broken gudgeon pin forcing him out. The only really bright spot, a magnificent victory (including setting a new class lap record of 101.58mph), came in the Junior TT on his four-cylinder MV. Sadly, the race was marred by the fatal crash of Tom Phillis, riding the new 285cc Honda four.

Junior (350cc) TT – 6 laps – 226.38 miles
1st   M. Hailwood (MV Agusta)
2nd   G. Hocking (MV Agusta)
3rd   F. Stastny (Jawa)
5th   R. Ingrim (Norton)
5th   M. Duff (AJS)
6th   H. Anderson (AJS)

On Friday 8 June, a combination of gearbox and clutch gremlins dropped Mike back to 12th in the Senior TT on his bigger MV Agusta. At the time, Geoff Duke questioned:

...why Mike, when handicapped by the lack of first gear, proceeded to throw away a certain second place by driving his clutch into the ground. I know that it must have been a great disappointment to him to find that, for reasons beyond his control, he was not able to do battle with Hocking, but there is always another day – and a championship to consider.

The 1962 Dutch TT and Mike on the EMC tails Honda-mounted Luigi Taveri. Mike finally finished fifth, with Taveri taking the race victory.

EMC

To trace the origin of EMC, one must go back to 1937 when Dr Joseph Ehrlich, then in his twenties, arrived in Great Britain from Austria seeking to further his career in the field of two-stroke engineering. Two years later came the first of his engines, but it took a further seven years of research to come up with a machine which would be a viable proposition in quantity production, and attract the city money that was needed to start the ball rolling. With the necessary backing acquired, Dr Ehrlich went into production in 1947 with his 350cc split-single two-stroke, which at the time was priced at a very competitive £157.

Operating from a factory in Park Royal, north-west London, EMC Ltd (Ehrlich Motor Company) produced a modest 10 to 12 machines per week. But even though the 80mph 350cc EMC – using an air-cooled single-cylinder engine with squared-off cylinder finning, 4-speed Burman footchange gearbox, telescopic front forks and duplex frame – had for its day an impressive specification (there was even an auto oiling system), sales never reached more than 500 units per year. The bike was simply too radical for the austerity of the immediate post-war era, and production was brought to a close in late 1952. The company folded in March 1953.

However, this was far from the end of either Dr Joe or EMC. The first EMC racer had appeared in 1946, with Les Archer riding a 250cc EMC to win the coveted Mellano Trophy in 1947.

The first in a long line of 125cc EMC racers was introduced in 1952, with use being made of an Austrian Puch air-cooled split-single two-stroke engine. The short open megaphone exhaust was responsible for an incredible din, and E.H. Burman, who finished sixth in the 1952 Ultra-lightweight TT, could be heard approaching from a distance of over five miles!

Disillusioned by the lack of success attained by his motorcycle manufacturing enterprise, Dr Joe then joined the Austin car company to assist with new vehicle development. While there he designed a twin split-single featuring four pistons for the then revolutionary Austin Mini. But Ehrlich's engine was deemed 'too revolutionary' by the Austin board and so never passed the prototype stage.

During the late 1950s, the British aircraft industry, due to a substantial fall-off in both military and commercial sales, was looking to diversify production into other fields. And like many others, the de Havilland company decided to move into the production of small capacity industrial engines, designing a 150cc two-stroke unit which proved a total disaster.

The man brought in to solve the problem was Dr Ehrlich. And in this he was successful, achieving results that de Havilland had previously thought unobtainable. Operating from the de Havilland works at Leavesden, north Watford, and promoted to small engine division chief, Dr Ehrlich proceeded to develop a series of small two-stroke engines. Based on a single-cylinder from the DKW three-cylinder, he adapted the design to suit a whole range of prototype vehicles, which included a 150cc 80mph bike, a 150cc scooter, a 150cc outboard motor and even a two-stroke dumper truck! The primary aim was to rival Villiers in commercial and motorcycle engine sales.

Then, in early 1959, the development team came up with a 125cc rotary disc induction engine of advanced design. This was clearly modelled around the existing MZ design. However, the liquid-cooled engine was equipped with a finned cylinder, as opposed to the bald MZ component, and this was produced at the local foundry, Browns of Hitchin.

In spring 1960 Dr Joe fitted this still experimental engine into one of the antiquated Puch frames that were last seen in the mid-1950s, but despite the indifferent handling early tests proved extremely promising.

All that was needed was a good rider, and Dr Joe found his man working as a toolmaker not 200 yards away in the main de Havilland factory. Rex Avery, an established Norton rider, was only too pleased to transfer to the small engine division and became the unofficial works rider.

The 54x54mm six-speed engine was a winner almost immediately and in original form put out a healthy 23.5bhp fitted with a 'C' (factory coding) barrel. This proved virtually unbeatable on the British short circuits with Rex Avery aboard throughout the 1960 season, at least when Mike Hailwood was not riding his works Ducati Desmo single.

During 1961 and 1962 Mike rode the 125cc EMC liquid-cooled two-stroke single, making his debut at the Spanish GP on 23 April 1961. After leading the race and setting a new lap record, Mike eventually finished fourth after the EMC's exhaust split. However, its potential was evident to everyone and, with a bit more good fortune, EMC could have been a major force, even at the highest level. Mike finished fifth in the 125cc World Championship table in 1962.

The original engine had an effective powerband of 2000rpm, but later engines, although giving 27bhp, had powerbands of only 800rpm, making them extremely difficult to ride. Another problem was vibration, which of course didn't help reliability.

The high point of the EMC single came in the 1962 Belgian GP, where Dr Joe's team finished a magnificent third, fourth and fifth (Paddy Driver, Mike and Rex Avery), with Mike taking third the following week in the West German Grand Prix. In 1963 the Japanese development went into overdrive, resulting in exotic designs such as a five-cylinder 125 Honda, a Suzuki twin and ultimately a 41bhp Yamaha V4. Dr Joe did build a twin to replace the single, but this proved unsuccessful.

During his stay at Leavesden, Dr Ehrlich produced, on a consultancy basis, designs for other factories. He also sketched out a 500cc liquid-cooled rotary disc induction square-four two-stroke. The drawing of this still survives to prove its existence on paper.

In 1965 the de Havilland group of companies was taken over by aero engine giants Rolls-Royce. This left Dr Ehrlich and his team high and dry, as one of the first moves Rolls-Royce made was to dissolve the small engine division. This meant Dr Joe now had to finance his own two-stroke research or retire.

He set up in his own small factory unit at Bletchley, Buckinghamshire. From there he carried out a number of development contracts, including racing outboard engines – and even an engine for a lawn mower! Then came a period in the 1970s when Dr Ehrlich turned his attention to Formula 3 racing cars, before returning once more in the next decade to his original love, motorcycles.

After a short-lived association with the ill-fated Waddon enterprise, Dr Joe was to taste perhaps his greatest moment of glory when English rider Andy Watts took his EMC-Rotax powered inline twin to a brilliant runner-up spot in the 1984 250cc British Grand Prix at Silverstone.

Dr Josef Ehrlich passed away in 2001.

Dr Joe Ehrlich with his development team at the de Havilland Engine Company in 1961. The man seated on the bike is racer Rex Avery.

Maybe, after such a superb 1961 TT, Mike was a bit frustrated by his lack of success this time around? Even so, the highlight of the week was generally agreed to have been the race-long scrap between Gary and Mike on their MVs in the Junior race.

Mike cracks two Mallory records

On Sunday 10 June, the Hocking v Hailwood battle continued, as *Motor Cycle News* commented: 'round three went in favour of Hailwood'. In fact it was Mike's day, as he set up new 350 and 500cc lap records on his MVs. Mike established an absolute motorcycle lap record in the 500cc race of 91.7mph, beating the old figure set the previous September by Hocking of 89.66mph, while the new 350cc one of 88.69mph smashed the previous figure of 87.41mph which he jointly held with Bob McIntyre. Mike also came second in the 250cc race on the Purslow Benelli. *MCN* again: 'Hailwood put up a magnificent fight, but his machine could not match the power of the faster Honda (ridden to victory by Jim Redman)'.

The next day, Bank Holiday Monday 11 June, a huge 50,000 crowd at Brands Hatch saw Mike drop his 350 MV and remount to finish the race. Mike had held the lead comfortably from Norton-mounted Phil Read for 17 of the 20 laps on the 2.65-mile circuit, when suddenly his machine spun on the exit of Druids Hill Bend, flinging him off. Unhurt, he quickly remounted and was still in the lead, but his gear lever had been bent and the MV jammed in third gear. He was eventually relegated to fourth spot. Mike's only other race at Brands was the 500cc event. In this he created a bit of history as it was the first-ever win at the circuit for a 500cc four-cylinder machine. Geoff Duke (Gilera) had been beaten in 1955 by John Surtees (Norton) and in turn Surtees (MV) had succumbed to Minter (Norton) a couple of years later. As *MCN* said in their 13 June 1962 issue: 'in this race nobody could approach Mike'.

Hocking quits

A week later, it was announced to a shocked audience that Gary Hocking, the existing 350 and 500cc world champion, had quit motorcycle racing. The reason why and what subsequently happened to Gary appears in a boxed section within this chapter. Gary had gone to see Count Agusta straight after the post-TT Mallory Park meeting for a discussion about the future. He then flew to his home in Bulawayo to meet his girlfriend Valerie Chorley before his decision was released to the press.

Gary Hocking was Mike's teammate at MV as the 1962 season began. However, Gary sensationally quit two wheels after the 1962 TT.

Paddy Driver (30) and Mike (2) during the 125cc Belgian GP at Spa Francorchamps. Both were riding British EMC liquid-cooled disc valve two-stroke singles.

Both Gary and Mike were due to travel to Italy and race at San Remo on Sunday 17 June, but industrial unrest at the Agusta works prevented machines being prepared. This meant that Mike, who had entered the 125cc race on an MV, did not compete, while on the Benelli single he was forced to retire on the seventh lap after one of his clip-on handlebars came loose.

From the unsuccessful San Remo trip, Mike spent a few days 'off duty' in the south of France with Paddy Driver and his wife Janet.

The big news at the Dutch TT, held over the Assen circuit in the north of the country, was that Mike's smaller MV four simply wasn't fast enough to stay with the 285cc Honda of Jim Redman. In fact, Mike found himself hounded in the early stages of the race by both Franta Stastny (Jawa) and Silvio Grassetti (Bianchi). The *Motor Cycle News* race report says:

Mike found himself with a real handful of trouble as he fought off Stastny's repeated challenges all round the 4.8-mile curves of the Van Drenthe circuit and tried hard to catch Grassetti at the same time. With the MV sounding rough and flat at times, Mike had to use all his skill to pass Grassetti three laps from home, but Redman was well up at the end of the 20-lap race and there was never any hope of catching him.

350cc Dutch TT – 20 laps – 95.75 miles
1st   J. Redman (Honda)
2nd   M. Hailwood (MV Agusta)
3rd   S. Grassetti (Bianchi)
4th   F. Stastny (Jawa)
5th   D. Minter (Norton)
6th   P. Read (Norton)

If Mike found the going tough in the 350cc event, the same could not be said of the 500cc race, in which the MV led from start to finish. Mike also set a new lap record of 89.76mph.

500cc Dutch TT – 20 laps – 95.75 miles
1st   M. Hailwood (MV Agusta)
2nd   D. Minter (Norton)
3rd   P. Read (Norton)
4th   A. Shepherd (Matchless)
5th   B. Schneider (Norton)
6th   T. Godfrey (Norton)

Mike also finished fifth in the 125cc event on the EMC. Mike commented that 'Assen is the finest semi-short circuit in the world'.

Spa Francorchamps

Start money became an issue for Mike. In the week before the Belgian GP at Spa Francorchamps he received a telegram saying 'regret unable to accept proposition to start MV 500'. Mike also went on to say:

> *...the Belgian GP circuit I think is far too fast and dangerous with its long sweeping bends, trees and houses all round it. It's the only circuit that I find really frightens me.*
>
> *...the EMC is going beautifully and the handling has been improved a lot. I really think we are now capable of putting the wind up the Hondas.*

Mike resolved the money issue and raced the big MV at Spa, this time winning from Alan Shepherd on his Matchless G50 single, with Tony Godfrey (Norton) third. Mike's fastest lap was 121.9mph, but even this wasn't fast enough to break the lap record. As for the 125cc race, EMC came third, fourth and fifth with Paddy Driver, Mike and Rex Avery respectively. On the final lap Mike's exhaust pipe broke off, letting Paddy Driver through to third. But it was still an excellent performance for Dr Joe and his tiny British team.

The following week, on Sunday 15 July, Mike rode the EMC to third place at the West German Grand Prix, held over the beautiful Solitude circuit just outside Stuttgart, watched by a vast crowd of over 300,000 spectators.

125cc West German GP – 9 laps – 63.8 miles
1st   L. Taveri (Honda)
2nd   T. Robb (Honda)
3rd   M. Hailwood (EMC)
4th   B. McIntyre (Honda)
5th   J. Grace (Bultaco)
6th   H. Anderson (Suzuki)

Solitude; length 7.1 miles.

The programme consisted of 50, 125 and 250cc solos, plus sidecars. Mike had been fastest in practice at Solitude on the EMC and could have done even better if he hadn't been slowed by a loose helmet strap, of all things.

Back in England

Next came three meetings back in the UK over two weeks during which Mike didn't win a single race. In fact, he had more than his fair share of problems – probably due to not having the services of a full-time UK-based mechanic. At Castle Combe his AJS suffered misfiring problems, while at Snetterton the AJS seized and he fell off the Norton. Then, at Oulton Park in early August, he was runner-up on the AJS in the 350cc race and third in the 500 on a Reg Dearden-loaned Norton. Sadly, this latter meeting saw the fatal accident of Bob McIntyre, who crashed in heavy rain on his Norton.

Only six days after Oulton Park came the Ulster GP and Dundrod on Saturday 11 August. Here Mike put on what *Motor Cycle News* said was: 'A cold-blooded demonstration of sheer skill and guts', as he 'hurled' the four-cylinder MV around the rain-swept Irish road circuit to win the 500cc race and push the lap record up to 99.99mph. In truth it was a remarkable performance, on roads that were wet in some sections of the course and dry

Mike on his way to victory during the 500cc Ulster Grand Prix in August 1962 with his works four-cylinder MV Agusta.

in others, and in a gusty wind that neared gale force, Mike lapped everyone except Alan Shepherd and Phil Read in second and third places. He also rode the 350 MV, but retired with engine trouble.

East Germany

At the Sachsenring, Mike showed that the latest two-fifty MZ was a match for the very best four-cylinder Honda machines, when during the 250cc East German Grand Prix the Englishman was locked in combat with Jim Redman's Japanese machine. At the end, although Mike shattered the class lap record, going round at 100.78mph, Jim got the flag by two-tenths of a second. But Honda had certainly been given a fright! Mike also finished runner-up (again to Redman) in the 350cc race, but it was clear that his MV was, as *Motor Cycle News* said: 'completely out-classed'.

Mike finished the day on a triumphant note, however, with victory in the 500cc race. He averaged 102.09mph and set a new lap record of 104.49mph. Alan Shepherd finished runner-up, with Austrian Norton rider Bertie Schneider third.

Clinching the 500cc crown

Monza, on Sunday 9 September, was very much about clinching the 1962 500cc world crown. But of course, Monza had other races: 50cc, 125cc, 250cc and 350cc. Mike had already been withdrawn from the 350cc contest – Count Agusta had finally thrown in the towel and did not want to be embarrassed on home ground. In the 125cc race Mike rode an EMC, but retired with a seized engine. He had no more luck in the 250cc event

Monza; length 3.57 miles.

when, after holding second spot for a while, his single-cylinder Benelli was outpaced and he eventually crashed without injury. The 500cc race, which Mike won to become 500cc champion for the first time, was really an anticlimax.

The Count had put Remo Venturi out on a second MV, and that was how they finished.

500cc Italian GP – 35 laps – 125.13 miles

1st	M. Hailwood (MV Agusta)
2nd	R. Venturi (MV Agusta)
3rd	S. Grassetti (Bianchi)
4th	P. Read (Norton)
5th	P. Driver (Norton)
6th	B. Schneider (Norton)

With MV showing no interest in contesting the final two rounds of the championship series in Finland and Argentina, Mike decided to enter his own 500cc Norton and a factory MZ in the 125cc race, there being no 250cc race at the Finnish GP at Tampere on Sunday 23 September 1962. However, he was injured while practicing on the East German machine, damaging an elbow, and ruled himself out of the racing. The crash had been caused by an engine seizure.

Back home in England the following week Mike was a spectator at Mallory Park. 'I shall not race until next year,' he said. His right arm was in plaster from the Finnish crash.

Gary Hocking rose to the top in motorcycle racing very quickly – winning his first GP in 1959 and then becoming double 350/500cc world champion in 1961. Then for 1962 he was Mike's teammate at MV, before retiring mid-year.

Gary Hocking

In the list of MV's world champions, Surtees, Hailwood, Agostini, Read and Ubbiali immediately spring to mind. Two important names are often forgotten – Cecil Sandford, who won the marque's first-ever world title (the 125cc) in 1952, and Gary Hocking, the brilliant Rhodesian.

Hocking reigned between Surtees and Hailwood and was double 350/500cc title winner in 1961. One reason why his Grand Prix career is less well remembered than others is because it lasted just four years from novice to double world champion. Another is because, unlike John Surtees and Mike Hailwood, he very rarely raced on the British short circuits. Yet Gary, who tragically died in a racing car accident after quitting

motorcycle racing in December 1962, gained a distinction achieved by neither John nor Mike: he became a full works rider in only his second GP year.

As the late Charlie Rous once said:

Welsh-born Hocking was quiet and did not waste words. But he was as tough as granite, and his seemingly shy manner hid extreme self-confidence and determination. With only limited racing experience, he firmly believed that he could beat anybody.

Gary Hocking was taken to Rhodesia (now Zimbabwe) by his parents as a nine-year-old in 1946, and stayed on in Africa when the family returned to the UK in 1955. His first motorcycle was a twin-port Jawa two-stroke, then came a couple of Triumphs, including a new Tiger 100. A friend from his school days, veteran race mechanic Nobby Clark, remembers the young Hocking winning 17 consecutive races on a dirt track at Umgusa on one of the Triumphs.

His first outing on a pukka race bike was on a 350cc Manx Norton, and this was followed by a stint in business with Jim Redman. After Redman left for Europe in March 1958, Hocking soon followed and was fortunate enough to receive backing from Manchester dealer Reg Dearden with a couple of Manx Nortons. In his first-ever race for Dearden, in the Dutch TT at Assen, Gary stunned the racing world by finishing a magnificent sixth in the 500cc, behind the MV fours of John Surtees and John Hartle, Derek Minter's Norton and the BMWs of Hiller and Dale. He went even better at the West German GP over the infamous 14.7-mile Nürburgring, where he finished third behind Surtees and Hartle.

Dearden's support continued into 1959 and then, after some impressive early-season results, including the non-championship Austrian and Saar GPs, Gary was eventually signed by the East German MZ squad.

In his first race on the air-cooled MZ 250 twin in the Swedish GP, he beat MV world champion Carlo Ubbiali by over a minute, and then went on to win the 250cc Ulster GP. This prompted Count Domenico Agusta to offer him a contract, but Hocking refused, saying he wanted more money. The Count was not accustomed to being refused, and this rejection, coupled with Hocking's pledge 'to continue beating you on the MZ', probably convinced the MV boss to give in and offer a new deal. This time it was accepted.

With the likes of Surtees and Ubbiali in the MV team, Hocking did not achieve instant results; in fact, for some time, he was allowed to race only the 125 and 250cc models, plus occasionally a special 285cc twin. Hocking raced a four-cylinder 350 for the first time at the 1960 Dutch TT, where he finished second to Surtees.

With the retirement of both Surtees and Ubbiali at the end of 1960, there is no doubt that during 1961 Gary had the field largely to himself. He made the most of the situation, winning both the 350 and 500cc titles. However, at the final round in Italy, Count Domenico drafted Mike Hailwood into the squad, creating a massive dilemma for Gary. Having already clinched the world championship, he did not need to win the Italian GP, but, as world champion, it would not help his reputation if Mike beat him. The rivalry was intense, for Hailwood had everything to gain and rode hard to win, and Gary was forced to meet the challenge head on. On this occasion, the Englishman came out on top after the Rhodesian came off. It was a message to Hocking that the easy days were over and that he was going to have a hard time in 1962 against Mike on an identical machine.

The showdown came at the 1962 Isle of Man TT, when Hailwood won the Junior (after Hocking was slowed by a misfire), but Gary got his revenge in the Senior event (when Mike suffered clutch slip). However, the death of his friend, Australian Tom Phillis, in the Junior (on a Honda) convinced Hocking that it was time to retire, and he never raced a bike again.

Gary Hocking's tragic death on 21 December 1962 is shrouded in mystery. He was practicing for a car race in Natal and the Lotus he was driving simply went straight on when it reached a bend. One source claimed that Gary died at the wheel from a heart attack. Another report stated that he was suffering from a blood disorder, which caused him to black out and crash. The truth is that no one really knows the cause for sure, and Gary Hocking's death will remain one of racing's mysteries.

Hocking leads Mike at the Race of the Year at Mallory Park in September 1961. They are riding MV and Norton machines respectively.

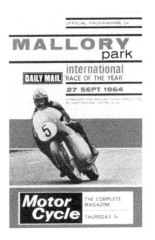

Off to South Africa

Actually, the 'no racing' didn't include South Africa, where Mike went ostensibly for 'a holiday', leaving England on 29 October, even though he was taking his 7R AJS and Manx Norton. When interviewed before his departure, he was quoted as saying that he had 'no definite plans for next year' and that he was 'still more than interested in having a go on four wheels'.

Also, in late October, it was announced that Alan Shepherd (who had finished runner-up on his G50 Matchless to Mike in the 1962 500cc World Championship) had been signed by MV. At the same time came the first hints that Gilera would be returning to the GP scene in 1963.

Once in South Africa, Mike, together with his travelling companion Paddy Driver, fell foul of the authorities. The South African authorities cabled the ACU in England requesting permission to withdraw the two men's national and international licences! The ACU said no, which the local press misinterpreted as a political decision.

At their first race meeting at the Swartcops circuit near Pretoria on 24 November, Mike won the 500cc race, but was beaten by Jim Redman

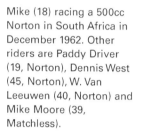

Mike (18) racing a 500cc Norton in South Africa in December 1962. Other riders are Paddy Driver (19, Norton), Dennis West (45, Norton), W. Van Leeuwen (40, Norton) and Mike Moore (39, Matchless).

(Honda) in the 350cc event. Then, on 2 December in Bulawayo, Southern Rhodesia, although he again won the 500cc race, he could only manage a fourth on his AJS 7R, behind Redman, Driver and Bruce Beale (the latter also on an AJS).

Finally, on 29 December in East London, South Africa, Mike suffered a day he would certainly not want to remember. Firstly in the 350cc race a stone flew up, breaking the glass on his goggles, then in the 500cc event the frame broke on his Norton. In both cases he was forced to retire. He flew back to the UK in mid-January and was reported in *Motor Cycling* as saying: 'I can't tell you what I'll be doing this year... I cannot make up my mind whether to race on four wheels or two'. He also dismissed rumours of a return to Honda as 'ridiculous' and confirmed that MV had made him an offer for the 1963 season.

Gilera changes everything

In the 9 January 1963 issue of *Motor Cycle News*, a massive front page headline simply said 'Gilera at Monza'. This concerned the fact that the famous marque, which had been out of racing since the end of 1957, was seriously considering a comeback in GPs for 1963. The man behind the Gilera comeback was former world champion Geoff Duke, who had won three of his six world titles on the Arcore fours. The Monza tests were to be carried out by Derek Minter and 'another rider', who was later revealed to be former Norton and MV star John Hartle.

It was not until 28 February that Geoff Duke, Derek Minter and John Hartle (together with Ralph Newman and Brian Heath of Avon tyres, plus journalist Charlie Rous) flew to Italy to test the four-cylinder Gileras.

Meanwhile, Mike was already in that country trying his skill on four wheels with a new ATS Grand Prix car. There were also rumours linking him with a ride on the 250cc four-cylinder Benelli – which, as events were to prove, were totally unfounded.

In early March 1963 everything was finally settled, with Gileras officially making a return under the Scuderia Duke banner with Minter and Hartle, while Mike finally put pen to paper and signed for MV Agusta. Mike's contract didn't stop him riding his own machines. Mike was also reported to have come to an 'arrangement' with the Italian ATS car firm, to drive one of their cars 'in the British Grand Prix and at a couple of other meetings prior to this'.

Mike also tested a 500 MV at Monza – and actually 'gatecrashed' the Gilera tests, as the only British journalist at Monza, *MCN*s Charlie Rous, was later to reveal.

Preparing a couple of 350 Gilera fours during the Monza tests in March 1963.

In early 1963 news came that Gilera, out of racing since the end of 1957, were to make a comeback. The first tests, at Monza in Italy early that year, were undertaken by Derek Minter (centre). Others in this photograph are Geoff Duke (team manager) and Charlie Rous (*Motor Cycle News* journalist).

The official Rous report of the Gilera tests from *Motor Cycle News* dated Wednesday 6 March 1963 reads:

> *Derek Minter came within 0.59mph of shattering John Surtees' Monza lap record when he lapped the 3.57-mile Italian circuit at a speed of 118.55mph on a 500cc Gilera four on Sunday. Surtees' 1959 record stands at 119.14mph, set on an MV four. Minter's was a staggering performance. He had not ridden for four months, he was alone on the track, and it was only a degree above freezing point, and the Monza track was affected by oil and rubber deposited on it by a Ferrari 3-litre car being tested at the same time – one of the drivers being none other than John Surtees!*

The question now being asked was 'who will be this year's 500cc champion?' (*MCN* 13 March 1963). As things stood the choice was between Mike and Alan Shepherd (MVs) and Derek Minter and John Hartle (Gileras). While in Italy Mike not only got in some testing, but also rode at Modena on 19 March, winning the 500cc race on his MV from teammate Grassetti.

Next Mike was linked with the Ducati Desmo 250 and 350cc twins, which the Hailwood équipe had sold to John Surtees. These were originally offered to John Hartle, but the Gilera deal – and 'other considerations' – meant Mike was offered the bikes. In addition, having made his plans for 1963 – works MV Agustas on one hand and private Ducatis on the other, and the prospect of an ATS racing car into the bargain – Mike announced that he had 'decided to sell up' his remaining personal machines, and thus he had for disposal two 7R AJSs, two 500 Manx Nortons and 'tons of spares'.

The week before the Mallory British season opener, after returning from Italy, Mike suffered a bout of flu and was not expected to ride at the Leicestershire circuit.

Leighton Buzzard entrant/dealer Syd Mularney was the man who ended up buying all the remaining Hailwood AJS and Norton machines. Not only that, but Syd said he would be keeping one of the 500 Nortons 'in top form' for Mike to ride in home events, when the world champion's MV commitments would allow. And in fact, recovering from flu just before Mallory Park, Mike rode the Norton to runner-up spot behind Derek Minter (Norton) in the 500cc race. On the AJS Mike retired with a blocked carburettor jet. But the really big news was his victory in a hotly contested 250cc final on the Ducati twin.

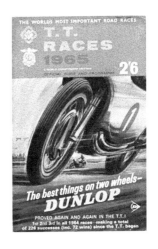

250cc Mallory Park – 15 laps – 20.25 miles
1st   M. Hailwood (Surtees Ducati)
2nd   D. Minter (Cotton)
3rd   R. Good (Ariel)
4th   C. Vincent (Aermacchi)
5th   R. Bryans (Benelli)
6th   B. Clark (Aermacchi)

Silverstone

The author can well remember Silverstone on Saturday 6 April 1963. It marked the British debut of the Scuderia Duke team. The main race of the day was the *Daily Express*-sponsored 500cc BMCRC Championship event. This brought the Italian fours of Derek Minter and John Hartle to the line, with all the top privateers mounted on British singles – including Mike on the now Mularney-owned Norton. Derek Minter won in convincing fashion, but teammate Hartle was made to fight every inch of the way by Phil Read, riding his own Allen Dudley-Ward prepared Norton, with Mike some way behind in fourth.

However, on the Surtees Ducati, Mike finished runner-up to Jim Redman's four-cylinder Honda, while Mike scored what *Motor Cycle News* described as a 'superb victory' in the 350cc BMCRC Championship race on the Mularney AJS, the machine only arriving 30 minutes before the start of the meeting.

Mike had been entered at Brands Hatch, Snetterton and Thruxton over the Easter Holiday period. However, the expected clashes between the MV rider and the Gileras at Brands Hatch never took place. Just about everyone had crammed into Brands on Good Friday. But then Mike crashed out in his first race (on the Mularney AJS), damaging himself too badly to race any more at either the Kent circuit or the other British venues that weekend. Once again it was Phil Read who 'gave the Gillies' more than a good run (*MCN)* at both Brands and Oulton.

It was very much a case of 'hoping for the best' as Mike put it, after his Brands Hatch accident, nursing a severely swollen left wrist and badly cut right arm, as he summed up his immediate racing plans. His father Stan said that in his mind 'the crash helmet had saved Mike's life'. Even X-rays could not detect whether or not one of the 34 tiny bones in his wrist had been cracked or broken.

Meanwhile, Derek Minter had broken both the Brands Hatch and Oulton Park lap records while winning at the two circuits over the weekend on his Gilera. He was expected to be the main opposition to Mike, who was defending his 500cc world title.

First blood to Gilera

The first clash between MV and Gilera came at Imola on Thursday 25 April – with first blood going to Minter and Hartle. Mike finished third. However, unknown to the other riders, spectators or press, Mike was still suffering the effects of the Brands crash, and his wrist caused problems in the long, nearly 80-mile race. This was also the first race between the two marques since 1957, and thus the annual International Shell Coppa d'Oro meeting attracted widespread press attention.

500cc Imola – 25 laps – 77.9 miles

1st	D. Minter (Gilera)
2nd	J. Hartle (Gilera)
3rd	M. Hailwood (MV Agusta)
4th	S. Grassetti (MV Agusta)
5th	R. Venturi (Bianchi)
6th	M. Duff (Matchless)

Already questions were being asked about Alan Shepherd's non-appearance at Imola, even though he had already ridden twice (as per his MV contract) in Italy that year on the Italian four-cylinder machine. Then, back in England on Sunday 28 April, Bill Webster, the man who had lent Mike an MV 125 for his first race six years before at Oulton Park and had thereafter been a close confidant, collapsed and died of a heart attack at the Mallory Park circuit.

From Imola, Mike travelled to Salzburg for the non-championship Austrian Grand Prix, which took place on Wednesday 1 May 1963. Here, racing his works four-cylinder MV, he led from start to finish and broke his existing course and lap records. While riding a water-cooled MZ 250cc two-stroke twin, he also shattered the lap record before retiring with what was described as 'mechanical trouble'. Mike said that he was 'particularly impressed with the performance of the 125 MZ'.

Giacomo Agostini

Born on 16 June 1942 at Lovere in the Bergamo region of northern Italy, Giacomo Agostini ('Mino' to his close friends, and 'Ago' to his thousands of adoring fans worldwide) got his first taste of motorcycling in his home village when, aged nine, he cadged lifts on the petrol tank of a 500 Moto Guzzi single owned by the local baker.

He pestered his father so much that, two years later, Papa finally relented and bought a 50cc Bianchi two-stroke. By the age of 14, Ago was racing off road on a 125cc Parilla motocrosser. Four years later, his apprenticeship was complete when he made his competition debut on the tarmac, on a 175cc Morini ohv single. He finished second to the existing Italian champion in the Trento-Bondone hill climb event.

By the beginning of 1963, Agostini was winning races all over Italy on a Morini 175 Settebello. This led factory boss Alfonso Morini to acquire his signature on an official works contract, making him back-up rider to the legendary Tarquinio Provini (formerly with FB Mondial and MV Agusta).

At the end of 1963, Provini quit Morini and signed for rivals Benelli.

Although both Giacomo Agostini and Mike were great rivals on the race circuit, off it they were great friends, sharing a mutual respect for each other's abilities.

Giacomo Agostini – 15 times world champion and 122 GP victories.

Ago was promoted to number one. Even before Provini's departure, Ago, now aged 21, had proved at the Italian GP at Monza in September 1963 that he had real class. He had lapped joint fastest in practice with Honda-mounted world champion Jim Redman and MZ star Alan Shepherd. In the race, the Morini youngster actually led in the early stages, before finally being overhauled and passed by both Provini and Redman. The following year, 1964, Agostini won the Italian Senior Championships on the Morini.

Count Domenico Agusta had always wanted a rider who would be able to win the 500cc world title, but he particularly wanted him to be an Italian. His belief that Giacomo Agostini was the right man led the Count to sign the gifted youngster in time for the 1965 season.

Agostini's first time out did not prove to be the dream outing that everyone had expected. In fact, it was just the reverse, and he crashed out, but all this was soon forgotten. His first win came early in the 1965 season, when he took the flag ahead of the field on one of the new 350 three-cylinder models at the Nürburgring, home of the West German Grand Prix.

During 1965, when Giacomo and Mike were teammates at MV, and then during 1966–7 when the two were in rival teams, both men shared a genuine friendship. In the latter two years the duels fought on the race circuits of Europe are now the stuff of legends. Probably the greatest of these battles came in the 1967 Senior TT, which Giacomo ultimately lost by default, his chain breaking after some two hours of intense action. However, Giacomo has always maintained that to him Mike was not only the greatest rider ever, but a true gentleman. But the Italian was a superstar in his own right. His achievements on the race circuit speak for themselves: a record 15 world titles, 13 on MVs, the other two on Japanese Yamaha machines. Added to his total of 122 GP victories, it seems like a record that will never be beaten.

Giacomo finally hung up his leathers in 1976, at the age of 35. But the ever-popular Italian superstar did not simply retire and vanish from the scene. During the early 1980s, he became manager of first the Marlboro Yamaha squad, and later Cagiva.

'Ago' lifting the front wheel of his three-cylinder MV at the international Cadwell Park meeting in September 1970. It was the Italian rider's first visit to the demanding Lincolnshire circuit.

Then came an incident which had a major bearing on the ultimate outcome of the 1963 500cc championship series, when, at Brands Hatch on Sunday 12 May, tragedy struck in what many consider to have been one of the greatest races ever.

Derek Minter (on his own Manx Norton) and the up-and-coming Dave Downer, riding Paul Dunstall's Norton 650cc Domiracer, crashed on the final lap – Downer fatally, Minter sustaining head and back injuries. This unfortunate affair was, without doubt, to weaken Gilera's chances, and, in the author's opinion, Derek would never quite regain the form he had shown before the Brands Hatch crash. The following week it was announced that Minter was to be out 'for at least four months', so 24-year-old Phil Read was signed by Scuderia Gilera, Geoff Duke commenting 'if Minter makes a wonder recovery and comes back this season, then I'll have three Gilera riders'. This statement came in the wake of reports that Phil was only a 'temporary replacement'.

At the same time, it appeared that Alan Shepherd was no longer an MV rider and was re-signing for MZ.

Isle of Man TT

With no 500cc races in the first two world championship meetings (Barcelona and Hockenheim), Mike did not turn out again until the Isle of

John Hartle during the 1963 Senior TT, when he finished second behind race winner Mike Hailwood.

Man TT. This was actually quite a wise move on Mike's part, as it allowed him time to fully recover from his Easter injuries.

In 1963 he only contested the Junior on Wednesday 12 June and the Senior on Friday 14 June – both on his four-cylinder MVs. Once again the smaller four proved it was more of a liability, with Mike retiring with engine trouble. So, in effect, he was left to concentrate on the Senior. And of course this meant doing battle with the Gileras of Hartle and Read. With a headline 'Mike Hailwood laps all week at over 100mph', the Gilera duo knew they were in for a real struggle.

'Hailwood 106.41mph' spat the *MCN* headline in the 19 June 1963 issue. 'John rode marvellously, but Mike was just fabulous,' commented Geoff Duke after witnessing Mike's Senior TT victory. The MV rider broke the lap record from a standing start, then set a new lap record of 106.41mph and a race-winning record speed of 104.64mph. Mike led from start to finish.

Mike, who started 10 seconds behind John Hartle on the Geoff Duke-entered Gilera four, said that as soon as he caught and passed John he knew he was alright.

With 4½ laps gone, Mike began to suffer gear selection problems – having to change them by hand. It affected the lower gears, making his victory even more amazing and finally settling the MV–Gilera argument.

Senior 500cc TT – 6 laps – 226.38 miles
1st   M. Hailwood (MV Agusta)
2nd   J. Hartle (Gilera)
3rd   P. Read (Gilera)
4th   M. Duff (Matchless)
5th   J. Dunphy (Norton)
6th   F. Stevens (Norton)

Just as it looked as if he was on his way to retaining his 500cc crown, Mike struck trouble during the 500cc race of the Dutch TT at Assen on Saturday 29 June 1963. Mike's retirement was due to piston trouble and came early in the race, leaving John Hartle and Phil Read to circulate on their Gileras. Hartle hoisted the 500cc race average from 87.48mph to 88.05mph, but didn't equal Mike's record lap for the 4.8-mile circuit, set the previous year on the MV.

This time Mike's smaller MV kept going, to finish runner-up behind Honda's Jim Redman in the 350cc race in Holland. Luigi Taveri on another Honda (a twin instead of a four) was third, with the Czech rider Franta Stastny (Jawa) fourth. There were no Gileras in this race, as they were all back in Italy for repair work following the TT.

In Belgium, eight days later, on Sunday 7 July, Mike made up for his Dutch TT failure by lapping everyone bar the second-place man Phil Read (Gilera). His performance was acclaimed as 'fantastic' and 'brilliant' by a couple of the leading sports journals. In the process of winning the 500cc event he set a new race record of 123.15mph and a new lap record of 125.54mph for the 8.75-mile Spa Francorchamps circuit. Mike led from start to finish and there was simply nothing the Gileras of Read and Hartle could do. John had to retire on lap 12 of the 15-lap race.

500cc Belgian GP – 15 laps – 131.41 miles
1st   M. Hailwood (MV Agusta)
2nd   P. Read (Gilera)
3rd   A. Shepherd (Matchless)
4th   F. Stevens (Norton)
5th   J. Ahearn (Norton)
6th   G. Marsovszky (Matchless)

There was no 350cc race in Belgium.

More records in Ulster

Mike made history in the Ulster Grand Prix at Dundrod on Saturday 10 August 1963 by achieving the first 100mph lap on the circuit. He also won his third 500cc championship race of the season at record speed – 99.29mph. Mike's actual lap record speed was 101.28mph.

This meeting also saw the return of Derek Minter. It was his first ride on the Gilera since his crash at Brands Hatch in May, and his first appearance on a 500cc machine at Dundrod since 1958.

However, no one could overlook Hartle, as he was something of a specialist at Dundrod. This showed at the start of the race, when Mike and John swapped places on the first lap. At Leathamstown the order was Hartle, Mike, Read, Minter. But at the end of the first lap Mike was back at the front of the field, never again to relinquish the lead.

500cc Ulster GP – 17 laps – 128 miles
1st   M. Hailwood (MV Agusta)
2nd   J. Hartle (Gilera)

3rd   D. Minter (Gilera)

4th   A. Shepherd (Matchless)

5th   R. Bryans (Norton)

6th   M. Duff (Matchless)

In the 350cc race, Mike once again finished runner-up behind Jim Redman's four-cylinder Honda.

The East German GP at the Sachsenring saw Mike not only set another new record – three Grand Prix wins in two days – but in the process stamp his authority on the 1963 season with what were, without doubt, the performances of the year. *Motor Cycle News* reporter Peter Howdle's headline read 'Wonderful Hailwood! Sensational triple victory at East German Grand Prix'.

Not only did Mike win the 250, 350 and 500cc races, smashing race and lap records in each one, but he achieved this on two entirely different types of machine. For the two larger classes he rode four-cylinder MVs, while in the 250cc race his mount was an MZ two-stroke twin from the locally-built (Zschopau) factory.

250cc East German GP – 15 laps – 81.3 miles

1st   M. Hailwood (MZ)

2nd   A. Shepherd (MZ)

3rd   J. Redman (Honda)

4th   L. Szabo (MZ)

5th   L. Taveri (Honda)

6th   S. Malina (CZ)

350cc East German GP – 16 laps – 86.7 miles

1st   M. Hailwood (MV Agusta)

2nd   L. Taveri (Honda)

3rd   J. Redman (Honda)

4th   G. Havel (Jawa)

5th   N. Sevastianov (CGKD)

6th   M. Duff (AJS)

500cc East German GP – 17 laps – 92.1 miles

1st   M. Hailwood (MV Agusta)

2nd   D. Minter (Gilera)

3rd   A. Shepherd (Matchless)

4th   M. Duff (Matchless)

5th   J. Findlay (Matchless)

6th   V. Cottle (Norton)

As expected, Mike clinched his second 500cc world road racing title at Tampere, Finland, on Sunday 1 September. On his 500cc MV, he hurtled round the twisting, tree-lined 2.25-mile circuit to lap the entire field at least once and pull away from second-place man Alan Shepherd (Matchless) by another 30 seconds after lapping him! Mike set up a new lap record and a new race average. He also closed the gap in the 350cc class by beating Jim Redman (who rode a production twin, rather than a four). Mike put in a new 350cc lap record of 75.85mph, together with a record race average speed of 73.33mph. And all this after taking to a slip road and dropping back to fifth place!

Monza

Then came the MV–Gilera clash on home ground. When they had last tangled in Italy, before the GP season had got under way, Mike had come off second best. What would happen now?

The expected and much hoped for challenge from Derek Minter never materialised. Nor, for that matter, did any challenge from any other member of the Gilera squad. So the 500cc Italian Grand Prix actually turned out to be one of Mike's easiest ever wins. While he circulated as regularly and consistently 'as an express train' (MCN), his main rivals fell by the wayside. Minter, after holding runner-up spot for nearly 10 laps, was passed by Remo Venturi aboard a 450cc twin-cylinder Bianchi. On the 13th lap, the British rider called it a day and retired. The 10th lap had seen Phil Read retire on his Gilera, while John Hartle crashed and was extremely lucky to suffer nothing more than a shaking up and a broken finger. Mike also set a new lap record at 119.91mph.

Monza also saw Jim Redman claim the 350cc title after victory on his Honda four. Mike retired his 'none too fast' MV with suspected engine trouble.

An interesting aside to the Italian GP was that the day afterwards Mike was back at Monza testing tyres, and was offered a ride on a Gilera. Mike agreed and was all set to dash round the circuit when his Italian mechanic, Vittorio Carrano, hastily put a stop to it. In truth, it was more than his job was worth to return to Gallerate having let Mike ride the Gilera!

Race of the Year

Billed as the 'Race of the Year', Mallory Park's meeting on Sunday 29 September 1963 saw over 50,000 spectators watch Mike and his MV beat rival Derek Minter and his Gilera by over half a minute as he won the £1,050 main race. Alan Shepherd (Matchless) was the only other rider not

The Gileras of Phil Read (6) and Derek Minter (4) during the Race of the Year at Mallory Park on 29 September 1963 – but Mike and the MV still won!

to be overtaken by Mike during 40 searing laps of the 1.35-mile Leicestershire circuit. However, the weather was cold and blustery. Mike chopped 34.8 seconds off the previous 40-lap race record set two years earlier by MV-mounted Gary Hocking.

Besides the big race, Mike also won the 25 lap, 33.7-mile 500cc event, this time with Shepherd second and Minter third.

The same week as the Mallory meeting, Mike announced that he was in fact sticking with bikes for 1964. Originally Mike had had every intention of quitting bikes for cars – being offered the chance to drive a Lola in 1964. However, he had received a 'tempting' offer from Count Agusta consisting not only of a sizeable financial deal, but also of hints about a possible MV Grand Prix racing car, which it was claimed should be ready for the 1965 World Championship series (this proved a red herring). Mike was reported as saying, 'you can't turn down an offer like that!'

On Monday 30 September (the day after Mallory), Mike flew to South America in the company of several other riders for the Argentine Grand Prix the following Sunday, 6 October 1963, where he easily won the 500cc race. He and Alan Shepherd had hoped to race MZs, but this proved impossible because of existing restrictions concerning visas for the East Germans.

After that, he flew to Italy to discuss exact terms and sign the new contract with the Count, which was duly completed. Mike had wanted to race the 350cc MV at Suzuka in Japan – that country's first Grand Prix – but the Count vetoed this plan. Instead Mike went to the Moroccan Grand Prix (a non-championship meeting), held on 3 November. With no MVs available dealer and race sponsor Tom Kirby came to Mike's rescue with AJS and Matchless machines. 'Uncle Tom', as he was affectionately known, already sponsored the likes of Paddy Driver, Lewis Young, Ron Chandler and Roger Hunter. The small British contingent 'had themselves a ball' as *Motor Cycle News* described in the 6 November 1963 issue.

There was little doubt, that, after winning the 350cc race, Mike would have notched up a double success at the sun-drenched but windy 1.3-mile North African circuit at Casablanca, washed by spray from rolling Atlantic breakers. But in the 500cc event Mike fell off in sight of the finishing flag, leaving his friend Paddy Driver to the victory. In both major races Swedish riders finished second – Bror Karlsson (AJS) in the 250 event and Sven Gunnarsson (Norton) in the 500cc class.

After returning to England, Mike flew off to South Africa, where his racing year began. As last year, he was to stay on Paddy Driver's farm near Johannesburg – but this time it really was for a holiday.

This superb model of the 1963 MZ 250, as raced by Mike and Alan Shepherd to their historic 1-2 success in that year's East German Grand Prix, was built by Ian Welsh of Edinburgh.

The one hour record

Less than 1½ hours before Mike was due to wheel his 500 four-cylinder MV to the start line of the United States Grand Prix at Daytona on 21 March 1964, the 500cc world champion smashed Bob McIntyre's 1957 one-hour record of 141.27mph on a 350 Gilera, set at Monza, with a fantastic 144.83mph.

But it was a record attempt that very nearly didn't take place at all. For a start, mechanic Vittorio Carrano's tools were missing, together with the spares for Mike's two MVs, which prevented any thought of an attempt until they were located – still at Malpensa airport, Milan.

Mike then had a rehearsal on the 2.5-mile high-speed Daytona Bowl and, from a push start, averaged 143mph for his first two laps, proving to his own satisfaction that Bob's record could be broken. Mike had been reluctant to go for the record, simply because he felt it should stand as a memory to his friend and rival. But even while they had been at Daytona there was talk from the Americans of a Harley-Davidson attempt, which eased Mike's concerns.

Count Agusta telegrammed Mike, advising him against the attempt, but

In 1964 the diminutive Argentinian Benedicto Caldarella (seen here in the white shirt with Giuseppe Gilera), gave Mike a run for his money at Daytona in February, but after that the challenge faded.

finally, after Stan Hailwood had intervened, he left the final decision up to Mike, on the understanding that only his spare bike could be used. The number one race bike was for the GP only. Stan Hailwood then recruited *Motor Cycle News* journalist Charlie Rous to act in the role of team assistant for the record attempt. Stan himself would hold out the pitboard for Mike to see as the attempt unfolded. Mike tried both anticlockwise and clockwise ways around the banked circuit, eventually opting for the clockwise route having put in a 147mph lap in that direction. Another worry was fuel (normal pump petrol was being used). Would the MV's tank, holding 6 gallons and 1 quart, hold out for an hour? At the finish Mike had less than 1 litre left, and he knew this because during his final two laps the MV engine coughed a couple of times.

After some 45 laps averaging 145mph, Mike began to slow down and once his average had dropped to 143mph, Stan gave him the 'hurry up' sign, so he turned on the power, put in his fastest lap at 148.27mph, and finally, after 58 laps, the hour was up and the record was his – at a new average speed of 144.83mph (233.03kph).

Caldarella's challenge

Only 90 minutes after his successful record attempt, Mike was on the start line for the 500cc United States Grand Prix. And, as he was to admit later, he had never (up to that time) had to work so hard for a race win since joining MV. This was because a previously little-known rider from South America stunned Mike, and the crowd, with his performance. That man was Benedicto Caldarella, a diminutive Argentinian aboard a Gilera four which had been loaned to the importers in his country for publicity purposes.

Caldarella led the world champion for the first six laps. Mike then went by, but simply couldn't pull away. The pair circled the banking and infield as if tied by an invisible rope, swapping the lead. But disaster struck the Gilera at half distance in the 41-lap, 127.1-mile race when its gearbox started to play up. Caldarella dropped behind Mike and two laps later pulled in to retire with his gearbox jammed in fourth gear.

From then on, Mike was able to almost cruise to victory, setting a record race speed of 100.16mph and a record lap of 103.3mph.

The United States Grand Prix was not only the opening round of the 1964 world series, but also the first ever stateside event qualifying for FIM status at this level.

Unlike in previous seasons, Mike was to have only four meetings in the whole year which were not World Championship status. Three of these came between Daytona and the second round of the championship defence.

First, at Modena (22 March), he crashed the 500 MV but remounted to finish fifth before winning at Silverstone on Saturday 7 April (again he only rode his big MV) in heavy rain. Finally, back in Italy, at Cesenatico on 29 April, he again won on the five-hundred MV.

Then came a break of some six weeks before he was back in the saddle, at no less an event than the Isle of Man TT. Even then he only rode in a single race; the Senior (500cc) on Friday 12 June.

A bout of tonsillitis meant that Mike's practising was limited. He had intended to compete in the Junior race, but illness had seen his idea axed.

With the Scuderia Gilera effort having ended the previous year and Benedicto Caldarella limiting himself to the Italian international and selected continental European GPs, even an off-colour Mike could still win the Senior TT, albeit at the slowest speed since his Norton days, at 100.95mph. As one journalist remarked, this was 'just about the same as his temperature 24 hours earlier!'

Dutch TT

The Dutch TT was on Saturday 30 June. Mike had two rides, winning the 500cc race and finishing runner-up to Jim Redman's four-cylinder Honda in the 350cc class on his smaller-engined MV. Then came the Belgian GP at Spa Francorchamps, where, as usual, there was only a 500cc race, which he duly won. But although it might appear to the reader that Mike was having a pretty easy life with the greatly reduced number of races, this was actually a false impression.

In 1964 Mike had at last begun to take a serious interest in four wheel racing. For example, between practicing mid-week in Holland and racing on the Saturday, Mike had flown down to Rouen to drive a Reg Parnell entered Lotus-BRM in practice for the French Grand Prix. Immediately after winning the 500cc Dutch TT, Mike had got behind the wheel of his E-Type Jaguar and driven 400 miles to Rouen to compete the next day in the Formula 1 event. Then it was back to Belgium for the bike Grand Prix.

In winning the 500cc West German GP on Sunday 22 July, Mike had made sure of retaining his title for a third year. It was his fourth world crown and he had only just turned 24.

His favourite GP circuit

Next came Mike's favourite circuit in the GP calendar, at the Sachsenring, home of the East German round. As he told

In 1962 Mike had led the 250cc East German GP on a works MZ, before having to settle for second behind World Champion Jim Redman (Honda). But a year later in August 1963 Mike took the MZ to victory at the Sachsenring with teammate Alan Shepherd runner-up. Redman was relegated to third.

Motor Cycling, this was 'because it has every type of bend, its still a genuine road circuit, the organisers and spectators are tremendous and there's a terrific atmosphere'.

The East German GP took place on 29 July. Mike was scheduled to race both his 500 MV and, for the third year running in the event, one of the locally made MZ two-fifty twins.

The 500cc race came before the 250cc. And as *Motor Cycle News* described:

> *...leathers peeled off to his waist, Hailwood was obviously itching to get cracking and cool off as the midday sun blazed down on the 500cc starting grid. He and 33 others were sweating uncomfortably when a red signal indicated a minute to go. Then off he went.*

And Mike 'screamed' round at an impressive rate of knots to notch up his sixth successive victory in the world 500cc series. Mike's time of 3 minutes 6.5 seconds with a lap of 103.32mph equalled his own in 1963 (104.40mph) but the circuit was now slightly shorter.

The undoubted highlight of the East German GP was always the 250cc race (because of the MZ participation). This year ran true to form. In training both Mike (MZ) and Bertie Schneider (Suzuki) cracked the old record. Next fastest were Redman (Honda), Shepherd (MZ) and Read (Yamaha). And with full works support on hand, Mike looked the favourite. But with Read and Redman fighting it out for the title, it was going to be difficult. And it was Read who was off like a rocket, leaving Mike and Redman behind on acceleration.

The first appearance of a Yamaha in East Germany had got off to a sensational start. Despite practice times it seemed impossible that the MZ could stay with the Yamaha, but that's exactly what happened. At the end of the first lap, Read was fractionally ahead of Mike, with Redman less than 10 yards behind. But at the end of the next lap, Mike led by over 80 yards – no wonder he had chopped five seconds off his two-year-old lap record on a similar bike. His speed of 102.66mph was little short of his 350cc record on the MV four.

Then came the big drama of the race. Cornering absolutely on – or even over – the limit and grabbing a fistful of throttle, Mike's rear wheel came level with the front and down he went. 'I can't remember what happened after that,' he said later in hospital. Phil Read went on to win, with Jim Redman runner-up (a position which was reflected in the final championship table at the end of the season). Mike had a gashed head, concussion and torn shoulder ligaments, and these injuries conspired to stop him riding in the Ulster Grand Prix.

Mike was fit again in time for the Italian GP at Monza on Sunday 16 September. However, he was not a happy man. Why? Well, the problem centred around Count Agusta's refusal to let him race the brand new, across-the-frame three-cylinder 350cc machine. *Motor Cycling* reported: 'I've seldom seen Mike so annoyed as he was at Monza'. For one thing, the Count was far from pleased with Mike for riding and crashing the MZ in East Germany. And he was also playing safe, wanting Mike in peak condition to race the 500 MV against a now fully recovered Benedicto Caldarella. Mike responded by beating the Argentinian Gilera star.

Next the Count arranged for the big MV to be flown over for the Race of the Year at Mallory Park on Sunday 27 September. Mike won both the Race of the Year and the 500cc events. The *Motor Cycle News* report hailed the meeting 'Gate of the Century!' reporting:

The largest crowd ever recorded at a short circuit race in Britain packed Mallory Park to bursting point on Sunday. The crowd literally mobbed 'Mike the Bike' as he set off on his lap of honour.

Race of the Year Mallory Park – 40 laps – 54 miles

1st	M. Hailwood (MV Agusta)
2nd	J. Cooper (Norton)
3rd	D. Minter (Norton)
4th	J. Redman (Honda)
5th	P. Dunphy (Norton)
6th	Bill Ivy (Monard)

Japanese Grand Prix

After Mallory, the only other meeting Mike contested in 1964 was the Japanese Grand Prix at Suzuka, on Sunday 1 November. With no 500cc race, and with the Count still not playing ball concerning the new 350cc triple, Mike organised a deal to borrow a pair of works MZs: a two-fifty, plus an overbored model (251cc) for the 350cc class. And despite the mere £70 'start money' which the Japanese organisers offered when there were at least £1,000 travelling expenses involved, Mike still decided to go, commenting that it was 'for a bit of fun'. In fact, as Mike Woollet so rightly

Mike taking his four-cylinder MV Agusta 500 to victory at the Mallory Park Race of the Year, 27 September 1964.

Another challenger to Mike during 1963 and 1964 was Remo Venturi and the twin-cylinder Bianchi seen here at Imola in April 1964.

said: 'the meeting was a farce, with just 24 competitors riding a total of 33 bikes in four classes'. As for Mike, his two-fifty MZ suffered plug trouble and struggled home fifth, while on the 251cc model he gave the winner Jim Redman (Honda) a race for his money, finishing second.

Once again, when interviewed about his plans, Mike seemed unsure. And he was definitely becoming sick and tired of playing games with Count Agusta. For example, he blamed his East German crash on the fact that he was 'rusty', because of 'having so few rides'.

But his continued success – and his visit to Japan – had triggered a wave of interest from Japanese manufacturers, notably Suzuki. Mike wanted to ride Suzukis in the smaller classes. However, once again the Count had different ideas and in January 1965 he summoned Mike to Italy. Yet again, the wily Count came out on top. This time he told Mike he was 'expanding' his racing programme. Not only would there be the new 350cc model, but he was also signing the young Moto Morini rider Giacomo Agostini as Mike's new teammate. Both riders would be 'doing a full season's racing'. So Mike signed another contract with MV – but although he wasn't to know it at the time, it would be his last season with the Italian firm.

Mike and Ago
And so, for 1965, there was a new MV duo, Mike Hailwood and Giacomo Agostini – Mike and Ago. This pairing were to be teammates and later, in different teams, bitter rivals on the track, but they were always truly great friends.

Giacomo was Italy's most promising youngster, who, as fully recounted in my book *Giacomo Agostini: Champion of Champions* (Breedon), had quickly come through the ranks to win the Italian Senior Championship in 1964 on a factory dohc Moto Morini – beating no less a man than Tarquinio Provini on the Benelli four. To Mike, Giacomo's arrival also signalled that, at last, the Count was really going to field the new, and so far unraced, three-cylinder machine.

Back home, on Sunday 7 February 1965, spectators at the Normandy MCC's February Cup Trial near Frensham Pond, Surrey, were astonished to

John Hartle

Stan Hailwood is on record as saying that John Hartle's 105mph lap from a standing start on the Scuderia Duke Gilera four in the 1963 Senior TT was one of his finest performances.

Hailing from Chapel-en-le-Frith in the English Peak District, John Hartle was born in 1933. In a career which lasted from the early 1950s until the late 1960s he rode a variety of machinery, including not only four-cylinder MV Agustas and Gileras, but also BSA, AJS, Norton and Aermacchi singles, plus Bob Geeson's REG twin. He was even a TT winner for Triumph aboard a Thruxton Bonneville.

For a couple of years after leaving school, John took a job in a local garage where, as he once described: 'I was required to delve into the internals of cars and lorries'. But his interest lay more with two wheels than four, and with a certain degree of what he described as 'hero worship' the young Hartle visited various trials and scrambles in which local star Eric Bowers was competing.

The lure of motorcycle sport proved too strong to resist and so in 1950, then aged 17, John joined Bowers's Chapel-en-le-Frith dealership. By this time Bowers had retired from active competition, but was sponsoring a couple of road racers, including Eric Houseley. John Hartle was recruited as a 'weekend race mechanic'. When Houseley subsequently won the 1952 Junior Clubmans TT on a BSA Gold Star, the young Hartle was there to look after the spanners and pitboard.

Monza Autodrome, March 1963. The Gilera racing team is reborn under the Scuderia Duke banner. A group of journalists from all over Europe watch as John Hartle prepares to fire up one of the four-cylinder models.

The following year, John made his own race debut at Brough airfield circuit in East Yorkshire on a BSA single alongside the likes of Houseley, Peter Davey and Ken Kavanagh (the latter on a works Norton). In September 1953 John found himself in the Manx Grand Prix, on an AJS 7R in the Junior and a Manx Norton in the Senior. But after refuelling the 7R in around 10th position, he braked too hard at Quarter Bridge and fell off. Undaunted he then remounted to come home 21st. In the Senior event he did better, finishing a respectable 15th on the Norton and, as a result of these two finishes, collected that year's Newcomer Award.

Even better was to come the following year, when not only did Eric Bowers provide new machinery (still an AJS and Norton), but also, after finishing third on the 7R in the 1954 Junior Manx GP, John led the Senior race in truly awful weather conditions until he ran out of fuel on the last lap. Later that same month he also had the distinction of finishing third behind Geoff Duke (Gilera) and Bob Keeler in the Hutchison 100 meeting at Silverstone.

These outstanding performances led to John being invited to join the Norton team alongside Jack Brett and John Surtees for 1955. A close friendship between John Surtees and John Hartle transpired and Hartle later joined Surtees in the MV Agusta team for the 1958 season. Prior to that he continued to ride for Norton in 1955 and 1956, while in 1957 he had the use of a fully streamlined Norton bike.

John's MV contract continued into 1959 and he rode for the Italian factory in the 1960 TT but was subsequently sacked, which John Surtees told the author he thought 'unjust'. There is no doubt that Lady Luck seemed to desert Hartle during his MV days – he suffered more than his fair share of crashes, breakdowns and even a fire.

After MV John went back to racing as a privateer on his own Norton machinery. He was recalled as a works rider for the Geoff Duke Scuderia Gilera squad in 1963. It was during this year that he became the main challenger to Mike Hailwood in the world championship series. But the combination of Mike and the MV simply proved too strong and the Scuderia team was disbanded at the end of 1963.

Then it was back to Norton, but by the mid-1960s John had switched to Italian Aermacchis, riding for the British importer, Syd Lawton. There followed a period riding factory-supported Triumph production bikes. In 1967, John set up a racing spares service business, but he was fatally injured while racing at Scarborough the following year, aged 34.

John Hartle, seen here leading Derek Minter at Silverstone in 1960 (both are Norton-mounted), was someone who raced against Mike from his earliest days in the sport.

Mike shaking hands with Lord Beaulieu at a presentation in 1964 of a works four-cylinder 250 Honda to the National Motor Museum.

On Sunday 7 February 1965, spectators at the Normandy MCC's February Cup Trial near Frensham Park, Surrey, were astonished to see Mike (250 Greeves) competing in the South Eastern event. He finshed only 13 points outside award standard, losing 67 points in all.

see Mike (250 Greeves) competing in the South Eastern event. Mike finished only 13 points outside award standard (losing 67 points in all). Besides Mike, Suzuki teamster Frank Perris was also entered. Mike let out a heartless laugh when Frank retired within a few yards of the start on his 80cc

Suzuki, a victim of electric gremlins. The trial itself was won by Terry Graves (250 Greeves) with 23 marks lost. While Mike was mudplugging in England, Giacomo Agostini had his first ride on an MV (a 500 four) at Modena on Monday 15 February.

MV bike developments

In the 24 February 1965 issue of *Motor Cycle News* came the first British photograph of the long-awaited three-cylinder racer.

The MV triple was appreciably lower than the existing 500 four. As the photograph revealed, two exhaust pipes were on the nearside (left) of the machine. The central exhaust ran between the front down tubes of the duplex frame. The third exhaust pipe was on the offside (right) and ran outside the frame. The double side single-leading shoe front brakes were of a smaller diameter than those on the four.

The original idea behind the three-cylinder MV had been the success enjoyed in 1962 by Honda with a larger displacement version of its 250cc four. This had at first an engine size of 285cc, thus allowing the Japanese company to enter the 350cc division. Soon, a fully-fledged three-fifty – actually 339cc – made its debut. And with the latter bike Honda were able to see off the ageing 350cc MV four which had made its debut as long ago as 1953 – a decade earlier. Even with Mike's brilliant riding abilities, the Italian bike was totally outclassed. And so began the first moves to design and build a replacement.

The result was the 343.9cc (48x46mm) across-the-frame triple, with its air-cooled twin-cam cylinders inclined forward some 10 degrees from vertical. Other technical features included a seven-speed gearbox, a quartet of 28mm Dell'Orto carburettors and a power output of 62.5bhp at 13,500rpm.

Model of the four-cylinder MV Agusta with which Mike Hailwood took the 500cc World Championship title in 1962, 1963, 1964 and 1965.

Improvements to the 500

There had also been some improvements to the 500 four, which previously, except for the addition of a six-speed gearbox, had been largely the same motorcycle as that raced by John Surtees until his retirement at the end of the 1960 season. These changes, as detailed by official Agusta sources, included 'considerable weight pruning, a lower tank, a new fairing and revised exhaust system'; there was no information regarding power figures.

As in the previous year, the first round of the 1965 World Championship series was the United States Grand Prix, staged over the 3.1-mile Daytona circuit in sunny Florida. Only Mike represented MV and, as *MCN* said: 'Mike didn't have to stress himself, nor did he'. In the 41-lap, 127.1-mile race he averaged 101.45mph – and finished over two laps ahead of the runner-up, Californian Buddy Parriott (Norton), who was another lap up on third-place finisher R. Beaumont (Norton). Mike's friend, the South African Paddy

For the 1965 season Mike was joined in the MV team by the Italian youngster Giacomo Agostini. Here Mike (left) helps fasten Giacomo's helmet strap. Team manager Nello Pagani is in the middle.

Driver, was unlucky, having to retire from a secure second place after 12 laps with a rattling big-end on his Tom Kirby G50 Matchless.

Then it was a case of Mike and the MV mechanics rushing back to Italy to contest a meeting at Riccione the following Sunday, 28 March.

Ago and Mike clash

The first clash between Ago and Mike came at Riccione. And for the first time since early 1963, Mike suffered a defeat on the 500 MV. And the man who put it across 'Mike-the-Bike' was none other than his new teammate, Giacomo Agostini.

Both the MV stars cleared off from the rest of the field right from the start of the 34-lap, 68.9-mile race and steadily began to lap the field. Agostini found the right line through one bunch of back markers, but Mike was slowed and lost a lot of ground, before putting in a record lap of 74.69mph in an attempt to catch his younger teammate. A fading front brake worked against him and he had to be content with second position.

A revenge for the defeat at Riccione came when the two met the following week on Sunday 11 April, with Mike coming out on top and, in the process, setting new lap and race records at an international meeting over the Cervia circuit on the Adriatic coast. Mike was never seriously challenged and both MV riders finished a lap ahead of third-place man Silvio Grassetti (Bianchi).

500cc Cervia – 35 laps – 73.9 miles

1st	M. Hailwood	(MV Agusta)
2nd	G. Agostini	(MV Agusta)
3rd	S. Grassetti	(Bianchi)
4th	G. Mandolini	(Moto Guzzi)
5th	R. Pasolini	(Aermacchi)
6th	F. Stastny	(Jawa)

It must have been disappointing for the 50,000 crowd at Brands Hatch on Good Friday 16 April 1965 that the promised MV was not available, and Mike was certainly annoyed about it. He explained to the stewards at Brands that, on signing with MV for the year, he had been promised a machine for 'about four meetings' in the UK that year. This, he understood, 'included these two meetings at Easter' (the other one being at Snetterton on Easter Sunday). It had not been until he was in Italy for the meeting at Cervia a few days before that he was told a machine would not be available for Easter. Instead: 'all machines were required for the Italian home meeting at Imola on Easter Monday'. This incident was to mark the beginning of a rift between Mike and the Count as the year went on.

But as *Motor Cycle News* was to report:

> *...the holiday weekend turned into a great personal triumph for the 500cc World Champion when, at Snetterton on Sunday, he won the 500cc race on a borrowed Norton at 91.88mph.*

The *MCN* race report dated 21 April 1965 went further:

> *Mike Hailwood, brilliant Mike Hailwood, showed why, precisely why, he is the world's greatest road racer at Snetterton on Sunday by outriding the cream of Britain's short circuit stars on a borrowed Norton (belonging to Syd Mularney).*

500cc Snetterton – 10 laps – 27.1 miles
1st   M. Hailwood (Norton)
2nd   D. Shorey (Norton)
3rd   D. Degens (Dunstall Domiracer)
4th   D. Minter (Norton)
5th   L. Young (Matchless)
6th   B. Ivy (Monard)

Mike's other races over that Easter weekend were:

Brands Hatch	AJS 350cc	12th (gearbox trouble)
Brands Hatch	Norton 500cc	retired
Snetterton	AJS 350cc	6th

A dash to Imola

Dashing straight to Italy after winning the 500cc race on the Norton at Snetterton on Sunday, Mike arrived just in time for the race at Imola the

Mike with the Mularney Norton at Snetterton, Easter Sunday 1965. He put in a brilliant performance to beat the cream of British racing on a borrowed bike.

Easter Sunday, 18 April 1965, and a mechanic is seen with Syd Mularney's 500cc Manx Norton.

next day. He had an overnight journey of some 200 miles from Milan airport to the race track, and he arrived at the circuit too late for practising, so he was forced to start from the back of the grid.

In his eagerness to get through the pack and into the lead, which he managed by the end of the first lap, Mike overshot a bend and, although he did not come off his machine, the mistake cost him a great deal of ground. This let MV teammate Giacomo Agostini, also riding a four, to pull away. However, riding at his brilliant best, Mike overhauled the entire field, including Ago, and recaptured the lead during the 17th lap.

500cc Imola – 30 laps – 100 miles
1st   M. Hailwood (MV Agusta)
2nd   G. Agostini (MV Agusta)
3rd   R. Pasolini (Aermacchi)
4th   J. Ahearn (Norton)
5th   G. Mandolini (Moto Guzzi)
6th   J. Findlay (Matchless)

350cc world champion Jim Redman and his Honda suffered a dramatic exit from the West German GP held on 24/25 April 1965 over the shorter

South Loop Nürburgring circuit in the Eifel Mountains. Seldom has the appearance of a new machine proved so controversial, but it was certainly the case with the new MV three-cylinder. Agostini was on the front row on the new bike, but Mike's triple had blown up in practice and he was forced to ride an old 'hack' four-cylinder machine and start from the back of a line-up of 48 riders. Redman and Agostini were soon locked in a fantastic battle, which ended when the world champion crashed out. Mike struggled round, finishing runner-up to his teammate. Ago's race average speed was 84.75mph, Mike's 81.66mph. This equated to being three miles behind in the 20-lap, 96.2-mile race; Mike finished soaked in oil.

The roles were reversed in the 500cc race: here Mike was the master. This was the first time since 1962 that two MV riders had really battled together, but the Englishman came out on top and in the process set new race and lap records (88.76mph and 89.73mph respectively).

Then, after almost a month's break, Mike suffered an engine blow-up on his 500 MV at San Remo, Italy, on Sunday 23 May. *Motor Cycle News* asked:

> *Are these big MV's growing old?… Their legendary reliability took a kick in the pants when Mike Hailwood blew up his fire engine after leading an international 500cc race at San Remo Italy, on Sunday. His teammate Giacomo Agostini won the race. Mike's trouble was a suspected broken valve. Enough to cause panic in the MV camp. After all, the Senior TT is only three weeks away.*

During practice for the Isle of Man TT races, Mike set the fastest lap of the week on his five-hundred MV Agusta at 104.97mph – from a standing start! It should be noted that this was the fastest practice time ever recorded up to that time. He also rode the 350cc triple for the first time, but experienced suspension troubles.

In the Junior TT on Wednesday 16 June 1965, Mike set a new class lap record of 102.85mph on the three-cylinder MV, before retiring due to a mixture of problems including engine oil leaks and chain problems. This left Jim Redman to win on his Honda, from Phil Read (Yamaha) and Agostini.

A heroic ride

In what his father Stan was later to recall as: 'one of Mike's greatest performances', Mike won the Senior TT in truly dramatic fashion. It was a rain-soaked race, and Mike came home with his clutch lever bent at a crazy angle, two megaphones flattened, the handlebars bent, his leathers torn and

Mike with the new 350 three-cylinder during the 1965 Junior TT. He set the fastest lap of the race at 102.85mph before retiring with engine trouble.

one carburettor out of action after a crash at Sarah's Cottage. There were many accidents, caused not only by the wet conditions, but also by gale force winds. As Mike described it himself:

> One minute I was on it and the next moment I was sliding up the road on my back. When I stopped, the first thing I saw was Agostini (who had crashed at the same spot earlier) and the other MV at the side of the road. Luckily, my bike wasn't too badly bent and I was able to get going again.

The damage still required a lengthy pit stop (taking 68.4 seconds). Incredibly, even after crashing, Mike was still 19 seconds ahead of Derek Woodman (Matchless) on the third lap and he still led the race by nearly two minutes. As one journalist described Woodman and Joe Dunphy (who were second and third at that time) chasing Mike: 'It was like the Battle of the River Plate – a brace of old British battlers going after the pride of the enemy's fleet'.

Then Mike had to pit again at the end of the fifth lap, his engine sounding 'haywire and erratic' *(MCN)*. One carburettor had shaken loose and was causing the throttle slide to jam. Mike's mechanic, Vittorio Carrano, worked furiously to remove the offending slide and a further 67.8 seconds ticked by before Mike was able to push-start his MV into action again amid cheers from the grandstand. His engine was effective on only three cylinders. So began a last-lap race between a 375cc three and a couple of lusty full-size 500cc singles.

The question on everyone's mind was: would the world champion be able to hold them off, particularly on that last long climb over the Mountain?

Then came more drama. One of Mike's other carburettors had stuck open, meaning that the cylinder was running flat out all the time. Poor Derek Woodman's Matchless retired on the Mountain, and somehow Mike's MV kept going to eventually cross the finishing line to win his third consecutive Senior TT, at the slowest full-distance speed since 1950, when Geoff Duke (Norton) won over seven laps at 92.27mph.

Mike's average speed for the six-lap 226-mile race was 91.69mph. The *Motor Cycle News* race report for the 1965 Senior TT said: 'He wouldn't give up!' and that summed things up perfectly.

Senior TT – 6 laps – 226 miles
1st   M. Hailwood (MV Agusta)
2nd   J. Dunphy (Norton)
3rd   M. Duff (Matchless)
4th   I. Burne (Norton)
5th   S. Griffiths (Matchless)
6th   W. McCosh (Matchless)

MZ 250 Twin

The first drawings for a two-fifty twin-cylinder MZ (an air-cooled rotary valve induction two-stroke) were made by chief designer Walter Kaaden during the winter of 1953–4. The broad strategy was to experiment on the existing 125cc single, then transfer the technology to the twin. At this point, it should be explained that the 250 was actually two 125s with crankshafts spliced to a common primary drive. However, in practice, it was not quite as simple as this, with the result that the larger bike was not ready until 1958 in a form suitable for Grand Prix events.

At the West German GP at the Nürburgring works rider Horst Fugner gave the MZ twin a fabulous race debut by bringing it home behind race winner Tarquinio Provini (MV Agusta). At that time official MZ figures quoted 36bhp. At the very next round, the Swedish GP at Hedemora, Fugner gave the new MZ its first victory. The man he beat was Mike Hailwood (NSU). However, no works MV Agustas finished the race.

During 1959 MZ signed Gary Hocking, and he gave the East German factory its next victory on the two-fifty in Sweden (Kristianstad), followed by the Ulster round (where Gary beat Mike – the latter now riding an FB Mondial). Subsequently Hocking was signed by Count Agusta. Mike made his MZ debut at Monza (on the 250) in September 1959, but could only finish a lowly ninth. The best finish the MZ 250 gained in 1960 was when Ernst Degner finished third in the last round at Monza.

In 1961, Kaaden and MZ concentrated on the 124 single, but, when Degner was leading the championship, he defected in Sweden, leaving MZ without a top line rider, except for occasional races by Englishman Alan Shepherd. This caused a political storm, which was to have severe repercussions for MZ, both on and off the track. Degner's exit also virtually ended MZ's success in the 125cc class, and it was to turn more and more to the 247.2cc (54x54mm) twin.

After years of work with air-cooled engines, MZ introduced a semi-liquid-cooled version of its 250 twin in early 1962. This had water jackets around the barrels only to disperse excess heat between the cylinders; the heads remained air-cooled. Another change was pressure lubrication of the main bearings, from the gearbox supply. Development work on a fully water-cooled version was already in hand, and by June 1962 such a machine was ridden in practice, but not raced, at Schleiz. This employed twin radiators.

For the 1962 East German Grand Prix at the Sachsenring, MZ not only had the services of Alan Shepherd, but also the 1961 250cc world champion, Mike Hailwood. Ranged against Alan and Mike in the 250cc race was the entire Honda works team, headed by Jim Redman. In front of over 250,000 wildly-excited spectators, Shepherd was the early leader. However, after he was forced out due to a broken crankshaft, Mike took up the mantle and went on to ride an absolutely fantastic race. The *Motor Cycling* report sums it up nicely:

> *...with never more than inches in it, the lap record was shattered time and time again, and in a breath-taking climax that had the whole crowd in a frenzy, Redman tenaciously held on to win despite a fantastic lap at 100.77mph by Mike.*

This lap was actually quicker than Redman's new 350cc record, set at the same meeting!

The performance of the latest MZ was on a par with, and sometimes superior to, the Japanese four-cylinder. For example, although the Honda was faster around the bend prior to the finishing straight, the MZ more than made up the distance on the straight itself.

At the beginning of the 1963 season, Mike broke the lap record before retiring due to spark plug trouble during the non-championship Austrian GP over the 3.12-mile semi-autobahn circuit near Salzburg on 1 May. But with problems of obtaining visas for its East German mechanics and Kaaden himself, MZ was frustrated once again in its efforts to mount a full Grand Prix challenge.

Without doubt, however, one of the very biggest news stories of the 1963 international race season came with Mike's sensational victory in the 250cc East German GP at the Sachsenring, on the latest version of the MZ twin.

The *Motor Cycling* race report read:

> *...two-hundred thousand East Germans rose to their feet shouting, cheering and waving flags as Mike Hailwood scored the most popular win of his fabulously successful career at the Sachsenring on Sunday. Piloting a locally built MZ two-stroke twin in the East German Grand Prix, Mike had spread-eagled the opposition to win the 250cc class at a record speed of 98.30mph.*

During the previous winter, Walter Kaaden and his team had lifted the power output to 48bhp at 10,800rpm. The maximum speed had risen to 155mph (timed at the Belgian GP in 1962).

A single, light-alloy radiator and finning on the water jackets were used. However, the fins were for strength, not cooling. A new crankshaft had also been introduced following Shepherd's retirement during the 1962 East German GP. Incidentally, this was the first time a 250 MZ had succumbed to a bottom-end failure. Instead, retirements had usually been caused by piston seizures.

As already related, early experiments had been carried out with sheet-metal jackets simply welded around the existing cylinder after the fins had been ground away, while the cylinder head remained air-cooled. For 1963, the change was made to water-cooling both the cylinder and head, using entirely new components. Water circulation was provided by the thermo-siphon method with no water pump. When the engine was running, heated water inside the cooling jacket would rise and flow up through a large-diameter hose to the top of the radiator, where it would displace cooler water that would flow downwards, through another hose, and into the cylinder jacket. MZ had also reverted to rearward-facing exhausts. With the exhaust ports at the front, any slight gain from having an increased exhaust-pipe length to play with was more than offset by the drop in power output and decreased reliability.

Another reason for positioning the exhaust port at the rear of the cylinder had been to improve piston sealing (with a forward-rotating engine, rod angularity during the power-stroke pushes the piston against the rear cylinder wall) as there had been a noticeable power loss with the relocated exhaust port. Most damning of all, however, was that the forward-port engines proved even more prone to piston seizures! This was probably caused by the reduced sealing effectiveness allowing some of the flame to blow down past the piston on the exhaust port side. This caused overheating of the piston and, additionally, burned away the lubricant on that side of the cylinder. Finally, the power output was increased from the 1962 figure of 46bhp, while fuel consumption at racing speeds was in the region of 22mpg.

As for Mike's MZ relationship, he was prevented from many more appearances on two counts: the first was simply the political situation as already described and the second was Count Agusta's open hostility to his riding other makes of machine while he was under contract to MV (a problem which had earlier been experienced by John Surtees).

However, Mike did race an MZ 250 in the 1964 East German GP (again at the Sachsenring) but crashed out while leading. Then, towards the end of the 1964 season, he rode MZs in the 250 and 350cc classes at the

Japanese GP, staged on the Honda-owned Suzuka circuit. He finished fifth in the 250cc race and second (on a 251cc MZ) in the 350 event.

What Mike's MZ rides did show was his incredible ability to ride virtually any type or capacity of machine – often on the same day – and still prove a winner. Very few other riders ever had this level of ability.

Mike hustling the new three-cylinder MV Agusta during the 1965 Junior TT.

Two days later, at Mallory Park, Mike had another victory on his 500 MV, but this time things were much easier – and the sun was shining! Mike let Bill Ivy (Kirby Matchless) lead for the first seven laps. He then caught him and cleared off to win comfortably by 200 yards. In a sporting gesture, Mike gave his winner's laurels to Bill, before the two did a victory parade lap around the Mallory circuit. It was a great show for the enthusiastic 25,000 crowd, and much appreciated by them.

The European GPs
Then came a bout of European Grand Prix. The first, the Dutch TT at Assen, was on Saturday 26 June – only six days after Mallory Park. Here Mike had to concede the 350cc race to Jim Redman's Honda after a race-long battle. As *Motor Cycle News* reported:

For 12 laps Mike hounded Jim in the 350cc race, and for a short spell even led him. Then with tattered boots and bleeding toes

Mike during practice for the 1965 Senior TT on his MV four, when he set the fastest lap of the week at 104.97mph – from a standing start!

bearing mute witness to the effort he had put into staying with the flying Rhodesian, Mike the Bike settled for an honourable second place. His MV three cylinder, on this showing at any rate, is not as quick as the Honda.

In the 500cc Dutch TT, Mike continued his unchallenged lead in the championship and won another victory.

Eight days later, on Sunday 4 July, Mike took a step nearer retaining his title when he won the 500cc Belgian GP and in the process set a new lap record for the 8.76-mile Spa Francorchamps circuit.

500cc Belgian GP – 15 laps – 131.42 miles
1st   M. Hailwood (MV Agusta)
2nd   G. Agostini (MV Agusta)
3rd   D. Minter (Norton)
4th   P. Driver (Matchless)
5th   F. Stevens (Matchless)
6th   G. Marsovzsky (Matchless)

In East Germany, Mike's 500cc victory on his MV clinched his fourth successive world title in the blue riband class – a feat never achieved before. Mike suffered engine trouble with his three-cylinder MV in the 350cc event, and retired.

It was a repeat performance a week later on 25 July at the newly introduced Czech GP at the Brno circuit, where the 350cc triple expired again. However, he won the 500cc race, finishing over a minute in front of his MV teammate, Giacomo Agostini.

As *Motor Cycle News* said in their 18 August 1965 issue, 'Hail the Mike'. Three brilliant wins on an assortment of machines totalling seven cylinders and 1500cc proclaimed Mike Hailwood 'Hero of the Hutch' on Saturday. The setting was the famous Hutchison 100 meeting at Silverstone on 14 August. The machines and races were:

350cc	AJS 7R single	348cc
500cc	MV Agusta four	499cc
Production	BSA Lightning twin	654cc

And this outstanding performance simply sealed Mike's reputation as a man who could win on any size, engine type or make of machine. In addition the weather was typical of the so-called British summer, as *MCN* put it:

> *Inevitably it rained, steadily and miserably for most of the afternoon. But not before a tremendous crowd* [including the author!] *had gathered round the 2.93-mile Grand Prix circuit.*

A monsoon at Monza

And if Mike thought it would be sunnier in Italy for the Italian GP at Monza on Sunday 5 September, he was wrong. The tail-end of the typhoon that had hit Italy the previous week landed right on the circuit for race day. The *Motor Cycle News* headline ran: 'Monsoons Drench Monza Classic'.

Mike looked set to score his first victory on the three-cylinder model in the 350cc class, but then the rain arrived and he slid off. Before that, Mike had set a new class lap record of 117.68mph. Uninjured, he later won the

In what his father Stan was later to recall as one of Mike's greatest performances, Mike won the 1965 Senior TT in dramatic fashion. In a rain-soaked race, and with his machine quite badly damaged after a crash at Sarah's Cottage, he still managed to win.

500cc race in pouring rain, which was actually so fierce it was bouncing off the track surface. Even so, Mike still gave the big MV enough throttle to put in the fastest lap of the race at 103.65mph – amazing!

Mike then returned to the UK for the lucrative end-of-season meetings at Mallory Park (Race of the Year) on 26 September, and Brands Hatch (Race of the South) on 10 October. Although he won the 500cc race at Mallory, wet conditions made his big MV a handful round the short Leicestershire circuit, and he could only come home fifth in the Race of the Year. Then at Brands Hatch he won the Invitation race on a Tom Kirby G50 Matchless, crashing while leading the 500cc on the same bike, and was slowed with clutch trouble on a Kirby AJS in the 350cc event, finally finishing fifth.

Even before he had left, together with teammate Giacomo Agostini, for the Japanese Grand Prix at Suzuka, questions were being asked about Mike's MV future. The firm he was being linked with was Honda. *Motor Cycle News* carried a story in their 6 October 1965 issue: 'Next season Honda are prepared to sign him as a fully fledged works rider, with the firm possibility of giving him a bike for the 500 class.' Yet another press story said that Mike could: 'Take his pick' from not only Honda, but also Suzuki, Gilera and 'presumably' MV. In fact, Honda did offer Mike a 250 six-cylinder model for the Japanese GP on Sunday 25 October. Although there were potentially many pitfalls, including his existing MV contract and oil companies (Mike was with Shell, Honda with Castrol), everything was eventually sorted out,

As *Motor Cycle News* said in their 18 August 1965 issue 'Hail the Mike'. This was in response to a trio of brilliant victories on an assortment of machinery totalling seven cylinders and 1500cc. That day at Silverstone his bikes comprised an MV 500 four, AJS 7R 350 single and, shown here, a BSA Lightning twin displacing 654cc in the production event.

allowing the now five-times world champion (four 500cc, one 250cc) to compete on the Honda in the 250cc race and MV in the 350cc event.

Then came the racing itself. In the 350cc race, Mike's job was to tail Giacomo Agostini home so that the Italian could win the 350cc world title. This Mike did until Ago's MV went sick (a broken contact breaker spring). Then Mike went on to win himself, with champion elect Jim Redman (Honda) runner-up – thus clinching the title. Mike then moved over to the Honda camp, riding the latest six-cylinder model as a 'private' entry. Once again, he stormed away from the field to win comfortably.

350cc Japanese GP – 25 laps – 93.27 miles

1st	M. Hailwood (MV Agusta)
2nd	J. Redman (Honda)
3rd	I. Kasuya (Honda)
4th	M. Yamashita (Honda)
5th	G. Agostini (MV Agusta)
6th	B. Smith (Honda)

250cc Japanese GP – 24 laps – 89.54 miles

1st	M. Hailwood (Honda)
2nd	I. Kasuya (Honda)
3rd	B. Ivy (Yamaha)
4th	M. Yamashita (Honda)
5th	H. Hasagawa (Yamaha)

When the racing was over, Mike was reported as flying out of Japan on Wednesday 27 October to Honolulu on his way to South Africa to decide whether to race for MV Agusta or Honda; his contract with the Italian concern expired in January. What would Mike do? No one seemed to know.

Back in Britain early in November, *Motor Cycling* reported that Mike had decided on the Honda route:

> *The clash of the giants is over. Honda have won the battle of the payroll from Count Domenico Agusta. Mike Hailwood signed to ride for the Japanese factory before leaving Tokyo for South Africa with his ex-rival and new teammate Jim Redman last week.*

Why Mike had chosen Honda instead of MV? Was it really simply money, or was there something else? That something else was the brand new five-hundred four-cylinder that Honda promised Mike. So it was roll on 1966!

Walter Kaaden

Walter Kaaden was a true engineering genius, and the man who had created the MZ two-stroke racers upon which Mike had put in some fantastic performances until banned from riding the East German bikes by Count Agusta.

Kaaden was also a man of the old school – humble, honest and loyal. Born on 1 September 1919, his father was chauffeur both to Dipl. Ing. Carl Hahn, who oversaw the famous DKW firm in the 1930s, and the company's founder, Jorgen Stafe Rasmussen. When only eight years of age, the young Walter was able to accompany his father and Rasmussen to the opening of the famous Nürburgring circuit. Doubling as a racing circuit and industry test ground, it was a vital tool in the development of motor vehicles in Germany.

Walter Kaaden entered the Technical Academy in Chemitz, some 15 miles from DKW's base at Zschopau. Chemitz was very much a centre of industry and commerce for the German state of Saxony, and many other pre-war motorcycle marques including Wanderer were based in this area.

World War Two broke out when Kaaden was 20, and his engineering prowess saw him arrive at the infamous Peenmunde research establishment on the Baltic coast, where he was to work under the likes of Werner von Braun. At that time Germany was leading the world in rocket design, and Kaaden is generally acknowledged to have built the prototype Cruise missile – the 4S293 – which today is on permanent exhibition at the Deutsches Museum, Munich.

After Peenmunde was virtually destroyed by RAF bombers in August 1943, the research centre was relocated and work on V2 rockets continued. Then, in May 1945, Kaaden was interned by the Americans before being handed over to the Russians. Zschopau, meanwhile, was in the sector of Germany controlled by the Communist authorities and Walter was eventually released in 1950. He then returned to Saxony, and soon entered employment with DKW's successors, MZ (Motorradwerk Zschopau).

From 1953 Kaaden took charge of the MZ racing development, and developed a series of engines where the carburettor was mounted to the side of the crankcase, to supply mixture by means of a disc valve mounted in the crankcase wall. He was also a pioneer in utilising the now widely-used square 54x54mm bore and stroke dimensions (on a 125cc single) with expansion chamber exhaust.

By 1961, the 125 single and 250cc twins were producing the equivalent of 200bhp per litre – an amazing figure for the time – and MZ looked capable of winning the 125cc World Championship. But it was not to be, for their chief rider, Ernst Degner, defected to the West to work for Suzuki (who were to win their first-ever world title the following year).

Kaaden had been approached earlier, but had refused Suzuki's advance, putting his family and country before personal freedom or wealth.

With the Cold War in full swing, MZ and Walter Kaaden were severely restricted in what they could achieve – for no other reason than the fact that obtaining visas for travel outside the Communist area was virtually impossible. But as Mike Hailwood was to prove, if MZ had had a level playing field it could well have provided a serious challenge to the Japanese juggernaut as the 1960s unfolded.

As it was, although Kaaden's research was to be reflected in all subsequent racing two-stroke engines, he and MZ were not to benefit.

Walter Kaaden died on 3 March 1996, but his technology acts as a constant reminder of what this man, dubbed the 'father of the modern two-stroke' achieved.

Chapter 7

Back to Honda

SO FOR 1966 Mike was back on Honda machinery. Previously, in 1961, when he had raced the Japanese bikes it had been as a privately entered rider – via the British importers Hondis Ltd, rather than as a full works man. Of course, even then he had still come out on top, winning his and Honda's first-ever World Championship on a 250 four.

Now he was returning, not only with a full works contract, but also as Honda's number one rider, in everyone's eyes, although officially this was never stated at the time. There had even been rumours that Honda had asked their team captain Jim Redman to take up a non-riding role. But Jim continued racing into 1966. In addition, Mike and Jim got on well and in fact spent much of the 1965 winter together, if proof was needed.

Perhaps more worrying for Honda was that Mike had said, in no uncertain terms, that he was less than happy with the roadholding abilities of the 250 six he had ridden in the Japanese Grand Prix in October 1965.

At the beginning of January 1966, Mike and Jim were requested by Honda to go to Japan for testing, both at that time being in South Africa. Mike was able to go immediately, whereas Jim informed Honda that he had outstanding entries for South African meetings. Aware of the FIM ruling concerning honouring entries, he was excused.

At the end of January Mike returned to England, having also fixed his racing programme for British short circuit meetings. He had been promised one 350 Honda four – with 'plenty of spares'. So Mike was 'confident' of appearing at all of the meetings he had arranged.

Mike also planned to ride in the 500-mile production race which, in 1966, moved from Castle Combe (where it had been held as a replacement for the out-of-commission Thruxton circuit) to Brands Hatch. However, he had 'no idea' which machine he would ride or who would partner him. Actually, the stumbling block was to centre around the new Honda CB450 twin – which was outlawed due to having double overhead camshafts and torsion bar valve springs. In the end Mike did not contest the event.

Nobody knew exactly what bike Mike would be racing in the 500cc class in the World Championship, apart from the Honda works – and they were

When Honda celebrated its first 50 years in business, it put Mike at the centre of its achievements.

HALF CENTURY. FULL THROTTLE.

One morning in 1954, Soichiro Honda gathered all of his employees and made an outrageous statement: Their tiny company, Honda Motor Co., was going to race at the Isle of Man. Race, and win.

Mr. Honda and his racers bring home the gold at the Isle of Man.

Freddie Spencer and his championship-winning 1985 NSR500 Grand Prix bike.

Now you have to understand that at this time, Honda Motor Co. made little 50cc stepthroughs and clip-on engines for bicycles. But you also have to understand that Soichiro Honda had the blood of a racer coursing through his veins, that in 1936 he set an automotive speed record at the All-Japan Speed Rally which

stood for almost twenty years.

So, in 1961, when Hondas won not one but two classes at the Isle of Man, the world may have been surprised, but anyone who knew Soichiro Honda wasn't.

Honda Motor Company was founded by a man who believed in racing. And in the fifty years we've been in business, we've actively pursued racing as a way to test our

The great Mike Hailwood heads towards victory.

innovations, to prove our designs, and develop our technology. Along the way, we've produced some incredible machines, and worked with some phenomenal riders. The lessons we've learned have directly influenced the way we build our bikes. And we've

also achieved quite a track record: championships in every class we've entered from Road Race and Off-Road to Motocross, Supercross and Flattrack, with over 100 National and World

Gary Jones and his number-one Elsinore.

Championships in all.

So the next time you walk into your Honda Dealer's showroom, take a second to look around. Because you're looking at the total of half a century of racing heritage and philosophy. And the vision of one man who

Four-time 500GP Champion Mick Doohan and his NSR.

knew that racing was the most important thing his company could do, and had the faith and skill and tenacity to back up that dream.

Celebrating the Dream HONDA

Dick Mann rode his Honda CB750 into history at the 1970 Daytona 200.

not saying. Typical of the rumour mill at the time was the following story which appeared in *Motor Cycle News* on 9 February 1966:

> *Honda aren't saying anything but a glimmer of gossip from the land of the rising sun suggests that they are definitely working on a vee-eight 500 for Mike Hailwood and that the engine is no wider than the 250 six. The engine of one prototype anyway, is fitted with one bank of cylinders horizontal and the other vertical rather than a definite V.*

As for Honda's rivals in the 500cc class, Count Agusta had already welcomed the competition, saying he was 'ready and waiting' for the Honda challenge.

The reason why Mike signed to ride for Honda for 1966: the new and unraced RC181 500cc four-cylinder. Although power was never a problem, handling certainly was, and it took all Mike's considerable skills to tame the beast.

Also in early February came news of a 'much lighter and slimmer 500cc MV four'. However, this was to prove only partly true, as the bike in question turned out to be a larger displacement for the three-cylinder that Giacomo Agostini and Mike had ridden in 1965.

While all these rumours were floating around, Mike had visited Daytona – not for motorcycle purposes, but for a 24-hour car race, as co-driver to Innes Ireland. But this proved a big disappointment, with Mike saying: 'the race was a flop; the gearbox packed up after 3½ hours, before I took the wheel'. Mike also said he expected the 350 Honda four to arrive from Japan by the end of February and that besides the British meetings already mentioned he planned to race the machine at 'some early Italian meetings'.

Agostini to go it alone

In early March, it was learned that Mike's former MV teammate Giacomo Agostini was to go it alone. Talking to journalist Carlo Perelli (an old friend of the author), Giacomo confirmed that he would be the only MV rider in the classics. Then, in mid-March, it was finally revealed that Mike Hailwood's Honda mount for the 500cc class would be a four-cylinder, with its cylinders in the traditional across-the-frame format. Mike showed off his new allegiance with his famous golden crash helmet now sporting the Honda motif.

When interviewed for a special *Motor Cycle News Ten Years Anniversary Supplement* in March 1966, Mike commented:

Where has all that old smooth style gone?… Things have changed a lot since I began racing. The most noticeable, to my mind, is the change in racing styles. When I started, chaps like Geoff Duke and Bob Anderson set the pattern with everything flowing nicely. Nowadays it's all ragged and nasty-looking. I suppose the improved grip of modern racing tyres has something to do with it. I can't really pin it down. Another change I deplore is that many riders no longer take the fastest line through corners but take a line which prevents overtaking. They even drive up the inside. I noticed this particularly when I came to Brands Hatch after last year's grand prix season on the continent. Some of the riding I saw made it more of a carve-up than a road race.

At the end of March 1966, the Honda team for the new season was officially confirmed as Mike, Jim Redman, Luigi Taveri and Ralph Bryans. As *Motor Cycle News* said, it was: 'A formidable quartet of reigning and former world champions for all five classes'. Mike was to concentrate on the 250 and 500cc, although, where it was possible, he would support Jim Redman in the 350cc class. Redman, in turn, would support Mike, again where possible, in the 250 and 500cc classes. FIM rules limited racing mileage to 310 in a single day.

The 1962 and 1964 125cc world champion, Swiss rider Luigi Taveri, was Honda's hope in this class with the high revving five-cylinder model and his Ulster teammate Ralph Bryans as second string. Ralph, the reigning 50cc title-holder, led the challenge again in this class, with Luigi in support.

The first works appearance of the team was to be the Spanish GP on 8 May, but Mike would be appearing with the 350 four at Brands Hatch, Snetterton and Oulton Park over the Easter weekend.

During late March, Mike was again away in Japan testing, including the brand new five-hundred four. Then in the 6 April 1966 issue of *Motor Cycle News*, Mike had this to say about how he saw things with two days to go before his first meeting at Brands Hatch:

Not since joining the MV team have I looked forward to a road racing season quite so much as this one and I will be plunging in at the deep end with three meetings on the trot at Easter. Fortunately Mr Honda had given me one of the 350 fours and it should be a really great weekend and the ideal rust remover for the start of the world championships. By the time Snetterton comes on Sunday, I reckon to have knocked a few spots off.

SNETTERTON RACE CIRCUIT
CIRCUIT LENGTH 2·71 miles

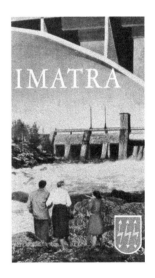

Snetterton during the early 1960s, prior to the introduction of the infamous Russell's Corner; length 2.71 miles.

...my biggest headache is in case I have machine trouble because I have neither spares nor tools, and, unlike MV, Honda won't allow me to ride any other make of machine. I need a few short circuit dices and hoped the fans would perhaps like to see the Honda four racing round, so I'm chancing it but I shall be a very relieved rider when the flag drops at the last Easter meeting.

The fact that only the bike had been sent by Honda seems strange: surely it must have come with the likes of alternative sprockets and jets. And what of the promised spares Mike had mentioned a few weeks earlier?

Mike foresaw a tough year ahead in the GPs:

...now that I am riding for Honda it means that I will be back in the most competitive class of all, the 250, as well as trying to hold on to the 500 title. The big class may not be as easy as some people think for Count Agusta will be trying hard to win again and the MV is a magnificent machine. The rider will be Giacomo Agostini and nobody should underestimate Ago. The 250 class is a real hot potato. Phil Read has been champion for the past two years and given a bit of luck with the new two-stroke four, he is going to take some beating. It is hard luck for Yamaha that Mike Duff is still in trouble and may not be fit until the TT. It will be nice to see him

Snetterton, Easter Sunday 1966, and Mike is seen attempting to pick up his four-cylinder Honda 350 at the infamous Russell's Corner. In the end so many riders crashed that the race had to be stopped.

back. I will be supporting Jim in the 350 class where again our biggest headache will be Ago. He is probably better on the MV three than the four and could cause a few sparks – in more ways than one. The TT will be one of the year's highspots and, nice though they are, I hope that I'm not eating the marshals' tea and jam butties somewhere out on the course during any of the races.

Two wins, one fall

Then came the trio of Easter meetings, which resulted in two wins and a fall. The victories came at Brands Hatch (Friday 8 April) and Oulton Park (Monday 11 April). In between came Snetterton. For 1966, the Norfolk circuit had deemed it necessary to put in a new corner (Russell's – after Jim Russell the local car driver). The purpose of this was to slow competitors as they exited the fast Coram Curve and then entered the straight past the pit area and startline. But the problem was that in the wet (as the author experienced when racing at Snetterton that same year) the new corner was like a skidpan.

As a spectator at the meeting on Easter Sunday 10 April 1966, I well remember the whole sorry incident, which saw not only Mike, but almost half the field become victims of Russell's Corner. The carnage was so severe that eventually the organisers had to stop the race as more and more riders fell.

Motor Cycle News printed a photograph entitled 'The Ravages of Rain-soaked Russell' in their 'Paddock Gossip' column in the issue dated 13 April 1966. This is what Robin Miller had to say:

> No, *this is not a paddock scene! It is the new Snetterton emergency centre for broken motorcycles set up rather hurriedly on Sunday. These, in fact, are the unhappy victims of Snetterton's dreaded Russell corner which became the subject of much unholy language on Easter Sunday. On the right is Dave Simmonds' Honda, in the centre Chris Conn's AJS (7) and on the left Tony Wilmott wheels his Norton away. At least eight riders fell at this point, including Mike Hailwood and Joe Dunphy. This was due in some measure to the rain and the rubber left from a car meeting on Good Friday. But the major source of the trouble was the corner itself. It is bad from every angle and although some improvement has been made since the hairpin was first introduced last year, it is still dangerous and, in my opinion, unnecessary. There are two alternatives. Either scrap it and revert to the old circuit or, at the very least, make it safe. At the moment there is a nasty ridge at the crucial point where the new surface joins the old, and at the exact spot where the bikes are flicked over on exit. If we must have the corner, let's have it widened and the new surface extended right out with, if possible, a slight camber.*

But in truth it was *three decades* or so before the dreaded Russell's was anything like safe. In between came so many revamps and redesigns that everyone, including the author, simply lost count.

Imola and Cesenatico

Next it was off to Italy for meetings at Imola (17 April) and Cesenatico (24 April). And as the *Motor Cycle News* race report said of the Imola event: 'Stars warm up for the World Classics in Italian sunshine'.

At the 3.12-mile Imola circuit, between Bologna and Rimini, after weeks of rain, the weather was like summer – a far cry from the cold, wet Easter weekend Mike had experienced back in Britain.

With just the three-fifty four, Mike only contested the 350cc race, but this

Bill Ivy rose through the ranks of club, national and GP racing to become one of the great riders of the late 1960s. He also shared with Mike a love of life, the pair becoming great friends before Bill's fatal accident while racing a Jawa V4 two-stroke in 1969.

Bill Ivy with his works 125cc Yamaha four at Cadwell Park in 1967, and a Japanese race mechanic.

Bill Ivy

Although they were never members of the same team (both rode at different times for Hornchurch, Essex, dealer/entrant Tom Kirby), Bill Ivy was a close friend of Mike Hailwood.

Born in Maidstone, Kent, on 27 August 1942, Bill Ivy began racing 17 years later on a 50cc Italian Itom two-stroke, sponsored by his employers, the Chisholm Brothers of Maidstone, at his local circuit, Brands Hatch.

That same year he broke the class lap record for the famous Kent circuit. Then came a series of rides including a 175cc Gilera single, a race-tuned Honda CB92 and finally Honda CR93s, both from Chisholms and Liverpool-based businessman Bill Hannah.

In 1965, Bill won the British Championship for the first time and decided to turn professional. A year later he took the prestigious King of Brands title away from Derek Minter and scored his first Grand Prix victory for Yamaha at Montjuich Park, Barcelona.

From 1966 Bill's brief but sensational career blossomed to the point where he was one of the very best Grand Prix riders of the post-war era.

Bill Ivy was 'a colourful, flamboyant character with a fearless riding style', as race journalist John Brown once described him, and as such he was very much in tune with the 'swinging sixties'.

The pinnacle of Ivy's career came in 1968 with the duels he had, both on and off the track, with Yamaha teammate Phil Read. The rivalry between the two culminated in Read ignoring team orders to win both 125 and 250cc world titles that year. This was, in Ivy's opinion 'over the limit' and he announced his retirement, which came just as Yamaha had decided to quit Grand Prix racing, at least with its ultra-specialised hi-tech four-cylinder models.

Probably Bill's greatest moment came when he set an incredible 100.62mph lap during the Ultra-lightweight 125cc Isle of Man TT in 1968. For everyone who was there, this was a magical moment in TT history. Only 11 years earlier Bob McIntyre, riding a 500cc four-cylinder Gilera, had become the first rider to set a 100mph lap for the ultra-demanding 37.73-mile Mountain Circuit, and only three years previously Phil Read had become the first to record a 250cc 100mph lap on his factory RD56 twin in 1965.

His style, sense of fun and his diminutive size all combined to make Bill very much a favourite with the fans. And although he was often at odds with officialdom, which as often as not landed him in a pile of bother, he was no real law-breaker.

In 1969 he returned to racing, with the infamous Jawa 350cc V4 two-stroke. But sadly, just as he had got to grips with the Czech bike – and in the process given world champion Giacomo Agostini and his all-conquering MV Agusta a run for their money on more than one occasion – Bill suffered a fatal accident during a practice seizure in terribly wet conditions at the East German Grand Prix on 12 July 1969.

For 30 years thereafter, the annual Bill Ivy Trophy meeting was organised by Bill's former club, the Racing 50, under the auspices of its chairman Jim Parker. The club later changed its name to its current one, the New Era MCC.

Bill leads teammate Phil Read in the 125cc Czech Grand Prix at Brno on 21 July 1968.

turned out to be a real cracker. Mike set the pace on his 'hack' Honda four. Although he rode brilliantly, Giacomo Agostini (MV) and Tarquinio Provini (Benelli) were on their very latest factory machines. The race finished Agostini first, Provini second, Mike third.

At Cesenatico Mike finished runner-up to Provini when Agostini's gearbox broke at the end of the race. The latter was disqualified from the results for receiving outside assistance when an MV mechanic helped him push the bike back to the finish line.

Although Mike had left MV for Honda, the 500cc world champion still had friends at the Gallerate-based factory. In trouble with the suspension of his 350 Honda, Mike asked MV if they could lend him some rear suspension legs to suit his Honda for the meeting at Cesenatico. MV responded gladly and while Mike had other troubles with his self-maintained machine, his suspension bother was vastly improved.

At the same time came the first reports that a 'completely new 500 MV' would be available for Agostini in 1966. Although no firm details were available, *Motor Cycle News* guessed, wrongly, that 'it could be a new lighter four cylinder, it could also be a development of the 1957 six cylinder'. For some reason no one seemed to go for the obvious – a larger version of the existing triple.

Record breaking in Austria

On Sunday 1 May 1966, Mike created an absolute lap record during his winning ride in the 350cc class of the Austrian Grand Prix, rushing around the new 3.25-mile autobahn circuit at Arbo, near Salzburg, at 82.4mph on his 350 Honda. At the start of the 350, Mike rushed away from the rest of the field. His ever-increasing lead could have been boring had it not been for his inspired riding, which kept the crowd on its toes.

350cc Austrian GP – 12 laps – 39 miles

1st	M. Hailwood (Honda)
2nd	G. Havel (Jawa)
3rd	F. Bocek (CZ)
4th	F. Stastny (Jawa)
5th	G. Visenzi (Aermacchi)
6th	A. Pagani (Aermacchi)

Seven days later Mike won his first World Championship Grand Prix race since signing for Honda. The scene was a sunny Spanish GP around the 2.3-mile Montjuich Park circuit in Barcelona. After smashing the lap record by three seconds in practice, Mike was firm favourite to win the 250cc race, but teammate Jim Redman had no intention of simply making up the numbers and rocketed away from the start. But disaster struck after half a lap. On a tricky downhill right-hander, with a hump in the middle, Jim crashed, his bike bursting into flames in spectacular fashion. Mike, who was close on his tail, only just managed to escape the mêlée, but from there it was a one-horse race. The challenge of the new four-cylinder Yamahas proved something of 'a damp squib' *(MCN)* as Phil Read's model suffered constant plug trouble while something more severe was suspected in Bill Ivy's case. Both eventually retired. Mike finished the race lapping every other rider at least once.

250cc Spanish GP – 33 laps – 77.68 miles

1st   M. Hailwood (Honda)
2nd   D. Woodman (MZ)
3rd   R. Pasolini (Aermacchi)
4th   J. Findlay (Bultaco)
5th   H. Rosner (MZ)
6th   R. Blanco (Bultaco)

At the second round of the 1966 250cc World Championships at Hockenheim in West Germany, Phil Read (100, Yamaha) led Honda team-sters Mike (directly behind Read) and Jim Redman (103). In the end Mike won from Jim, with Phil third.

Honda clean up at Hockenheim

Honda machines won four of the five solo races at Hockenheim, the 1966 venue for the West German Grand Prix on Sunday 22 May, with Luigi Taveri winning the 125cc, Jim Redman the 500cc and Mike scoring a double in taking victories in both the 250 and 350cc events. Ralph Bryans finished runner-up to Suzuki-mounted Hans Georg Anscheidt in the 50cc encounter.

250cc West German GP – 23 laps – 96.66 miles

1st   M. Hailwood (Honda)
2nd   J. Redman (Honda)
3rd   B. Ivy (Yamaha)
4th   D. Woodman (MZ)
5th   F. Stastny (Jawa)
6th   G. Beer (Honda)

350cc West German GP – 23 laps – 96.66 miles

1st	M. Hailwood (Honda)
2nd	T. Provini (Benelli)
3rd	B. Beale (Honda)
4th	S. Grassetti (Bianchi)
5th	G. Havel (Jawa)
6th	F. Bocek (Jawa)

Mike scored another double Honda victory in the next round of the world championship series, the French GP at Clermont-Ferrand, on 29 May 1966, as *Motor Cycle News* reported: 'A fantastic display of riding by Mike Hailwood, shattering the lap record by 10 seconds, highlighted Sunday's French Grand Prix'. The 500cc world champion was simply 'unapproachable' as he scored his third 250 win on the trot and his second 350 victory to notch maximum points in both classes. *Motor Cycle News* again:

> *His performance in winning the two solo classes, 250 and 350, was simply breathtaking and overshadowed magnificent rides by Jim Redman and Phil Read in the 250 and dashing Giacomo Agostini in the 350. The extent of his dominance can be gained by comparing the increase in both record laps: 250cc new 80.96mph (old 1964 Read and Redman 77.31mph); 350cc new 80.93mph (old 1960 John Surtees 75.44mph).*

Mike with the 349cc Honda four he rode in non-championship races during 1966, at the international Brands Hatch meeting on 30 May that year. He won both his heat and the final (1000cc class).

After the French round, Mike took in a couple of British short circuit races at Brands Hatch, where he won the 1000cc race on 30 May, and at Mallory Park, taking the 350cc on 19 June. Both victories were aboard his 350cc Honda four.

Why, you may ask, was Mike at this meeting, which was during the period usually taken up with the Isle of Man TT practice and racing? The answer is simple. It was due entirely to the infamous Seaman's strike, which meant that the TT immediately preceded the Manx Grand Prix races later that summer (TT late August, MGP early September).

Dutch TT

Both Mike and Jim Redman were entered for all three races – 250, 350 and 500cc at the Dutch TT.

Engine from the three-fifty Honda four which Mike rode in British short circuit meetings in 1966. The machine was used by Honda squad in the period 1963–1965.

Two of Mike's rivals and friends during the mid-1960s were Suzuki's Frank Perris (far left) and Yamaha's Mike Duff (left).

The total mileages at the Assen circuit did not exceed the FIM maximum, and Honda wanted to ensure victory. Honda had flown over new, lighter frames for the 350s in an attempt to improve handling; these employed 19-inch front and 18-inch rear tyres.

After shattering the lap record by more than four seconds in his first race on the Honda 500 four, Mike fell off the bike at Assen (after suffering gearbox problems) on a slow left-hander. Before his fall, he raised the record from 90.23 to 92.30mph. Not only this, but with a brand-new 455cc three-cylinder MV Giacomo Agostini took over the lead. However, gearbox trouble and a brilliant ride by Jim Redman foiled the Italian factory's hopes of beating Honda. Jim snatched the lead in the closing minutes of the race to win by two seconds.

In 'scintillating form' *(MCN)*, Mike had earlier walked away from the opposition in the 250 and 350 races. These results left Mike a clear leader in both these classes, having scored maximum points in every race he had contested. Conversely he took just a single point in the 500cc title chase – the class in which he was the reigning world champion.

Spa Francorchamps, 3 July 1966, and Phil Read (Yamaha) leads Mike on the Honda six during the 250cc Belgian Grand Prix. Hailwood won the race, with Read second.

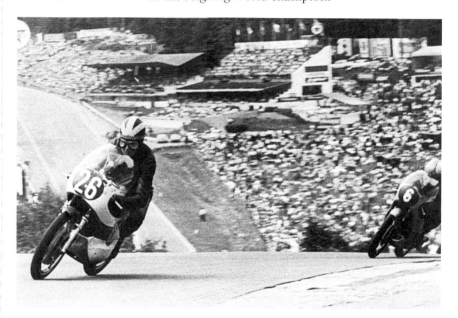

Eight days after Holland came the Belgian round at Spa Francorchamps on Sunday 3 July. This circuit, the fastest in the GP calendar, caused both Mike and Jim Redman problems with the 500 Honda, which was doing well over 170mph on the bumpy Masta straight. Both riders had difficulty holding their machines on the road.

After winning the 250cc race at Spa from Phil Read and Jim Redman, everyone looked forward to the possibility of Mike repeating this in the 500cc race. However, the hitherto invincible big Honda was, as *Motor Cycle News* described in their 6 July 1966 issue, 'sunk with all hands in a torrential downpour'. This flooded the circuit, causing competitors all sorts of problems, but worst hit were the Honda team. Jim Redman crashed, breaking an arm, while Mike was forced to retire suffering from exposure and gearbox problems. The man who benefited from all this was Giacomo

Agostini (riding the old four-cylinder bike to a superb, if extremely wet, victory). This meant that Ago now led the 500cc title race. His only real challenger, Jim Redman, was never to race again, announcing his retirement later from his South African home.

Many riders, including Mike himself, were of the opinion that the race should have been stopped. 'It was one of the worst races I have been in,' he said, 'it was impossible to see and the water was inches deep in places'.

Graham signs

On the eve of the East German GP at the Sachsenring, Stuart Graham, the 24-year-old son of the first 500cc world champion Les Graham (1949, AJS) was signed by Honda (as a temporary replacement for Jim Redman, who, at that time, was expected to resume racing once he recovered from his injuries). Stuart was put straight in the team and rode Jim Redman's six-cylinder two-fifty to fourth in East Germany.

Phil Read

Phil Read, born in Luton, Bedfordshire on 1 January 1939, has always been someone who has courted controversy. But on the other hand, there is absolutely no doubt that he has also been one of the truly great riders of not only his era, but also of all time. In fact, as even Phil agrees, if it had not been for a certain Mike Hailwood, Phil would now be even more highly regarded.

Besides Giacomo Agostini, Englishman Phil Read provided Mike Hailwood with his stiffest competition in the mid-to-late 1960s. Phil is seen here aboard his works four-cylinder Yamaha during his battle with Mike in the 1967 250cc TT, which Mike won.

One of Phil's problems has been a will to win above everybody else, which has not always endeared him to fans. Also there has been the small matter of his private life, both relationships and business interests, which have often caused difficulties. The press have also played a part by publicising Phil's dealings with certain rivals (for example Bill Ivy and later Giacomo Agostini) and events (notably the Isle of Man TT). All this has polarised public opinion. The author has known Phil on a personal level for many years – and we have always got on well. In addition, there is absolutely no disputing Phil's record of seven world titles – equal to no lesser man than John Surtees.

Phil began racing a BSA Gold Star (encouraged by his mother) in 1957, but his big break came when he won the Senior Manx Grand Prix on a Norton in September 1960. Then, again on a Norton, he won the Junior 350cc TT the following June. Other superb performances during the remainder of 1961 marked him out for future stardom.

During 1962, he mainly confined his activities to the British short circuits, winning many races, and there is little doubt that these performances, added to his victories in the Isle of Man, were responsible for prompting Geoff Duke to sign Phil to ride Gilera fours following Derek Minter's serious crash prior to the first round of the World Championship series, in which the latter, together with John Hartle, had been picked to take on Hailwood and the MV. Another factor was Phil's riding at Silverstone, in April 1963, when he had split the Gileras of Minter and Hartle in the 500cc – a sensational result which was also an embarrassment to the Scuderia Duke squad.

Ultimately the Gileras were to prove something of a disappointment (they had been mothballed since 1957), but Phil Read had been able to display his talents to a wider audience. This was to provoke an offer from Yamaha to race their works RD56 two-fifty twin, Phil having his first outing for his new employer in the Japanese GP at Suzuka during October 1963.

In 1964, Phil was top man in the 250cc World Championship, giving Yamaha their first world crown. It was the first time a two-stroke had won this particular title. Phil's victory also broke a three-year period where Yamaha's bitter rivals Honda had ruled supreme.

In 1965, Phil retained his title, then for 1966 Honda signed Mike Hailwood. This meant that both Yamaha and Honda had world-class riders in the 250cc class, and the machinery was awe-inspiring. Honda had a dohc six, whereas Yamaha had a brand new disc valve V4. Mike ended up champion, but Phil suffered teething problems with his new bike.

These problems were resolved in time for the 1967 season, and that year Read and Hailwood fought out one of the closest championships in the history of the sport. Phil actually had a higher total of basic points, and at first was awarded the championship. Later the FIM awarded it to Mike, because he had scored an extra victory. Phil also finished runner-up to teammate Bill Ivy in the 125cc championship.

In 1968 Phil won back both the 125 and 250cc titles. But even though both Honda and Suzuki had pulled out, this was no easy task, as a bitter rivalry erupted between Phil and Bill Ivy. In an effort to ensure peace, Yamaha had ruled that Phil could win the 125cc, with Bill being lined up for the 250cc crown. However, the two men had other plans, resulting in

SUNDAY 18th JUNE 1967   Programme 2s 6d

MALLORY PARK

INTERNATIONAL POST T.T.

MOTOR CYCLE RACES   Organised by the Easo Midland Centre A.C.U. for Mallory Park Circuit Ltd

SUNDAY JUNE 18TH 1967

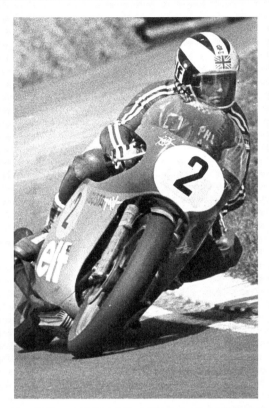

a season-long battle. At its end, Phil had won both titles, but in the process not only upset Ivy and Yamaha, but also many race fans. For many years thereafter, Yamaha were none too happy with the man who had given them their early successes, although all this now seems in the past with Phil being a member of the official Yamaha squad at the prestigious Centennial TT at Assen in 1998.

Meanwhile, on a privately entered, production Yamaha, Phil won the 250cc title again in 1971, on a machine tuned by the German, Helmut Fath.

In 1972 came news that Phil would be joining MV Agusta. At first this was to ride in the 350cc class, but for 1973 this was broadened to include the blue riband 500cc too. This brought Phil into conflict with MV's number one rider, Giacomo Agostini. As I described in my book *Giacomo Agostini: Champion of Champions* (Breedon Books): 'the move was like putting a fox into a hen house'. Phil and Ago simply didn't hit it off. And this was the main reason why Giacomo joined rivals Yamaha for 1974, after Phil won the 500cc championship in 1973. With Ago's departure Phil went on to retain the 500cc crown in 1974, but he was not to be found in the 350cc results that year, for the simple reason that MV withdrew from the class. Giacomo Agostini took the title for his new team.

In 1975, a fierce battle developed between Phil and Giacomo for the 500cc championship. Phil lost, with the Italian rider finally coming out on top, even though he had to wait until the last round to know the outcome of the titanic struggle.

Phil left MV at the end of 1975. Later, in 1977, he won the Formula 1 title in the Isle of Man on a Honda. Then came Mike's famous comeback in 1978, with these two great riders battling it out for the F1 crown around the Mountain Circuit in June 1978 – and, as is fully described in the main text, Mike came out on top.

Today Phil still rides regularly in historic racing events and the fast, neat style he used to win his world championship titles is still very evident. And, as the author has discovered, he saw Mike Hailwood as the man who prevented him winning an even higher number of titles.

Later, during the 1970s, Phil Read rode for the Italian MV Agusta team, winning the 500cc World Championship title in 1973 and 1974.

250cc East German GP – 15 laps – 76.6 miles
1st   M. Hailwood (Honda)
2nd   P. Read (Yamaha)
3rd   M. Duff (Yamaha)
4th   S. Graham (Honda)
5th   H. Rosner (MZ)
6th   F. Srna (CZ)

The works Honda 350 four with which Mike won the 1966 World Championship title. This was a much improved machine compared to the earlier model he raced at non-championship events.

In the bigger classes Honda had another bad day. In the 350cc race a piston shattered on Mike's machine, while more mechanical woes hit the big four in the 500cc race when a crankshaft broke. Agostini won the 350cc race, but after breaking the 500cc lap record the Italian crashed out, missing the chance to all but seal the 500cc title.

Champion of champions

So read the *Motor Cycle News* headline of 27 July 1966. The text went on 'Triple win at Czech GP' and continued:

The wonder man who now shoulders the full burden of Honda's title hopes in the 350 and 500cc classes proved that he must now be recognised as the greatest rider of all time.

This all came as Mike not only did the triple, but in the process also became the 250cc world champion. After an incredible display in the 250cc race with Phil Read, and beating Agostini in the 350cc, Mike then turned out in a downpour for the 500cc event. Handling the big Honda like the master he was, the reigning 500cc world champion battled through the spray to lap the entire field except second-place man Agostini (MV three-cylinder) who was then leading the championship. It was Mike's first 500cc victory in 1966.

250cc Czech GP – 9 laps – 78 miles
1st   M. Hailwood (Honda)
2nd   P. Read (Yamaha)
3rd   H. Rosner (MZ)
4th   M. Duff (Yamaha)
5th   G. Marsovsky (Bultaco)
6th   F. Stastny (CZ)

350cc Czech GP – 11 laps – 95.3 miles

1st   M. Hailwood (Honda)

2nd   G. Agostini (MV Agusta)

3rd   H. Rosner (MZ)

4th   F. Stastny (Jawa)

5th   R. Pasolini (Aermacchi)

6th   A. Pagani (Aermacchi)

500cc Czech GP – 13 laps – 112.6 miles

1st   M. Hailwood (Honda)

2nd   G. Agostini (MV Agusta)

3rd   G. Marsovsky (Matchless)

4th   J. Findlay (Matchless)

5th   J. Ahearn (Norton)

6th   E. Hinton (Norton)

The 500cc title is lost

At the Finnish Grand Prix, held at Imatra on Sunday 7 August, Mike lost his 500cc world crown when Giacomo Agostini won the 500cc race. Mike had been the holder for the previous four seasons. It was a particularly sweet moment for the Italian factory as, earlier in the year, it had appeared an impossible task after Redman and Honda's initial successes. Even so, Mike could be pleased with not only finishing runner-up to Ago, but also with winning the 250 and 350cc races.

A week later, on Sunday 14 August, Mike was taking part in the Mellano Trophy meeting at Brands Hatch. However, this meeting was not without its troubles. The 350cc four that Mike used for the meeting arrived back from overhaul in Amsterdam minus one or two rather important parts, including the clutch!

This gave Mike and his mechanic Roy Robinson some anxious moments, but after using Jim Redman's 250 four during morning practice, they fitted a new clutch and eventually got the 350 on the track. In the main race of the day, however, the bike let Mike down when an oil seal went in the gearbox; this was after he had won the 350cc race.

In the Ulster Grand Prix at Dundrod on Saturday 20 August 1966, Mike won the opening 112-mile 350cc race on his works Honda four (not the same bike as the one used for non-championship events) and drew the full appreciation of the crowd as he built up a winning two-minute lead over Ago and his MV. From the start Ago had led, but Mike was well ahead after the first lap of the 7.5-mile circuit, a position he maintained to the finish.

This resulted in him winning his second world title that year; a magnificent achievement, bringing his championship tally to seven.

350cc Ulster GP – 15 laps – 112 miles
1st   M. Hailwood (Honda)
2nd   G. Agostini (MV Agusta)
3rd   T. Robb (251cc Bultaco)
4th   G. Havel (Jawa)
5th   D. Simmonds (Norton-Honda)
6th   P. Dunphy (Norton)

Much of the racing had been in wet conditions, but a measure of luck came to the 500cc race. The rain eased and a slight breeze throughout the 90-minute lunch break conspired to dry the roads somewhat. Mike rocketed away from the start on his Honda four, with Agostini on the 420cc MV three next, followed by a horde of single-cylinder bikes, plus a couple of works Jawa twins. Patchy roads or not, Mike turned in a first lap of 99.49mph with Agostini doing his utmost to remain within striking distance. The ground those two put between themselves and the other competitors was, *Motor Cycle News* reported, 'staggering'. And at the end only these two remained on the same lap, Mike setting a new lap record of 105.03mph, breaking his own record set in 1963 (on the MV four) of 101.28mph.

500cc Ulster GP – 15 laps – 112 miles
1st   M. Hailwood (Honda)
2nd   G. Agostini (MV Agusta)
3rd   F. Stastny (Jawa)
5th   J. Findlay (Matchless)
5th   C. Conn (Norton)
6th   P. Williams (Matchless)

The delayed TT

Next came the delayed TT. The press was full of stories about the possibility of Mike winning all the four races he had entered – 125, 250, 350 and 500cc – all on Hondas. Since 1961, Mike had won seven TTs. Three wins would equal Irishman Stanley Woods's record of 10, and four would break it.

But Mike came close to disaster within a couple of miles of the opening TT practice session on Monday morning, 21 August. He was just entering the first right-hander into Union Mills when a rider who, according to Mike, was cruising on the outside of the course, swerved in front of him. The world champion was forced against the high kerb on the inside edge, punching the fairing and megaphone of the 250 Honda six, the machine almost taking control as it crashed towards the opposite wall. 'I didn't have time to see who it was,' said Mike in *Motor Cycle News*. 'I was too busy trying to keep the bike on the road'. It was not a happy lap for Mike or Honda. At the Mountain Box a connecting rod came through the crankcase, putting out of action Honda's sole remaining 250 six – but new machines were being flown in from Japan. As if all this wasn't enough, Ralph Bryans's five-cylinder 125 caught fire near Kirkmichael and was completely burned out.

Record speed from a standing start

On Sunday 28 August, Mike took one of the newly delivered six-cylinder Honda 250 models round the Mountain circuit at the almost undreamed of speed of 104.29mph in the process of winning the Lightweight TT. And this sensational lap was from a standing start!

From then on, as the opposition dropped by the wayside, Mike slowed down to win at an average speed of 101.91mph – still quicker than Jim Redman's 1965 lap record (also achieved on a six-cylinder) of 100.09mph. Teammate Stuart Graham was runner-up, but the surprise of the day was provided by Peter Inchley, who brought his Starmaker-engined Villiers Special into third place at a speed of 91.43mph. This was the first time since 1950 that a British 250cc machine had finished in the top three at the TT.

Phil Read and Bill Ivy on the V4 Yamahas both put up 100mph laps before retiring. Interestingly, through the *MCN* speed trap (on the downhill stretch between Creg Ny Baa and Brandish), Mike's machine was recorded at 139mph, against 141.2mph for Read, 142.9mph for Graham and Ivy's quickest at 149.4mph. By comparison Inchley's Villiers single clocked 118.4mph.

Mike's machine finished in perfect condition, except for a very slack chain and a well-worn rear tyre.

Lightweight (250cc) TT – 6 laps – 226.38 miles

1st	M. Hailwood (Honda)
2nd	S. Graham (Honda)
3rd	P. Inchley (Villiers Special)
4th	F. Stastny (CZ)
5th	J. Findlay (Bultaco)
6th	W. Smith (Bultaco)

Mike receives the Senior TT Trophy at the prize-giving ceremony on 3 September 1966. He also set a new lap record for the 37.73-mile course of 107.07mph.

On Wednesday 31 August, Mike rode in the Ultra-Lightweight (125cc) and Junior (350cc). On his five-cylinder Honda, Mike finished the former race in sixth, averaging 95.07mph for the three-lap, 113.19 mile race and the first Honda home (Bryans was seventh, Taveri eighth). But the two-stroke opposition was simply too powerful.

Ultra-Lightweight (125cc) TT – 3 laps – 113.19 miles

1st   B. Ivy (Yamaha)
2nd   P. Read (Yamaha)
3rd   H. Anderson (Suzuki)
4th   M. Duff (Yamaha)
5th   F. Perris (Suzuki)
6th   M. Hailwood (Honda)

In the Junior event, Mike's four-cylinder Honda suffered a broken valve and retired; victory went to the MV-mounted Giacomo Agostini.

Ralph Bryans

Born in Belfast, Northern Ireland, on 7 March 1942, Ralph Bryans was brought up in his native city and worked as a laundry boy with a firm of dry cleaners before becoming a motorcycle mechanic.

His first 'motorcycle' was actually a Power Pak (a motorised cycle), which his father had passed on to his son when he had purchased a 16H Norton. The first race Ralph saw was the 1957 Ulster Grand Prix when he was 15 years of age. Two years later, at 17, he took part in his first race – the Tandragee 100 – and he beat all the opposition to win the 200cc class on his 197cc Ambassador, averaging 55mph. He was so excited that after crossing the finishing line, he turned the bike around and rode back in the opposite direction to see if it was over. Needless to say, the officials did not share his enthusiasm!

His second race, the Cookstown 100, brought disillusionment, because he fell off. However, he then spent the winter months building a Triumph Terrier-engined Bantam-framed special.

In 1960 he crashed again while leading at the Tandragee races, due to a split oil tank. But he later came back to win at Kirkstown. His performances had been noted by insurance broker Jim Wilson, who provided Ralph with a 350 Norton. On it, in 1961, he won his third race, the Irish 25-mile Championship event at Kirkistown.

After spending the winter months grass track racing, Ralph extended his racing in 1962. This included finishing third in the North West 200 and winning at Cookstown. Then, as he admitted later, 'with £30 in my pocket, I boarded the boat with the Norton for the Isle of Man'. But after riding the bike to the start, the big-end went on the first lap of practice. Ralph continues: 'I spent the weekend fitting a new big-end, which I couldn't pay for, but fortunately my employer, Mr Chambers, paid my hotel bill'. But things didn't go any better in the race and he retired on lap two when a piston circlip came adrift.

He also had a lucky escape in the Carrowdore 100 when the gearbox seized at 125mph, Ralph commenting, 'I slid on my backside for 140 yards

Fourth in the 1967 250cc World Championship, Ralph Bryans provided valuable support to Mike in the Honda team.

– we measured it afterwards'. His only injury was a broken bone in his hand.

In 1963 Ralph Bryans started to show real form. And this was helped by being provided with the famous Joe Ryan 'Fireplace' Norton (Ryan was a fireplace manufacturer), together with a Honda CR93 and a 250 Benelli from Fron Purslow (the latter bike was the one ridden by Mike Hailwood the previous year).

Ralph won on his debut at Mallory Park in the 125cc event – which raised his profile no end. But it was that year's Ulster Grand Prix which really led to stardom. In the 350cc race he was third behind Jim Redman and Mike Hailwood, ahead of men like Alan Shepherd, Mike Duff and Luigi Taveri. Little did Ralph know, but in a few short months he would be joining the Honda works team.

Ralph takes up the story: 'I signed to ride Bultacos and then in December [1963] I had a letter from Jim Redman asking if I would be interested in riding Hondas'. Bultaco kindly agreed to release him and, in March 1964, Ralph flew to Japan where he tested, and later signed, for Honda.

He also moved to Ayr in Scotland, this being due to racing entrant Glen Henderson. In 1964, Ralph finished the season runner-up in the 50cc World Championship and fifth in the 125cc class. The following year, 1965, he went even better, taking the 50cc title (a first for Honda) on the fabulous 22,000rpm twin-cylinder machine. He followed this up by coming third in the 125cc and second in the 50cc stakes in 1966. Then, in 1967, he partnered Mike Hailwood in the 250 and 350cc classes, finishing fourth and third respectively on the six-cylinder Honda machines.

Originally signed by Honda to ride their 50cc twin (on which he won the championship in 1965), Ulsterman Ralph Bryans went on to ride 125 and 250cc models.

The big one

But the big one was most definitely the Senior race. Although Mike ultimately won his ninth TT, he was the first to admit it was one of his hardest races ever. There were two problems – the evil handling nature of his 90bhp five-hundred Honda and the performance of his great rival Giacomo Agostini. Both Mike and Ago smashed the existing lap record (set up by Mike at 106.4mph on the four-cylinder MV in 1963), with Mike going round at 107.07mph and Ago at 106.68mph.

After the race, Mike admitted to almost coming to grief several times. For example, on the first lap, he said:

> I thought I would have a go at taking Bray Hill, a ½ mile from the start in Douglas flat out, I hit the bottom with such a bump the next thing I was heading for the wall on the far side and I had to stand up to pull it back.

And so it continued for the next 220 miles, including a brush with the kerb at Union Mills and numerous slides, especially when part of the course became wet in the second half of the race (thus preventing a new race record speed).

At the finish, the rear tyre of Mike's machine was practically bald and the rear chain was stretched to its limit. At this stage in his career, Mike was just beginning to lose his hair – many more races like the one he had just taken part in could only hasten the process.

Senior TT – 6 laps – 226.38 miles

1st	M. Hailwood (Honda)
2nd	G. Agostini (MV Agusta)
3rd	C. Conn (Norton)
4th	J. Blanchard (Matchless)
5th	R. Chandler (Matchless)
6th	F. Stastny (Jawa)

Many agree that the 1967 Senior TT was one of the greatest ever races. For the majority of the event Mike and Giacomo Agostini on the three-cylinder MV (seen here) were only seconds apart. Mike won after Ago's chain snapped.

Winning and losing in Italy

In Italy, at Monza on Sunday 11 September 1966, Mike won the 250cc race, setting the fastest lap – a new record at 116.93mph, but in the 500cc event, after also setting a new outright lap record of 123.67mph, Mike was forced to retire on the sixth lap after his big Honda gushed smoke and clanked to a standstill with broken exhaust valves. The day really belonged to the new 500cc world champion, Giacomo Agostini, who won both the 350 and 500cc races on home ground. *Motor Cycle News* simply said: 'Giacomo Magnifico!'

Then it was back to England and Cadwell Park, in the Lincolnshire Wolds, for the circuit's big race of the year on Sunday 18 September. Mike, not having ridden at the track for seven years, made a dramatic comeback. On his 250 six-cylinder Honda he was the fastest competitor and pulverised the absolute lap record. Mike knocked no less than 5.2 seconds off the 250 time, 3.8 seconds off the 350 record and 1.2 seconds off the 500cc record.

It was generally agreed that it was a great day's racing – probably the best since the new, longer circuit had opened. Mike said: 'I found the course a bit different from my old days on Nortons'. The *Motor Cycle News* race report, dated 21 September 1966, read:

> *...in true world champion style, he demoralised his opponents by lapping the Lincolnshire circuit in 1m 44.8s. – a speed of 77.29mph which will take a long time to beat.*

Mike's record lap came in the 250cc race when he tailed Phil Read, on a works Yamaha twin, before clearing off to win in impressive fashion. Both riders broke the class record as they established a commanding lead. Then, in the main race of the day, the 20-lap Invitation event, Mike scored his second victory of the day – again with the style of a champion.

Invitation Race Cadwell Park – 20 laps – 45 miles
1st   M. Hailwood (250 Honda)
2nd   J. Cooper (500 Norton)
3rd   D. Shorey (500 Norton)
4th   P. Read (250 Yamaha)
5th   R. Gould (500 Norton)
6th   M. Uphill (500 Norton)

Seven days later, on Sunday 25 September, came the eagerly awaited first clash on the British mainland between Mike and his big rival Giacomo Agostini. On results alone, Giacomo came out on top, winning the 350, 500 and Race of the Year events.

But, as one commentator said, it was a 'lucky, lucky Ago', as in the only race in which the two met, the Race of the Year, Mike and his 250 Honda six led the Italian by some 13 seconds with only six laps of the 1.35-mile Leicestershire circuit to go when a valve stem pulled out from one of Mike's inner tubes.

Mike had been drawn on the back row of the grid (the positions being chosen by ballot) and was two rows behind Giacomo and five rows from the front, and yet by Gerrards Bend on the first lap he was 20 yards ahead of the field. And Mike continued as he had started, leading the race until he was forced out. At the time fellow racer Frank Perris (who had quit Suzuki and was a spectator) commented:

> I have never seen Mike so near the limit before, with his front wheel drifting around Devil's Elbow. This is the type of race, with all the odds against him, where he always shows what a fantastic rider he is.

With Honda boycotting the Japanese GP at the Fisco circuit (it had previously been staged over the Honda-owned Suzuka track), Mike's final meeting of the 1966 season came at Brands Hatch on 9 October, but it wasn't a happy one. A con-rod on his two-fifty six broke. This, and other problems with his Honda machine at British short circuits that year, prompted John Webb, managing director of Brands Hatch combine (which also included Snetterton and Mallory Park), to write to Mike saying that his start money for 1967 would be: 'subject to you guaranteeing the race worthiness of your machinery'.

News from Japan was that Honda were again to compete in all five solo classes in 1967 and that they were hoping for the clean sweep which had eluded them in 1966. But the Castrol competition manager brought the shock news that Honda would not be requiring 'new boy' Stuart Graham's services in 1967.

Honda quit the smaller classes

It was not until the very eve of the new racing season in mid-March 1967 that the dramatic news came that Honda was to cut its Grand Prix efforts. Essentially what this meant in practice was that the Japanese company had decided to drop the 50 and 125cc classes altogether. This left Luigi Taveri, now aged 37, without a ride, whereas Ralph Bryans was transferred to the 250cc to back up Mike. But this left Mike with the prospect of having to race the 250, 350 and 500cc machines virtually by himself. When he returned to England from Italy to his Heston, Middlesex, home after collecting his new Iso Grifo sports car, Mike admitted he didn't 'relish' the task.

Also, at around the same time, Mike hoped to sign a contract to race at some 10 British short circuit meetings in 1967. The first two of these came at Mallory Park on Easter Sunday 26 March, where he encountered handling problems with his 350 Honda, and the following day at Oulton Park, where in the 250cc race Mike crashed and remounted – and still won and also took a victory on the 350cc Honda.

His final 'warm-up' meeting prior to the start of the 1967 Grand Prix season came at Imola, Italy, on 25 April, where he won the 250cc event but was forced to retire with a broken brake lever on the 350 Honda.

Mike's problems continued at the Spanish GP at Barcelona on 30 April when he suffered a puncture while leading the 250cc race. Yet more grief followed at the second round of the world series, the West German GP at Hockenheim, where he struck ignition trouble in the 250cc race and a broken crankshaft while leading the 500cc, before finally having a debut victory in the 350cc race on the new 297cc six-cylinder Honda. As described within the boxed section in this chapter, this latter bike was essentially a larger displacement of the existing six-cylinder 250 design.

One of the problems with the Honda models was their less-than-perfect handling, with the 500 four as the biggest culprit. In an attempt to improve matters, Mike commissioned Rhodesian Colin Lyster to build a new frame for the big Honda. This machine, together with a three-fifty four-cylinder model which Lyster had modified back in March, had Italian Cerani front forks and twin hydraulically-operated front disc brakes. These efforts were unofficial and not funded by Honda, but did have their blessing.

The story behind the Lyster-Honda was that it used an Italian-built frame, similar in layout to that used by both Bianchi and Paton on their twins. The complete frame was designed and built in 16 days. The 500 machine (like Hailwood's 350 four) was fitted with Ceriani forks and double disc front brakes.

Meanwhile, Honda were said to be building a strengthened frame themselves for the 500.

The Lyster-Honda 500 made a winning debut with Mike aboard at the Rimini meeting in Italy on 14 May. Earlier the same day, Mike had won the 250cc class on his six, but had been beaten in the 350cc event by Renzo Pasolini on a works Benelli four.

500cc Rimini – 28 laps – 57.45 miles
1st   M. Hailwood (Lyster-Honda)
2nd   A. Bergamonti (Paton)
3rd   P. Williams (Arter-Matchless)

4th   J. Findlay (McIntyre-Matchless)

5th   D. Minter (Norton)

6th   K. Carruthers (Matchless-Metisse)

At the following weekend's French GP at Clermont-Ferrand, on 21 May, Mike suffered gearbox trouble on his two-fifty Honda, but still managed to finish third. Mike had the satisfaction of setting a new class lap record for the demanding circuit at 83.42mph (breaking his own record of 81.02mph set the previous year). The race was won by Bill Ivy from Phil Read on their V4 Yamahas.

A triple at Brands

At Brands Hatch on Bank Holiday Monday 29 May, Mike scored a hat-trick of victories on his 'private' Hondas, winning the 250 and 750cc events on the 250 six, and the 500 on his Lyster-framed 500 four.

Next came the Isle of Man TT. So it was a case of rushing straight over to the Island, having missed the first day of practice.

Less than 24 hours after smashing his 250cc lap record in TT practice, Mike

Mike's 500 Honda four in the paddock at the 1967 Isle of Man TT.

escaped injury in a road accident when a month-old Ferrari car driven by friend and fellow racer Bill Ivy crashed at high speed. Both Mike and Bill got out unscathed, which was more than could be said for the car, which was extensively damaged.

1967 marked the 60th anniversary of the TT – and it was also the second year that Mike scored three TT wins in a week (the other time had been back in 1961). In doing this, Mike also beat the record previously held by Stanley Woods, who had won 10 TTs in pre-war days. Mike's trio put his total up to 12.

All Mike's wins were great achievements, but it was the 500cc race that caused the most drama. Mike and Giacomo Agostini (MV three-cylinder) were neck and neck when Ago's bike lost its rear chain. Many believed that Ago would have won this titanic battle without the technical problems. Mike also had the distinction of setting new lap records in each of his three races:

250cc   104.50mph

350cc   107.73mph

500cc   108.77mph

It should be noted that he used six-cylinder machines in the 250 and 350cc races, and a Honda own-framed four-cylinder in the 500cc.

At the Post TT meeting at Mallory Park on Sunday 18 June, after winning the 250cc race, Mike was a non-finisher on his 350 four-cylinder machine in the 750cc race, due to valve trouble.

Back to GP duties

It was then back to GP duties, and in a little over a month Mike took in no fewer than five meetings:

> Dutch TT, Assen, 24 June: three races, three victories (250, 350 and 500cc); record laps in 250 and 500cc.
>
> Belgian GP, Spa Francorchamps, 2 July: runner-up behind Ivy (Yamaha) in 250cc and Agostini (MV) in 500cc.
>
> East German GP, Sachsenring, 16 July: won 350cc race, retired in 250cc (engine trouble) and 500cc (gearbox trouble).
>
> Czech GP, Brno, 23 July: won both 350 and 500cc races and new lap records; 250cc 3rd behind the Yamahas of Ivy and Read.
>
> Finnish GP, Imatra, 6 August: won 250cc race; crashed in 500cc after aquaplaning in heavy rain.

The punishing schedule did not stop there, and after a fabulous four wins in four rides performance at Brands Hatch on Sunday 13 August, in which he broke the 250 and 500cc lap records, Mike left for the Ulster GP at Dundrod on Saturday 19 August. Here he scored another glorious double in his two races (250 and 500cc) and set two more lap records.

After Ulster came more British short circuit action at Snetterton on Sunday 27 August and at Oulton Park the following day. In both cases Mike won the 250cc, although at Snetterton he retired in the 500cc race with engine trouble. All three races saw him establish new class lap records.

In the Italian GP at Modena on Sunday 3 September, Mike struck engine trouble with his 250 six-cylinder model, and finished runner-up to Agostini in the 500cc race.

More record breaking at Mallory Park

At Mallory Park on Sunday 17 September, Mike won all his three races – the 250, 350 and Race of the Year – and smashed the lap record in all three.

On 24 September, he won the 250 and 500cc Canadian GPs at Mosport, again setting new lap records in both. He then flew across the Atlantic to be in England at Brands Hatch the following day! He certainly didn't suffer from jet lag, going on to win both his races (350cc and Race of the South) with the same 297cc six-cylinder machine, also breaking the lap record.

Brands Hatch, 13 August 1967, and Mike tails team-mate Ralph Bryans during the 35th International Hutchinson 100 meeting. Mike won both the 250cc and 750cc races on his Honda six-cylinder machines (249cc and 297cc respectively).

The 1967 season was then ended in winning style at the Fuji circuit, the home of that year's Japanese GP, staged on 15 October.

It had been a truly memorable year for Mike; he won each of the three classes he entered (250, 350 and 500cc) at both the TT and Dutch TT. He had almost as many record laps as he had victories wherever he went.

Mike returned to Brands Hatch for the Race of the South meeting on 1 October 1967. Here he is pictured before the start of the 750cc event with mechanic Nobby Clarke.

Mike's favourite Honda was without doubt the 250 and 297cc six-cylinder, with which he won three world titles (250cc 1966 and 1967; 350cc 1967).

Six-cylinder Hondas

Honda's legendary six-cylinder two-fifty and '297' models had their origins in the drawings of a 24-year-old engineer, Soichiro Irimajari, in February 1964. Employed in Honda's massive Research and Development establishment, Irimajari was one of Japan's finest young engineering graduates and had already played a leading role in the development of the amazing 50cc 8-valve twin.

Thanks to this tiny engine, Honda had realised that the only way to outstrip the two-stroke opposition was ever more cylinders, together with multi-valves and higher revolutions. Soichiro Irimajari gave the new two-fifty, soon to be coded RC165, six cylinders and 24 valves. Other features of the engine included bore and stroke dimensions of 39x34.8mm, magneto ignition, a compression ratio of 12:1 and a seven-speed gearbox.

Within 90 days, a prototype engine had been assembled and the same period again saw a complete motorcycle ready for team captain Jim Redman to test. Jim flew out to Japan after the Finnish GP in August 1964.

Monza, the setting for the Italian Grand Prix in early September, was chosen for the bike's debut – mainly because at that time the handling was poor, even if the engine performance was extremely competitive. Because the company didn't have time to change its entry, the bike appeared in the race programme as a four. As secrecy was all important, it was even flown to Italy with only four exhausts fitted!

At Monza, the paddock was alive with rumours of a new Honda, but still most people didn't expect to see anything other than an updated four – certainly not a six. Even when it was finally unveiled, Redman wasn't keen to rev the engine in practice and give any indication of its full potential. So it wasn't until the actual race that he discovered the engine wouldn't take full throttle, and was forced to accept a third place, rather than the hoped-for victory. The cause was vapour lost in the Keihin carburettors at high temperatures – solved for the next outing by inclining the entire engine forward and modifying the streamlining to improve cooling at the rear of the engine.

In addition, in an attempt to improve the handling characteristics, the wheelbase was lengthened by some 90mm (3½in) and a new front fork assembly fitted. Redman proved the modifications worked by winning the final round of the 1964 GP season on Honda's home ground, Suzuka, at record speed.

However, this victory was to prove something of a false dawn, as the 1965 season yielded only a single victory (Isle of Man TT).

Then came 1966, and, with the signing of Mike Hailwood, a transformation came about for the Honda six-cylinder series. Not only did it now have the undisputed master of the sport aboard, but changes carried out to the engine, new oil coolers (fitted in the fairing) and modifications to the chassis

The jewel-like 297cc six-cylinder engine, showing across-the-frame layout, open frame design, dry clutch and massive cylinder head with centrally mounted spark plugs.

also improved the handling and roadholding qualities of the machine, now coded RC166. Mike won 10 of the 12 rounds to take the 1966 250cc world championship title (the other two he didn't contest) – in other words 10 wins from 10 starts!

In 1967 the engine was enlarged to 297cc (41x37.5mm) and the bike coded RC174. Mike took that year's 350cc title (and retained his 250cc crown) with six wins out of eight in that season's 350cc championship series.

To keep the smaller six competitive against Yamaha's new V4 two-stroke, the rev limit was increased to 18,000rpm. Unfortunately, this drastically shortened engine life. And there was a spate of valve breakages. Earlier Honda engineers had spent considerable time ensuring that the weight of the engine's internal components was as low as possible. They even tested a desmodromic valve system, but discovered it didn't give any real benefit. Instead, the solution was four valves-per-cylinder, using very small coil springs. Engine width of 356mm was no more than the four-cylinder model it replaced. Like other Hondas of the era, the engine acted as a stressed member of the cradle frame. Mike Hailwood suggested a new frame based on the Featherbed Norton, but, on the six, this proved impractical. Instead, Honda beefed up the original layout by using stronger tubing and additional gusseting, the latter hidden away under the fuel tank. In addition, the six featured a new front fork assembly, together with the sturdier frame and British Girling rear shock absorbers (the latter instead of Honda-made components), which helped cure the handling glitches. It is also worth mentioning that the new front forks, employing an abundance of aluminium and titanium, helped reduce the weight at the front end

During the main 750cc *Evening News* Race of the South on 25 September 1967, Mike covered the 20 laps of the Kent circuit in a time of 36 minutes, 22 seconds with an average speed of 87.44mph.

Although he failed to regain the 500cc crown after a bitter season-long struggle with Agostini, most observers thought he could have won had his bike been more reliable – even with the awful handling. As at Monza (the final round) with the title won and only two laps from the finish, his gearbox refused to function when he had half a lap lead over Ago. But even so, he still managed to win the 250 and 350cc titles – bringing his World Championship title score to nine (three 250cc, two 350cc and four 500cc). At the time, this put Mike equal with Carlo Ubbiali as the top-scoring rider since the world series began in 1949.

Even though to most people Mike had had an incredible year of success, the most important critic – himself – was not satisfied, or happy. Why? The reason was simple: Honda's 500cc machine. It was good to win the 250 and 350cc titles, but to Mike the 500cc was the real prize – and for the last two years this had gone to Agostini and MV Agusta.

Telling Honda straight

Mike told Honda that he would not sign for them again until they assured him that a new *and* competitive bike for this class would be forthcoming for 1968. He had also moved from his home in Heston, Middlesex, to South Africa. At the time Mike commented:

Actually, I'll probably spend no more time there than I have in the past eight years when I've always had two months during the winter with Paddy and Janet Driver on their farm near Johannesburg. I've also started a building company with Frank Perris in Durban.

During the winter Mike stayed in South Africa, taking in a couple of meetings at Pietermaritzburg (26 December 1967) and Killarney, Cape Town (14 January). In both cases, riding a 250 Honda six, he won and set up new lap records.

Back in Great Britain, Mike had been awarded the MBE and also been voted Sportsman of the Year by the Sports Writers Association.

As 1968 began there was still no news from Mike or Honda as to their plans. Then, in early spring, both Mike and teammate Ralph Bryans were summoned to Japan. When they returned, the world was given the shattering news that Honda had decided to quit GP racing. Both Mike and Ralph had also signed a contract which forbade them from riding for rival teams. In return, Honda made 'a large financial settlement' and gave them both machines on which they could contest a limited number of non-championship meetings. Maybe the reason both did this was because not only were Honda quitting, but Suzuki were too. Effectively, this only left Yamaha (who in any case would retire at the end of 1968) and MV Agusta. At the latter Giacomo Agostini was already firmly established, with the Count having achieved his lifetime ambition of having an Italian 500cc champion on an Italian motorcycle.

The 1968 season

And so came the 1968 season, with Mike beginning his season at Rimini in Italy on 24 March with a victory in the 350cc race on the 297cc six. In the 500cc he crashed his 500 (now with a British Reynolds frame), but remounted to finish runner-up behind Agostini on the latest MV three-cylinder. Before that, as *Motor Cycling* reported, 'Agostini simply could not live with him'.

The European season ended for Mike at Brands Hatch on Sunday 6 October, with wins and record laps in both his races (350 and 1000cc) on the 297cc six. In between he had ridden at Cesenatico, Imola, Cervia, Cadwell Park, Mallory Park (twice), Brands Hatch, Snetterton, Oulton Park and Riccione; plus the Italian GP at Monza, where he crashed a works Benelli four in the 500cc race and the Monte Generoso Hill Climb in Switzerland, where he had also crashed, breaking his collar bone on 7 July.

Mike riding the Reynolds-framed Honda four in the 500cc race at Cesenatico, Italy, on 7 April 1968. He finished runner-up. The machine had been converted as a private venture in an attempt to cure the handling gremlins which had plagued the big Honda throughout its life.

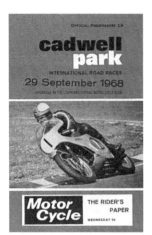

Technique

How did a star rider like Mike Hailwood achieve his success? Well, to be the best in motorcycle racing then and now demands a fairly long list of requirements. The big difference between greatness and just being good is down to technique and the will to win.

Mike's great friend and rival Bill Ivy once described the reason for his success in the following terms:

> I think the answer lies first and foremost in his will to win; this is why he is so hard to beat. He refuses to give up or even yield a single inch. If you want to take any ground off him, you really have to earn it. He gets into, through and out of corners quicker than anybody I have seen; he is amazing.

Certainly this 'will to win' is of paramount importance. A tigerish, never give up spirit. However, the really great rider also knows that it is not enough to lead races, and set fastest laps – the foremost requirement is to finish in the highest possible place. However, as Mike once said: 'if you don't fall off occasionally you are not trying hard enough'. That narrow strip between success and failure is not very wide!

Mike, together with Murray Walker, published *The Art of Motorcycle Racing* in 1963. And for anyone interested in how Mike went about achieving his success on the track it makes interesting reading. A large part of the book is devoted to riding techniques – as Mike said: 'the control of the machine when racing'. The following are some of the important points covered:

Physical and mental requirements
Temperament and personal qualities
Concentration, anticipation and judgement
Learning the course and practicing
Perfecting your starting techniques
Cornering – Mike said of this: 'the ability to take corners at the greatest possible speed is the hardest of all riding techniques to acquire'
Braking and the use of the gear box
Surface and camber
Weather conditions – riding smoothly in wet or damp conditions
Slipstreaming
Passing
Body movement
Style
Tactics

Mike himself was an admirer of style, notably mentioning riders such as Geoff Duke and Bob Anderson. But, as Bill Ivy said:

> ...he [Mike] is not the neatest rider. Technically he does all sort of things wrong. He sticks his knees and elbows out, his head bobs all over the place on corners. He feels for the corner with his body (this was before knee sliders were introduced); he moves

about all over the machine until he finds a comfortable position from which he can get the most out of the corner.

Mike also considered it was important to:

...relax as far as possible. Trying too hard seldom results in you going any quicker and often causes you to fall off, whereas a relaxed attitude improves your concentration and therefore reduces your lap time.

Also Mike considered the ideal way to win a race was by 'the narrowest margin, not the widest margin possible'. But 'this has to be very carefully judged and in easing up you should spare the machine, not yourself'.

Mike also advocated going 'as hard as you can, right from the beginning of the race'. The reason for this was quite simple: 'at the start of an event you are fresh and better able to produce a big effort'. This was the reason Mike invariably led from the front rather than having to play 'catch-up' as some of his rivals did (notably Derek Minter, who almost always made a bad start).

Mike was not just someone who could ride in one form of racing, but he was just as good on short circuits, purpose-made Grand Prix courses or pure road circuits including the Isle of Man. The same applied to size and types of machine; although later he admitted that he had 'grown out' of riding Ultra-lightweights (50 and 125cc).

As John Surtees described, Mike was not one who could go to bed early prior to race day, and he feels Mike's reputation as 'a man about town' largely stemmed from the fact that 'had he lain in bed, he would have sweated himself to pieces'. John also recalls that Mike was a 'bag of nerves before the start'. However, this was in anticipation rather than from any sort of fear! Mike could also eat a hearty breakfast – something a lot of racers simply can't do on race day.

In the very early days, Mike had the particularly bad habit of tending to look over his shoulder, not once but many times during a race. After setting up a new record in the 200cc class at Brands Hatch, Mike received a letter from the then MV importer and former racer, Ron Harris. This told Mike (then 18) that he was: 'losing valuable seconds in so doing and, in addition to the time factor, it is also dangerous and you may well run into a tumble'. However, instead of throwing this letter away, Mike kept it in a scrapbook, not as a reminder not to keep turning his head around, but to help him retain a 'sense of proportion'.

Mike Hailwood was never a prima donna – if anything he was a very shy man – but once astride a motorcycle he was able to transform himself into a winner.

When he began racing many observers thought it was simply Stan's cheque book which did the business, but as Mike's career blossomed so he silenced the critics by continuing to progress to become a worthy world champion. At that level only skill, judgement and determination are good enough.

Away from the circuits, Mike hated any form of routine. Many, including his father Stan, would describe this as impatience. But this

never showed in his racing. He also had to contend with Stan, who, as described in Chapter 4, was a hard driver, who never let Mike rest on his laurels. As Mike admitted to being 'a naturally lazy person', the author is sure that without Stan's drive, Mike wouldn't have been able to develop and display his true skills. And I don't mean the money – but the 'driving' from father to son.

Ted Macauley said: 'Stan Hailwood, with his wisdom and energy, had been the pushing power behind the champion'. This is absolutely true. And without Stan, Mike would, left to himself, probably not have pushed. It's an amazing fact. But once pushed – launched would be a better word – the good ship Mike Hailwood set sail to make use of his inner ability, talent and strength. Even Stan Hailwood could not have 'manufactured' a champion, he only 'encouraged'.

A true champion is born one, but technique hones the ultimate performance.

A happy Mike with a cheque for £1,050, his spoils for taking victory in the Race of the Year at Mallory Park on his Honda 297cc six on 22 September 1968.

During 1968 (including his South African outings in January and December) Mike scored 20 victories. But somehow, with the restrictions Honda had made, Mike was largely out of the limelight.

In 1969, Mike rode at Killarney, Cape Town, in January (winning on his 297cc Honda), at Riccione (runner-up to Agostini on his 500 Honda) in late March and finally the Race of the Year meeting at Mallory Park in September, where he rode a Seeley G50 to third and fifth places.

These rare performances were down to the fact that by now Mike was tired of racing bikes and determined to race cars. The Riccione meeting was

Mike and Colin Seeley, with the Seeley G50 Mike rode in a few meetings in 1968 and 1969.

entirely a financial one, Mike having been offered around 4 million lire (about £2,660 at the time and much, much more today), said then to be the most appearance money ever offered in motorcycling history.

Racing a BSA triple at Daytona

In 1970, Mike had a solitary race at Daytona aboard a works BSA 750 Rocket Three triple and led the 200-mile race until he was forced to retire through the engine overheating.

Then, in 1971, he returned to Daytona and again led the race until a valve broke.

At Silverstone, in August, he rode a 350 Yamaha (after testing the new 750 Ducati), and put up an excellent performance with a pair of fourth places (350 and 750cc races). A week later he rode a 350cc Benelli to finish runner-up behind Agostini (MV) at Pesaro in Italy. Finally, on 19 September 1971 at Mallory Park, he rode the same Yamaha he had piloted at Silverstone, finishing fourth in the 350cc race but retiring in the Race of the Year with broken piston rings.

Then Mike was effectively banned from racing on two wheels by his car racing contracts. And so began a five-year retirement from the sport which had established his name. Most thought this would be the end of his motorcycle career. They were wrong.

Mike at Daytona on 15 March 1970 with the BSA Rocket 3 he rode at the American classic. He was destined to retire after leading the race with an overheated engine. Then in 1971 he returned to Daytona with the BSA, but suffered a broken valve, again after leading the race.

Another motorcycle Mike raced in 1968 was the works Benelli 500 four. But the results were somewhat disappointing: a crash in the Italian GP at Monza on 15 September, and a third at Riccione on 29 September.

Finally, in August and September 1971, Mike had some entries on a 350 Yamaha TR2B at Silverstone and Mallory Park, putting up good performances, often against machines of twice the engine size.

Chapter 8

The comeback

In 1974, after a successful spell with Team Surtees, Mike joined the Yardley-McLaren squad to race a McLaren M23 Formula 1 car. He started the season well, but in the German Grand Prix at the Nürburgring, on the 12th lap, Mike's car crashed heavily, breaking both Mike's legs and shattering his right ankle. He underwent several operations and months of rehabilitation, but the accident left Mike with a permanent limp, effectively bringing his car racing career to an end. No one expected him to return to his two-wheel exploits, but that is exactly what happened.

Down under

Mike and his long-time partner Pauline had retired to their home in South Africa for the winter at the end of 1974, and, in the spring, Pauline says, he 'surprised me by finally asking me to marry him. I was over the moon'. So on 11 June 1975, Pauline and Mike married at Maidenhead Registry Office

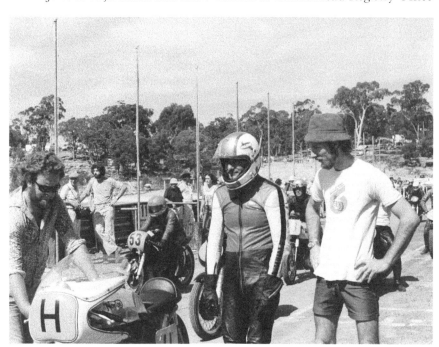

Mike (centre, in helmet), about to ride the ex-Kel Carruthers 499cc Manx Norton in Australia in early 1977.

Sydney's Amaroo Park, the scene of Mike's first outing in 1977, on a 499cc Manx Norton in a classic bike event. Later that year he shared a 748cc Ducati 750 SS with Jim Scaysbrook.

in Berkshire. In early 1976 the two newly-weds moved to New Zealand to begin a new life.

Then, in January 1977, Mike accepted an offer to take part in an historic race meeting at Amaroo Park, Sydney, Australia, where he rode a 499cc Manx Norton belonging to Barry Ryan (owner of a large Sydney dealership and a true stalwart of the local racing scene). He finished runner-up to the Australian Jim Scaysbrook. Three months later he was back in Australia for another historic race at Bathhurst. This time he finished third on the same Norton he had ridden at Amaroo – and the man who won was Scaysbrook again. Following this, Mike competed a couple more times on the British bike, this having been brought to Australia by Kel Carruthers during the 1960s, being an ex-Chris Conn bike. It was equipped with a Shaftleitner six-speed gearbox and Oldani front brake. It was raced by Max Robinson before being sold to Barry Ryan and is now owned by Bill Stone.

The Castrol 6-Hours

Then in June 1977 came the shock announcement that, together with Jim Scaysbrook, Mike had agreed to share a square-case Ducati 750 Super Sport in the Castrol 6-Hours production bike race on Sunday 23 October 1977, at Amaroo Park, Sydney. This event was acknowledged as one of the world's toughest marathon races because of strict regulations that prohibited riders from modifying their machines beyond stock 'showroom' specification.

The man behind the move to get Mike back on the track was Sydney radio announcer Owen Delaney. Owen and Mike had become friends

Mike lifting the front wheel of the Ducati 750 SS during the Castrol Six Hours at Amaroo Park, 23 October 1977.

following a radio interview the previous January, and it was Delaney who had been instrumental in bringing the multi-world champion to Bathhurst that April (when he rode the Norton). It was at Bathhurst that the subject of the 6-Hours was raised, and Mike was asked if he would like to compete in the marathon. He had replied: 'it sounds like a lot of fun – as long as people don't expect me to win'.

Even with the handicap of running a smaller displacement machine than the majority of the other forty teams, Jim Scaysbrook and Mike weren't held back at Amaroo Park. On the Ducati V-twin they completed 350 laps of the 1.21-mile circuit to finish sixth overall – an excellent result – and at the end Mike said he had enjoyed his ride 'very much'.

In retrospect, it was the 1977 Castrol 6-Hours at Amaroo Park which set in motion a truly remarkable series of events, a racing comeback that is unparalleled in racing history.

Night of the Stars

The significance of this was revealed the following January, when Mike made a surprise appearance in front of 16,000 ecstatic fans at the annual 'Night of the Stars' organised by *Motor Cycle News* in London. He announced the exciting news that he would be riding factory Yamahas as well as an 864cc Ducati V-twin in the Isle of Man TT races in June.

A couple of weeks later, in their 25 January 1978 issue, *Motor Cycle News* was able to bring further details from the official launch of Team Martini Yamaha. This took place on the 16th-floor Martini Terrace at New Zealand House in London's Haymarket, where Mike was quoted as saying: 'Nobody must expect miracles, but we're not going to the Island to swan about'.

Mike's wife, Pauline, says:

One of the 1978 NCR Ducati 900 Formula 1 racers outside the Italian works in Bologna before delivery.

1978 NCR 900 Ducati

In retrospect, the 1978 NCR 900 Ducati Formula 1 V-twin was one of the Italian company's better efforts and was to provide Mike with a very special moment, not only in his motorcycling career, but in world motor-cycle racing in general.

The bike, one of a small batch built by NCR that year, was essentially based around the existing series production 900 Super Sport of the era, but with considerable special attention, one-off components and modifi-cations. The engine retained the stock 864cc (86x74.4mm) displacement and was claimed to put out around 89bhp at the rear wheel – around 5bhp more than Roger Nicholls's 1977 TT bike. Good for 9,000rpm, the engine had been gas flowed and fitted with larger valves, the inlet going up to 43mm (39mm) and the exhaust to 39mm (36mm). The compression ratio of the three-ring forged slipper pistons was 11:1, compared with 9.5:1 on Nicholls's 1977 machine. Combined with a considerable amount of lightening of the engine's internals, these changes provided more useable power at lower engine revolutions. The standard ignition was discarded in favour of a British Lucas Rita transistorised system. An air-cooled clutch was the most obvious difference in the transmissions, but the gearbox had also been modified, with not only the gears drilled for lightness, but also dogs removed from fourth gear to provide a slicker shift.

Much care had been taken with the left-side mounted gearchange operation on Mike's bike – this may seem strange, but there were two almost identical Sports Motorcycles-entered 1978 NCRTTF1 bikes, one for Mike and the other for Roger Nicholls, the difference being that Mike's had been specially adapted because of his existing foot problems. Unlike the production 900 Super Sport of the period, both these machines employed bottom ends based on the earlier 750, rather than later 900-

The 864cc bevel 90 degree Ducati V-twin with Desmo cylinder heads. Other features included Dell'Orto carburettors, five-speed gearbox and a frame constructed by Daspa in chrome-moly tubing.

Mike with one of the two NCR Ducatis entered by Sports Motorcycles in 1978, before being tested at Oulton Park prior to the TT that year.

type engines. This not only meant that the air-cooled clutch and straight-cut primary gears similar to the 1973–4 Imola racers could be used, but also that as standard the gearchange was on the offside (right), rather than the nearside (left). This meant that because Mike's right foot had been

badly damaged in his 1974 Nürburgring car crash, the gearchange had to be transferred to the left. This was achieved with a crossover shaft inside the swinging-arm pivot and not the totally different method used on the production roadsters. As already mentioned in the main text, the frame was a special component manufactured by Despa and although based on the standard frame was much lighter; there was also a wider swinging arm to allow the latest racing tyres to be fitted. Finally, as on the Imola racers, the TTF1 bikes used fibreglass petrol tanks with a translucent strip that provided an instant reading of the fuel level, and an oil cooler was also fitted.

I knew it was pointless asking him not to do it, so I just went along with it. He was under enormous media pressure and many doubted the wisdom of his decision to race, but I knew that with the right back-up he could do it.

How it all came about

So how did all this happen? Well, while on holiday in Britain the previous summer, Mike had visited the ACU (Auto Cycle Union) headquarters to discuss the possibility of making a return to serious two-wheel racing – notably the Isle of Man TT. He had also attended the British Grand Prix at Silverstone where, purely by chance, or so the story goes, he came across the Sports Motorcycle racing team boss, Steve Wynne, and rider Roger Nicholls with the Ducati V-twin. Mike remarked that it 'looked like my kind of bike', to which Steve Wynne replied 'if you fancy a ride you have only to ask'. And so, with their little chat over, Mike disappeared.

Some weeks later (after his Australian 6-Hour ride with Jim Scaysbrook), Steve Wynne received a telephone call from Mike's close friend, *Daily Mirror* journalist Ted Macauley, asking if a Ducati could be made available for the 1978 TT. That Mike genuinely wanted to ride the Italian bike is proved by the fact that his fee was a nominal one of £500. So it was most definitely a case of love rather than pure financial gain. There are two other considerations: Mike already had experience of the Ducati V-twin, and Roger Nicholls on the Sports Motorcycles machine had failed by only a few seconds to beat the might of the Honda factory team with riders of the calibre of Phil Read and Stan Woods in the 1977 Isle of Man Formula 1 TT.

Following Ted Macauley's request, Steve Wynne, via the British Ducati importers Coburn and Hughes, got the factory involved. The cost of this plan totalled some £10,000, which involved a three-way split between the factory, Coburn and Hughes and Sports Motorcycles (Steve Wynne has always maintained that the other two parties didn't cough up and he had to foot the entire bill). The two machines were built by specialists NCR (Nepoti, Caracchi and Rizzi), a small company which was based near Ducati in Bologna and had an official link from 1972 until the early 1990s to work under the direct control of Ing. Fabio Taglioni. NCR could, in fact, be described as Ducati's official racing arm. And the motorcycles they constructed were decidedly 'works specials', with everything lightened inside the engines, dry clutches, sand cast crankcases and special Dell'Orto carburettors modified by Malossi to 41mm. The frames, manufactured by the Bologna company Daspa, were much lighter than the production version, and had a special wide swinging arm so that modern slick tyres could be used. Power output was a claimed 87bhp at 9,000rpm. Mike's bike was painted red, white and green – not to represent the Italian national flag, as many would suppose, but to advertise the Castrol Oil Company, Mike's main sponsors. Besides the Sports Motorcycles staff, Ducati would also supply two mechanics (Franco Farné and Giuliano Pedretti).

The death of Stan Hailwood

Although Mike was looking forward to the prospect of racing again on two wheels at the highest level, he found 1978 a bittersweet year none the less. His biggest sorrow was the death of his father, Stan, aged 75, in Barbados on 4 March that year. As described in Chapter 4, Stan had left Britain during the mid-1960s and set up two homes, one in Barbados and the other in Cannes. After being taken ill in Miami in December 1977, Stan had been flown to his Barbados home, where Mike had visited him en route to New Zealand in January 1978, a few weeks before he passed away.

Without doubt, Stan would have been proud at what was shortly to follow, even though the first signs were none too encouraging.

Bathhurst, spring 1978

'Hailwood humbled,' shouted the *Motor Cycle News* headline in its 5 April 1978 issue. This came in response to Mike getting lapped three times in his world debut on a TZ750 Yamaha in the Australian Grand Prix at Bathhurst during a 30-lap race over the Mount Panorama circuit on Easter Monday 26 March. However, it should be pointed out that all was not what it seemed – the Yamaha suffered plug problems in a rain-lashed race. Some 10 days later in a 3-hour production race at Adelaide Mike teamed up with Jim Scaysbrook and the 750cc Ducati to finish seventh, after the pair had twice run out of fuel.

This latter race produced the unforgettable sight of Mike, high up on the banked speed bowl section of the Adelaide circuit, passing some of Australia's finest riders with effortless ease. Even though he hadn't achieved anything similar with the Yamaha, his Ducati performance was a taste of what was to come.

The Australian trip also included a stop off at Mike and Pauline's home in New Zealand, and then it was back to the UK, arriving at Heathrow airport on Tuesday 25 April 1978, to prepare for his big comeback in the TT series.

Mike was scheduled to go to the Island at the end of the month to begin refreshing his memory of the fearsome 37.73-mile Mountain circuit, the toughest in the world. Although barred by his Isle of Man contract from racing in any pre-TT meetings in Great Britain, Mike hinted that if he was satisfied with his TT performances, he would also ride in the Mallory Park Post TT international races on Sunday 11 June.

But before visiting the Isle of Man, Mike did some mainland testing, having his first outing at Oulton Park on 2 May, with the Sports Motorcycles factory NCR-built Formula 1 bike. He adjudged his Oulton laps as 'very satisfying'. And it was after this test session at the Cheshire circuit that he finally felt confident enough to conclude a deal to race in the Mallory Park Post TT meeting. There he would pit himself against Phil Read in a nostalgic duel in the TTF1 race – media interest was so great that it was being said that the event might even get live television coverage.

A clue as to why Mike had agreed to race at Mallory, before he had ridden the Ducati in anger, was given by racer Barry Ditchburn for *Motor Cycle News* after a track test of Mike's bike the same month at Oulton Park:

> *The Hailwood Ducati is the first bike I've ever ridden hard against the stop coming out of Esso (a super-elevated wall-of-death-like right-hander). And as I came out of Knicker Brook I thought how good it will be down the Cronk-y-Voddy straight… The last time I raced a four-stroke twin was back in 1969-70 when I rode a Westlake-Triumph. And the fantastic engine braking of the big Duke brought memories flooding back… Handling was taut but good enough to make me feel at home on the bike immediately… but the bike's great attribute is the flexibility of the engine… It*

During the 1978 TT Mike used this Yamaha XS1100 to relearn the circuit. He is pictured here at the Ramsey Hairpin. Besides Ducati, Mike also rode for the Martini Yamaha team that year.

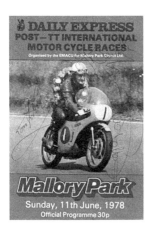

seemed the sort of engine which never needs maximum revs. I took it to 8,500 rpm in top, and although it never dropped below 4,000, the engine was at its best around 6,000rpm.

This meant that it was virtually impossible to arrive at a corner in the wrong gear. Ditchburn put it this way: 'the power of the Ducati is beautifully progressive. You don't get the kick of the Yamaha – just real gutsy strength'.

However, there are always things which testers don't like. In this instance there were two.

...suspension was a bit stiff for me but the special Girling shockers are claimed to be 100 percent better than the original Marzocchi's... I would not have the bars as steeply raked as Hailwood, but the bike was not tailored for me.

Overall, Mike's Ducati came through the test with flying colours. Barry Ditchburn concluded:

The Ducati is deceptively fast. There was no fuss or vibration and it never felt it was really moving. It may not be the quickest in the world, but the big Duke is a sheer pleasure to ride. I think it has ideal power characteristics for the Isle of Man. I don't know about Hailwood, but, on last year's performance alone, the bike is a potential winner.

Media interest

For several weeks prior to Mike's comeback in the TT, the world's motorcycle press devoted more column inches to him than everyone else combined. This prompted the following comment from the man himself in *Motor Cycle*, dated 29 May 1978:

The trouble with my comeback is that it's all got a bit too serious. This was not my original intention. I just wanted to race in the TT again. Maybe I should have done it incognito.

And the following week, on the eve of the races, again in *Motor Cycle*, Mike commented:

And I must admit that to bring the whole thing down to earth I played a nasty little joke on my old friend Ted Macauley, who has put in such a lot of work behind the scenes to organise the whole effort. I rang him up and told him I'd fallen off and broken my leg! Of course, I couldn't keep it up. I just burst into laughter after a few seconds of awful silence. He told me he had seen all the colours of the rainbow and broken into a cold sweat as he'd seen the whole carefully built plan, which now involves so many people, crumble. Makes you think, doesn't it?

Jim Scaysbrook

Jim was born into a motorcycling family. His father Charles was a very successful trials and motocross rider who rode for the New South Wales Matchless distributor for many years. Jim began riding competitively in 1964, aged 16, in local scrambles and progressed to the senior ranks. By 1973 he was in the top five Australian motocross riders and went to the US to ride in the Trans AMA series. He says: 'This was a fairly humbling exercise, but valuable experience, racing against the likes of Roger de Coster, Adolf Weil, Sylvan Goebers and Gerrit Woolsink.

Jim returned to Australia the following year and concentrated on business interests, which included a Honda dealership and an accessory import company. He even tried speedway at this stage, 'but thankfully did not pursue that one'. Then, in 1975, as part of a business deal Jim acquired a 1961 AJS 7R, which was 'in pretty good shape', which he rode at the Bathhurst Historic 'demonstration' at Easter 1975. As Jim related to the author recently: 'I loved the experience of racing a real classic and managed to buy a 630cc Seeley G50 engine that I put in the 7R frame'.

As Jim relates below, this was the motorcycle that he first raced against Mike and was responsible for their subsequent friendship.

Mike and Jim returning to the pits at Amaroo Park after finishing first and second in the main race.

Mike during his winning ride in the NCR Ducati 900 in the 1978 Formula 1 TT. The 'greatest comeback in racing history' is what many observers said of the ride.

Mike on the winners' rostrum after his historic 1978 Formula 1 TT victory – which also meant he was F1 champion as well. The other rider is John Williams.

Jim's experiences with Mike-the-Bike

I first met Mike at the historic meeting at Amaroo Park in January 1977. I won the main race and Mike the second, and I was delighted and a bit overwhelmed when he sauntered over to our tent after the meeting and joined us for (quite a few) drinks. Mike was my boyhood hero, although he was only eight years older than me. I remember as an apprentice photolitho camera operator I spent a goodly measure of my meagre pay on a subscription to UK *Motor Cycle News* and hung on every word of the race reports of Hailwood/Honda versus Agostini/MV. It never occurred to me that I would get to know Mike so well.

A few months after that great day at Amaroo, Mike came over from New Zealand to ride at Bathhurst and I picked him up at Sydney airport. We drove the three hours from Sydney to Bathhurst in my Ford utility, with my G50 and heaps of camping gear in the back. Mike had a hotel room in Bathhurst, but I think during the whole four or five days he only slept there once or twice. On the first night we all passed out around the camp fire on Mount Panorama.

That year, 1977, the organisers of the Bathhurst meeting made the usual 'demonstration' for historic bikes into an official race. It had always been a race, just not officially! Practice was very wet, and my G50 must have swallowed a gut full of water, because when we went to start it for the race on Saturday it had no compression whatsoever. We got it fired up and I went to the line – fortunately it was a clutch start, I think in deference to Mike's bung leg – and I got to the front inside the first lap. Compression or no, the bike seemed to be going alright, and I kept an eye on Mike behind me as he battled with Dennis Fry. On the last lap I got into a huge slide at McPhillamy Park, which is a flat out left hander on top of the mountain. Somehow I recovered, but the reason for the slide was that the rear tyre was covered in oil – pumped out by crankcase compression. I should have stopped but it was all steeply downhill from there to the finish line so I pressed on but the motor siezed at the end of the straight. Fortunately I was able to coast over the line before Fry and Mike caught up.

That night, Mike and I and a bunch of friends went to dinner in a local restaurant, which had a very extensive cellar. The owner of the restaurant insisted on showing Mike the cellar and Mike returned laden with bottles of red wine. None of us felt too good the next day, but our race for the weekend was over and we sat back on the mountain section and watched the GP races on the Sunday before driving back to Sydney.

Soon after this came the contact with Owen Delaney that led to the ride in the Castrol 6-hour race and several other events. It was one thing having fun on historic bikes, but the Castrol 6-hour was the biggest and most prestigious event in Australia. All the top riders were signed up for various teams, and everyone took it very seriously. Everyone except us, that is.

Fast forward to 1980, and I went back to the IOM with a brand new TZ500 Yamaha. This was undoubtedly the worst bike I ever raced. At this time Mike had his shop in Birmingham with Rod Gould, and entered me for the TT. The TT was nothing special in terms of results, but we had a great time staying with Mike and Pauline at their home in Tamworth-in-Arden. When we heard of Mike's death just nine months later, a whole

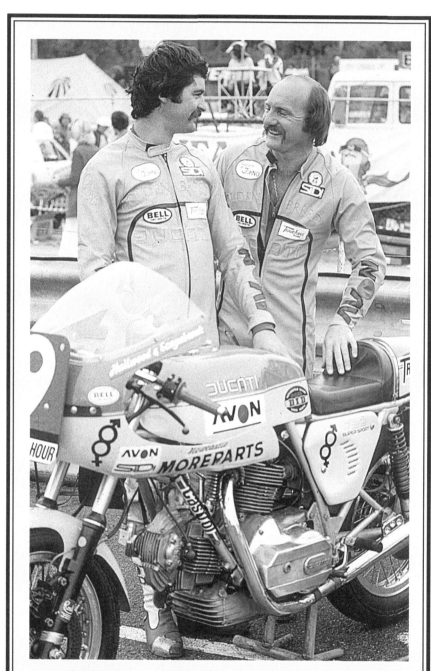

Jim Scaysbrook on the grid for the 1978 Castrol 6 Hour Race with Mike and the Ducati 750SS. Jim says 'We barely made it to the grid after a horror practice'.

group of us went straight to the Spanish restaurant that we had gone to several times with Mike. We sat at the tapas bar and toasted his memory in a very emotional night. For me, the fairytale of racing with and becoming good friends with my hero is still hard to believe. In my line of work, I meet plenty of so-called 'superstars'. Most are forgettable people, preoccupied with their own importance or obsessed with money and the trappings of wealth. Mike Hailwood may have been a brilliant racer, but he was also a great bloke.

Even with the massive publicity, so-called experts thought success highly unlikely. It had been 11 years since the name S.M.B. Hailwood had graced a TT programme. And racing over the ultra-demanding 37.73-mile course was different to anything else. So the cynics used these criticisms against Mike, although, to be fair, several were extremely lavish in their praise afterwards. In any case, it was expected that if the 'old man' (Mike was then 38) was going to do anything, it would be aboard one of the three Yamahas he was also entered on, rather than the lone Ducati.

But just how wrong those so-called experts were. Throughout his TT practice sessions, Mike and the Ducati continued to amaze, ending up with a fastest lap of 111.04mph – unbelievable but true. How could a man, the world asked, who had last raced on the circuit more than a decade ago, put up such a mind-boggling performance? In retrospect, it was probably a combination of things – that famous Hailwood will-to-win, course knowledge, determination, fitness (yes, Mike had worked on that too), and, with the Formula 1 event, the most suitable bike for the task at hand. It says a lot that the Ducati went faster than the Grand Prix Yamaha four-cylinder Mike used in the Senior (500cc) TT, on which he achieved a best practice lap of 107.57mph. And bear in mind too that the Yamaha was a full factory machine of the type conceived for the likes of Saarinen, Agostini and Cecotto. Even on the 750 Yamaha his best practice lap was only just faster than the Ducati speed at 112.36mph.

Mike's greatest gamble

Record crowds had jammed the Isle of Man for Mike's return and before the Formula 1 event, held on Saturday 3 June 1978, fans were claiming the best vantage points some *seven* hours before the race began. But their determination was rewarded as they witnessed a history-making race. As the *Motor Cycle News* headline said, simply: 'Mike Hailwood lands a fairy-tale comeback victory'. The report went on:

> *With tears of emotion streaming down his cheeks Mike Hailwood climbed the winner's rostrum for the thirteenth time in his legendary TT career after six record smashing laps with a 900 Ducati in Saturday's Formula 1 World Championship race.*

It was unreal… fantastic… but he had done it. Mike had won the greatest gamble of his life with a devastating victory that captured the imagination of the thousands of fans who waved him to his tenth world title. And in the process, he had stunned his rivals with a race record of 108.51mph and a

Lucas leads in the Isle of Man!
Mike Hailwood's '78 Formula 1 TT winning Ducati pictured
above closing on Phil Read's Honda.
Victories like this have been the proving ground for Rita
electronic ignition.

Rita electronic ignition

Lucas

Four wheels

In the first half of the 20th century there were many cases of successful motorcycle racers moving into motor racing, including the likes of Tazio Nuvolari, Piero Taruffi, Achille Varzi and Bernd Rosemeyer. However, during the latter half of the same century there were far fewer – John Surtees, Johnny Cecotto and Mike Hailwood being the only really successful ones to have made the transition.

Mike's dominance of the motorcycle game convinced him that he could make the switch, so in 1963 he purchased a Formula Junior Brabham. The omens looked good, as in his very first race he finished fifth. This was followed by some excellent results in the few other races he was able to take in that year, limited as he was by his two-wheel commitments.

Then, in 1964, Reg Parnell invited Mike to join his Formula One Lotus-BRM team in Grand Prix racing. Unfortunately, success was not forthcoming, because by that time the Lotus 25 car was already three years old, and its engine design unreliable. So he took part in the occasional sports car event so as to keep his hand in, driving cars such as E-type Jaguars and a selection of Italian Ferraris.

It is also worth noting that at this stage of his career Mike was owner of an exotic Iso Grifo, using the latter to travel not just in Great Britain, but also around various continental European countries (this car was subsequently sold to Liverpool dealer/sponsor Bill Hannah during the late 1960s). For those who don't know, the Grifo was an expensive Italian-made supercar powered by an American V8 engine displacing some five litres.

At the beginning of 1968, Mike decided to retire from Grand Prix motorcycle racing (brought about by Honda's decision to quit as outlined in Chapter 7). Although Mike was to continue to ride Hondas for a few months at lesser events, he had effectively switched his main attention to the four-wheel sporting scene, including taking in the South African Springbok series by co-driving Ed Nelson's Ford GT40.

For 1969, Mike was signed by the John Wyer team to drive Ford GT40s and Mirage-BRMs in the World Sports Car Championship series. He often led these races, but was usually forced out through technical problems, while the rival 3-litre Porsche models proved both faster and more reliable. But he and co-driver David Hobbs did finish an excellent third in the prestigious Le Mans 24-hour race. Mike also campaigned a works-supported Lola T142 in the Guards Formula 5000 Championship, taking third in the series despite, as one journalist described it, 'having an ill-handling car'.

Mike remained in Formula 5000 for 1970, driving the works-based Lola T190 entered by Jackie Epstein. After the chassis had been sorted out he really made the Lola competitive, winning at the Salzburgring in Austria and at Silverstone, while taking runner-up positions at Brands Hatch, Mallory Park and Snetterton. He also drove a Gulf-sponsored Porsche 917 at Le Mans, but this outing ended when he spun in torrential rain, badly damaging the front of the car.

It was with former bike racer and world champion John Surtees that

Mike was to gain his biggest four-wheel success. John signed Mike at the end of 1970, to drive the Surtees TS8 in the following year's Rothmans Formula 5000 Championship. As described more fully in *John Surtees – Motorcycle Maestro* (Breedon Books), the TS8 proved very competitive and Mike picked up victories at Silverstone (twice) and Mallory Park (twice), together with other podium finishes. These results placed Mike runner-up in the championship.

Mike (seated in the car) and presenter Eamon Andrews on BBC Television's *This Is Your Life*, 26 November 1975.

Towards the end of that season, John Surtees gave Mike a drive in a Formula One Surtees car at the Italian Grand Prix, where after leading the race on more than one occasion he finished fourth. This resulted in a full-time contract with the Surtees team for the 1972 season, to race both Formula One and Formula Two cars. In the Matchbox Toys-sponsored Surtees TS10, Mike enjoyed a fine year in Formula Two, winning at Hockenheim, Rouen, the Österreichring, Mantorp Park and the Salzburgring to comfortably win the European Formula Two Championship title. In Formula One, he finished only four events in his Surtees-Ford TS9B, but he scored World Championship points on all four occasions by finishing runner-up in the Italian round, fourth in Belgium and Austria and sixth in France; giving him eighth place in the championship table with 13 points. Mike also finished second in the Race of Champions at Brands Hatch and was leading the International Trophy at Silverstone until forced to retire.

Of course, Mike was no stranger to John Surtees – they had known each other for many years. In addition, in the two-wheel world Mike had followed in John's tracks at MV Agusta. Both Mike and John were truly great competitors, but in terms of temperament and personality they were very different. For example, whereas John was described as being 'as cold as ice' before a race, Mike was someone who, as John remembers, was 'a bag of nerves before the start'.

John also found that working with Mike 'brought a certain simplicity and honesty' – qualities that were often sadly lacking within the car fraternity, where personalities and politics often ruled supreme. There is no doubt that Mike himself did not appreciate this side of the four-wheel sport.

John Surtees describes Mike in the following terms: 'very honest, so you could work with him, but you needed to understand Mike and the vehicle and put them together to get the best results'. Also John says: 'Mike had the ability to carry through what he had started'. One has only to study photographs of John and Mike together to realise that they were totally at ease in each other's company.

Mike stayed with Surtees for 1973, but the Formula One car was none

Mike and his Lola Formula 5000 car at Snetterton; summer 1969.

too competitive and Mike either retired or finished well down the pack in all his outings. In long distance events he drove the Mirage Cosworth V8, winning the prestigious Spa 1000 Kilometres with Derek Bell as co-driver. He also came home fourth in the Austrian 1000km race and fifth in the Dijon 1000km and Watkins Glen 6-hour races.

For 1974, he quit the Surtees équipe and joined the Yardley-McLaren team to race a McLaren M23 in Yardley sponsorship colours. Mike began the season well, but during the German Grand Prix at the Nürburgring, on the 12th lap, he crashed heavily, breaking his leg in three places and effectively signalling the end of his car racing career.

But it was an event in 1973 for which Mike will most be remembered in car racing circles. This was when he was awarded the George Medal (the presentation took place in 1974). This award, one of Great Britain's highest civil awards for bravery, was presented for Mike's actions during the South African Grand Prix when he saved the life of driver Clay Regazzoni.

During the race Dave Charlton, while braking for the Crowthorne Bend, lost control of his Lotus and Mike (driving the Team Surtees) was unable to avoid it.

Clay Regazzoni's BRM and Jackie Ickx's Ferrari struck Hailwood and the impact caused Regazzoni's monocoque to split, resulting in his car bursting into flames.

Seeing Regazzoni unconscious and surrounded by flames, Mike leapt into the blaze and released the driver's safety harness. As his overalls caught fire, he retreated.

Marshals got the blaze under control and Mike returned to pull Regazzoni to safety. Clay escaped with only minor burns.

Mike's wife Pauline was later to reveal that when Mike reappeared in the pits after the incident he didn't say anything about it. Afterwards, when it became common knowledge, he just brushed it off as 'something anyone would have done'.

lap record of 110.62mph. He had set a scorching pace, during which he forced favourite Phil Read to push his works Honda to destruction. Not only this, but Mike's race average was only fractionally slower than his old record lap of 108.77mph on the Honda 500 four-cylinder with which he had won the Senior TT back in 1967.

Except for an instant on lap one, Mike led the race throughout. But it was the way he caught and passed Phil Read and the Honda that made the crowds delirious. Mike had started 50 seconds after Phil and pursued him so relentlessly that before the halfway mark the Ducati rider was leading on the road! On lap three, at Ramsey, the pair were neck and neck, but by the Bungalow Mike was 100 yards ahead of the Honda team leader. It was, as *Motor Cycle News* reported: 'the most exciting comeback the TT has ever seen'.

And, with the battle at full pitch, the pit crews prepared to refuel their charges. Mike took on 3 gallons in 41.2 seconds, but Phil was quicker. The Honda fired instantly, but the Ducati needed an extra push to help the limping Hailwood. The situation on the road was reversed, but the Honda was in trouble. Puffs of tell-tale smoke told their own story as Mike hounded his rival throughout lap four. As they began their fifth lap, Phil was still a few yards ahead on the road – but not for long! His engine smoking badly, Phil was behind through Union Mills. With his leathers smothered in oil, he finally threw in the towel at the 11th milestone after a couple of hair-raising slides and it was all over. With some 60 miles left, Mike couldn't afford to slacken the pace until well into his last lap, which was still completed at a speed of 105.84mph. On that last lap Mike cut the revs right down and said that he: 'cruised'.

Daily Mirror journalist Ted Macaulay – not only Mike's friend, but also the man largely responsible for his comeback in the TT.

Mike Hailwood about to push his Martini Yamaha into life at the start of the 1978 Senior TT.

Mike with his 500 Yamaha at Governor's Bridge during the 1978 Senior TT. He was openly critical of the poor support he received from Yamaha.

Mike on the start-line of the Post TT race at Mallory Park in June 1978, where he recorded another race victory, proving that he could ride both long and short circuits with equal brilliance.

How fast could he have lapped the Ducati? Mike's reply was: 'Certainly over 112mph, maybe more'.

Roger Nicholls, on the sister bike to Mike's, retired after the sight glass of his oil sump shattered, and was thus unable to repeat his runner-up position of the previous year.

A great victory

A sea of fans and photographers greeted the winner at the finish of the 226.38-mile long race, which was followed by ceremonies on the rostrum and photographs of the event. Afterwards, Mike made his way back to his hotel and the first man to knock on his door was none other than Phil Read. He still had his leathers on and had come to congratulate Mike. It was a very sporting gesture and afterwards both riders went down to the bar for a well-earned drink, Mike to celebrate, Phil to wash away his disappointment.

Next on the TT list was Monday's Senior, but Mike's hopes were dashed by a broken steering damper after the first lap. He had opened the race with a burst of 108.54mph and was riding well enough to have climbed the winner's rostrum again, but the broken damper badly affected the Yamaha's handling; then on the last lap he ran short of fuel and limped in 28th.

In the 250cc race, Mike finished a subdued twelfth – maybe his biggest disappointment of the week – but looked set to do well in the Classic (not what it would appear, but in fact an open unlimited event) until he holed a piston on his TZ750 when 10 seconds behind race leader Mick Grant (Kawasaki). Mike was none too pleased with the bikes the Japanese company had provided and went as far as commenting: 'Yamaha were a disgrace compared to the Sports Motorcycles effort'.

Back to the short circuits

Following his Island heroics, Mike returned to the British mainland for the Post TT meeting at Mallory Park on Sunday 11 June – only two days after his final TT race that week.

Following a poor start, Mike and the Ducati overcame not only both factory Hondas (Phil Read's engine problem having been rectified), but also the additional challenge of British Formula 1 TT champion elect John Cowie, proving that it wasn't just in the Isle of Man that he was still a force to be reckoned with. Mike was also able to take on and beat the current crop of British short circuit stars.

Even an accident at Donington Park on Sunday 9 July could not dim the superb performances achieved at the Isle of Man and again at Mallory Park.

Mike's final British meeting in 1978 was the international event at Silverstone, where the speed advantage enjoyed by the latest Japanese machinery was simply too much. Even so, Mike brought the Sports Motorcycles-entered NCR Ducati V-twin home in third place, itself no mean achievement.

Later that year, on his return to the southern hemisphere, Mike once again shared the 750 Ducati with Jim Scaysbrook, hoping for a repeat of their earlier successes together with this motorcycle. But it was not to be, with the pair posting a retirement after Jim crashed the Italian V-twin out of contention in the 6-Hour production race at Amaroo Park, Sydney, on 22 October.

Mike (second from camera) on the start-line at Silverstone, where he finished third in the Formula 1 race on 12 August 1978. Others in the line-up include Stan Woods, Ron Haslam, John Cowrie, Asa Moyce and Tom Herron.

Mike flat out on the Ducati at Silverstone, where the Italian V-twin was outpaced for speed.

In this photograph, taken in the summer of 1978, Mike looks tired and worn, a result of the years of racing and the pressures involved.

Mike (left) looks on as Murray Walker interviews Tom Herron. John Cowrie is on the far right of the picture.

And so 1978 came to an end. The big question on everyone's mind – including Mike's – was would he be back the following year?

Chapter 9

Final years

THE YEAR 1978 was supposed to have been a 'one-off' return and, certainly as regards the magnificent Ducati TT victory, it would have been best to have left it that way. But Mike's incredible comeback had been so well received he simply wasn't allowed to leave the scene as quietly as he had originally intended.

Also, after it had been shown that Mike's will to return was strong, the organisers were keen that Mike should continue and offers of machinery were made for the 1979 season. Some, like offers to appear in the GPs, were turned down by Mike because he, more than anyone, knew his limitations.

In the end he decided to return to the TT again, followed by a limited number of selected UK short circuit meetings. As for bikes, he had taken up offers from Suzuki and Ducati. The Ducati offer came immediately after his TT win, whereas the Suzuki deal was tied up in November 1978.

Before these new commitments came a couple of outings down under (Mike was still living in New Zealand). The first came at Wigram in New Zealand on 11 February 1979, when riding a 7R AJS he finished fourth in a classic bike event. Then, some six weeks later, he tackled another 3-Hour production race with his friend Jim Scaysbrook at Amaroo Park, Sydney, on 25 March. However, the faithful Ducati 750 Super Sport had given way to a new four-cylinder Honda CB 900F. The new bike didn't mean a better performance, because the pairing could only finish 14th.

Return to Europe

Then Mike returned to Europe. His first port of call was the Ducati factory in Bologna. This included a test session at Misano on the latest 864cc V-twin, which the factory (via NCR) had built especially for Mike. However, this ended disastrously when he came off the bike at high speed following gearbox problems. It was potentially quite a serious accident, and Mike was knocked unconscious for a few seconds. The whole incident unnerved the Ducati senior management and their government bosses in Rome to such an extent that the factory could no longer officially support the TT effort. This meant that the operation was run much as it had been the previous year,

Mike's 1979 Ducati TT effort never matched that of 1978. A practice crash in Italy didn't help, and in the race Mike was only able to finish fifth on a poorly prepared bike.

except that Coburn and Hughes were not in the frame, with Sports Motorcycles dealing directly with the Bologna factory.

Compared to the 1978 Yamaha set-up, or for that matter the problems associated with the 1979 Ducati operation, the Suzuki effort went much more smoothly. Essentially Mike was to race a works square four two-stroke in the Senior (500cc) and Classic (Unlimited) TTs (plus the latest Ducati in the Formula 1 event). His Suzuki was to have the full support of the British-based Texaco Heron team (who were effectively running the GP squad at the time).

Mike had his first test session on the Suzuki at Donington Park in May, after which he was able to report:

> *...what a nice surprise the Suzuki is turning out to be. Both Barry Sheene and Steve Parrish (the other Heron-supported riders that year) warned me it didn't handle, had a hinge in the middle and was generally a bit of a handful... but to my delight it was fine.*

Mike was very satisfied with his Suzuki, but the same could not be said of the 1979 Ducati. During TT practicing the handling was not a patch on the previous year's machine, so the frame was changed to the older one. This then showed up another problem – lack of top-end speed. Quite simply the latest Hondas were considerably quicker than the machines used 12 months before. Even so, Mike's bike was definitely slower than before and his lap time proved this. In addition, in the race held on Saturday 2 June, he hit a number of problems. First, after battling hard to gain third place, he entered the sixth and final lap with first gear missing. Then the exhaust broke and, finally, the battery came loose. This problem caused the bike to cut out entirely a few miles from the finish line. After coming to a halt, Mike somehow managed to repair his machine, restart and finally, almost in a state of collapse, come home fifth in a race won by Honda-mounted Alex George.

In this photograph it is possible to see the problems experienced with grounding-out of the fairing in the 1979 Formula 1 Ducati machine.

A Suzuki victory

Two days later, on Monday 4 June, Mike, despite covering a mere five laps in practice on his works 500cc Suzuki (a 1978 bike), achieved his 14th and last TT victory. It was a magnificent record-breaking performance. During the first lap of the Senior (500cc) event, Mike in his own words 'took it easy', getting the feel of the motorcycle, which was entirely different from the Ducati he had ridden only a few hours before. Then, increasing his speed, he went round at a record 111.75mph, before really getting his head down and charging around the Mountain course to set a new lap record of 114.02mph to win the race.

Fellow author and former journalist Mick Woollet, reporting for *Motor Cycle*, said:

In contrast to his Ducati problem, Mike won the 1979 Senior TT on a Suzuki RG500. He is seen here at Creg Ny Baa. His race average speed was 111.75mph, with a fastest lap of 114.02mph.

The Suzuki square-four disc valve engine, showing the installation of the carburettors, radiator, exhaust header pipes and dry clutch.

Hailwood has done it. On Monday mighty Mike blasted his way to his fourteenth TT win... yet this incredible superstar was completely relaxed at the end of the six-lap race.

Mike went on to say that there were: '...no problems at all. The Suzuki was perfect, it went like a dream. I'm looking forward to it racing again in Friday's Classic'.

Battle of the giants

Alex George had replaced Phil Read as Honda's top man for the 1979 TT. And having already shown his worth a 'battle of the giants' was expected between Alex and Mike. The former rode his Formula 1 winning machine, the 996cc Honda four-stroke megabike; the latter was aboard his Senior TT winning 500cc Suzuki square four two-stroke. After five nail-biting laps the pair entered the sixth and final circuit with Mike ahead by less than a second. Then, baulked on a couple of occasions by slower riders, Mike lost the lead, while Alex went on to win at the fastest TT-winning speed up to that time of 113.08mph. Mike acknowledged his rival's performance, saying: 'Alex went too quick for me. I didn't want to stick my neck out any further. That's the first time I've ever finished second in the TT'. Mike, writing in his own column in *Motor Cycle*, said:

In 1979 Ducati brought out its 900 Mike Hailwood replica to celebrate Mike's 1978 TT success. This sportster was in reality a customised 900SS, rather than an authentic reproduction of the TT winner.

I have finally and irrevocably retired from TT racing – about time too. After all, I will be 40 next year and it is hard for me to believe I rode in my first TT exactly 21 years ago – in 1958.

His old friend Ted Macauley described things from a different angle:

...at around five minutes past five on Friday evening, 8th June, Mike Hailwood's dejection was at its lowest ebb. For a time split of only 3.4 seconds had robbed him of a glorious victory in his last Isle of Man TT. By ten past five the grey mask of despair had slipped away and Mike was back to his chuckling, romping best, squirting champagne and pouring praise – enjoying Alex George's Classic triumph as much as the winner himself.

This was typical of Mike, someone who showed throughout his long career what Ted Macauley once described as: 'absolute resilience'.

Last rides

Mike's last scheduled rides were at Mallory Park on Sunday 10 June and, finally, Donington Park on Saturday and Sunday 7 and 8 July 1979.

In his last TT, the classic described above, Mike's Sports Motorcycles teammate George Fogarty (father of Carl) had written off the Formula 1 bike Mike had raced in the Island, which was scheduled to be ridden by him at Mallory and Donington.

So instead Suzuki came to the rescue and loaned Mike a Paul Dunstall GS1000, but at Mallory he suffered brake problems and, never being in contention, retired from the Formula 1 race.

At Donington Park, after suffering a high-speed crash in practice, he subsequently did a lap of honour with circuit owner Tom Wheatcroft in a

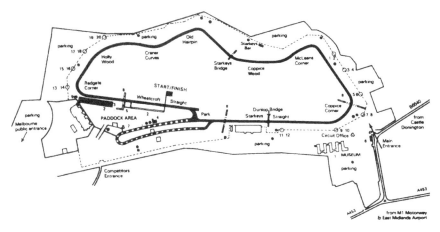

Donington Park; length 2.5 miles.

pre-war supercharged Bentley, but was unable to race. Why? Well, he had suffered a badly broken collarbone – but being the man he was, despite the pain he endured, he thought he owed it to the fans to put in an appearance. Hence the subtitle of this book: *'The Fans' Favourite'*.

Going into business

All along it had been planned that Donington Park was to be Mike's final appearance and so it was. Together with his wife Pauline and their daughter Michelle and son David (born 10 June 1971 and 16 May 1974 respectively), Mike had moved back to England to live in spring 1979.

Straight after the TT Mike got stuck into the task of arranging his future career: opening a motorcycle business with showrooms in Tyburn Road, Birmingham. Mike replaced his leathers with overalls to prepare the site for opening later that summer. Together with his partner in the new venture, former 250cc world champion and Yamaha team manager Rod Gould, Mike commented:

> *Getting the business off the ground has taken up a lot of time and concentration – and the time has come when motorcycle racing, for so long the main love of my life, will have to take a back seat.*
>
> *...I have a wife and family to look after and a totally new life and way of life to organise. Rod and I both have a lot of work to do before we can call ourselves a success in business.*

When asked how he saw the Hailwood and Gould company progressing, Mike continued:

> *Expansion? It's a little too early just yet – but my father set our family's precedent in the field. He built up King's of Oxford until it was just about the biggest chain of motorcycle shops in the land and it would be terrific if I could do the same.*

But as the author knows only too well, the motorcycle trade was just about to enter a crippling recession which was to last until well into the 1980s and hurt many existing, previously prosperous businesses, let alone newcomers such as Mike and Rod. Quite simply, they could not have picked a worse time to enter the fray.

But there were a couple of bright patches in this gloomy picture. The first was the drawing power of the Hailwood name. I know of several customers who bought bikes from Hailwood & Gould simply because they were able to say 'Mike sold me my bike'. The other was the arrival in 1979 of a new Ducati production model, the MHR (Mike Hailwood Replica). In many ways this was perhaps Mike's greatest tribute. How many people can say they have had a vehicle named after them!

Even though, in reality, the machine bore little resemblance to Mike's 1978 TT winner, except for having a V-twin engine and a green, white and red paint job, it proved a great commercial success for the Bologna company. Also, with Mike's name associated with it, the Hailwood & Gould dealership benefited from a mini sales boom.

However, this boom didn't last and by the spring of 1981 things were looking bleak for both the dealership and the motorcycle trade in general. And I can speak from personal experience of both my own company and Mike's situation, as in my role of Ducati spares importer at the time I visited the Hailwood & Gould deal-

Rod Gould, the 1970 250cc world champion and Mike's business partner in the Hailwood & Gould dealership venture. He is seen here on a 250 Yamaha at Cadwell Park that year.

ership and met Mike on several occasions. But I never felt Mike was either happy or suited to the routine of running his business.

The fateful day

One fateful Saturday evening, 21 March 1981, Mike set out from his home in Tamworth-in-Arden with his two children to collect a fish and chip supper. On the way a truck made an illegal U-turn on a stretch of dual carriageway at Portway, and in the process struck Mike's Rover SDI car.

Mike and Pauline's daughter Michelle, then nine, died instantly, but their son David (six) received only minor injuries. Mike, a few days short of his 41st birthday, suffered terrible head injuries from which he died in Birmingham Accident Hospital on Monday 23 March 1981.

His friend and car racing legend Stirling Moss said of Mike: 'He was one of the real characters. It's ironic that he should go like this'.

Pauline Hailwood, when interviewed by *Classic Bike* in October 2002, was to recall:

An advertisement for Hailwood & Gould, *c.*1980. The business was ultimately a casualty of the recession which hit the industry at the beginning of the 1980s.

RACE LEADERS

Twenty top 3 placings in World Championships including eleven 1st's means that choosing the right machines for the job came right for Mike Hailwood and Rod Gould.

Their experience is available to you when deciding on the make and model for your needs. An ever present range of models from HONDA, SUZUKI, YAMAHA, DUCATI, TRIUMPH and BSA are on display.

Many customised clothing and accessories always available backed up with a comprehensive spares department.

Take a 'CHAMPION's' advice and talk bikes with Mike Hailwood and Rod Gould.

hailwood &gould

60-98 TYBURN ROAD, ERDINGTON, BIRMINGHAM B24 8LA TEL: 021 327 0276

Mike Hailwood replica

In all the years of watching him race and being afraid of him getting hurt, I never imagined that I would lose him – and our little daughter aged nine – in a road accident, the result of another driver's dreadful error. Our son Dave, then six, was also in the car …thank God he was saved. I was devastated; all our lives were changed forever. Mike was my life and I still love and miss him and Michelle terribly. There are always fresh flowers by their photos in the sitting room, and in many ways Mike is still in my life, and always will be.

Pauline and David now live in Spain.

Chapter 10

A place in history

NEVER IN the history of motorcycle racing has there been a more popular champion than Mike Hailwood, and after his tragic death this became even more apparent. Normally, with death and the passing of time, memory fades. This has certainly not been the case with Mike. No more fitting tribute could have been made than that which appeared in the 1 April 1981 issue of *Motor Cycle News*, penned by the late Norrie Whyte:

> *In no sport has there been any competitor held in the same esteem as Stanley Michael Bailey Hailwood, MBE, GM. Throughout the racing world, the fans, the competitors, the organisers, the mechanics, the trade, the press – even the poseurs he detested – are united: 'Mike-the-Bike was the Greatest road racer of all time'.*

Mike's 1967 297cc Honda six on display at Silverstone in August 1980. As always Mike's name brought in the crowds.

The Ducati museum in Bologna, with its Hailwood Room, in 1998.

Actually, to my way of thinking, this should also have said 'loved', for that was how the world of two wheels saw the man, who now, a quarter of a century after his fatal accident, is seen as a true legend.

Mike bridged gaps like few others – in any walk of life. He came from a moneyed, privileged background, but at heart he was very much a down-to-earth man. Money never really came into it, except for the backing he received from his millionaire father, Stan. Mike raced bikes simply because he liked racing bikes. But instead of boasting about his success, he would simply shrug and say, 'It's the thing I'm best at'.

Besides his will to win there was Mike's great ability to ride any bike – in his time he straddled everything from a 49cc Itom single-cylinder two-stroke to a 1000cc Dunstall-Suzuki GS1000 four-cylinder superbike. Not only that, but he could switch capacity sizes and makes at the same meeting on the same day – and give an equally breathtaking winning performance. He was also just as good in wet or dry conditions.

Before his Nürburgring car crash in 1974 which left him with a damaged right leg and foot, the fact that the gear lever was on the offside or nearside didn't matter. Like Jim Clark, the equally respected car racer, Mike altered his style to suit the machinery.

Anyone studying the appendices at the back of this book can't fail to be impressed by the sheer number of races Mike contested, the variety of the bikes and the differing circuits. Mike probably had more experience – track time – than any other racer ever. He also liked new challenges. Once he had achieved success he wanted to move on to ride new bikes and face fresh hurdles.

Nobody is perfect, and Mike was certainly no engineer or mechanic, like John Surtees for example. He also does not seem to have inherited his father's head for business. But he was certainly a fast learner when it came to circuits. For example, Mike didn't bother to serve an Isle of Man apprenticeship in the Manx Grand Prix, the traditional route to TT success. Instead, he jumped straight into the TT itself – and not just in one class. Oh no! Mike arrived at the 1958 event with a bike for every solo class: 125, 250, 350 and 500cc. He was then only 18, had a mere 14 months racing experience behind him, and was entering a World Championship event for the first time.

It could have been a disastrous debut. Just think about it. Ambitious, and surrounded by the publicity his success (and his father!) had generated, it would have been so easy for the youngster to go too quickly and land himself in a pile of trouble on the unforgiving Mountain circuit, potentially putting his life at risk. But in reality he rode like a veteran, and finished all four races. He came home 13th in the Senior, 12th in the Junior, seventh in the 125cc and a fantastic third in the 250cc race, beaten only by Tarquinio Provini and runner-up Carlo Ubbiali on works MV Agustas. Quite simply this was an incredible performance. Mike went on to score 14 TT victories, a record only broken, after the event had lost its World Championship status, by Joey Dunlop.

A 1985 Ducati MHR (Mike Hailwood Replica) on display in an enthusiast's home, together with a painting of Mike and his 1978 TT-winning bike.

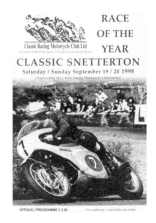

Trying to list all Mike's successes is a difficult – and lengthy – task! Simply listing his main achievements – his 14 TT victories, 10 world titles (four 500cc, three 250cc, two 350cc and the final one, the Formula 1 in 1978) and 76 Grand Prix victories – does not tell anything like the full story.

In a career which began on 22 April 1957 at Oulton Park and ended on 10 July 1979 at Donington Park – and included almost a decade of near inactivity on two wheels – Mike rode in well over 700 races, winning over half of them.

As for the bikes he raced, these include: British (AJS, Norton, Triumph, BSA, Matchless, Seeley, EMC), Italian (MV Agusta, Ducati, Paton, Itom, FB Mondial, Benelli), German (NSU, MZ) and Japanese (Honda, Suzuki, Yamaha).

Mike also tested many other machines and rode James, Greeves and Triumph off-road. At the height of his career each year he covered approximately 10,000 miles racing, 10,000 on the road and 160,000 miles in the air.

When asked in 1968 'Of the bikes you have ridden, which was your particular favourite?' Mike replied:

> *Every rider likes the machine which brings him success. In my case it's the MV 500 because it was a beautiful bike with no vices, amazingly reliable and so easy to ride.*

Mike also disliked the huge publicity he generated through his performances on the race circuit. He certainly wanted time and space to himself, commenting:

Another enthusiast's way of remembering Mike – a converted four-cylinder Honda CB500 seen at Oliver's Mount, Scarborough, in 2003, dressed out to look like Hailwood's works model of the late 1960s.

> *...after a race I usually want to relax or enjoy myself with friends without continual interruptions. This applies even more when I'm away from the circuits. I feel everyone has a right to a private life and it drives me mad if people continually want to break into it.*

Interestingly, it took Mike three attempts to pass his motorcycle test. He reckoned the reason was because: 'I'd already been riding for about ten years and was a bit over-confident'.

Mike also set a new one-hour world record

in 1964 on his five-hundred MV Agusta at Daytona. But his main concern was that in doing so he was taking the record away from his old friend, the late Bob McIntyre. This also shows Mike as a very feeling, caring person.

As Robin Miller, the former editor of *Motor Cycle News* was to recall following Mike's death in 1981, he had: 'a boyish grin, wide as the back of an Isle of Man ferry', and a 'marvellous sense of humour and barbed wit, often employed to deflate paddock poseurs'. Certainly Mike was the last person anyone could describe as a poseur himself; if anything he found it difficult to see what all the fuss was about.

Robin Miller again:

...the greatest tribute, however, comes from his fellow riders. Not just the Agostinis and Reads, but the Mick Chattertons and Terry Grotefelds. He was one of them, felt at home in their company, and they in his. They spoke a common language in a sport where people live for the day.

The author (left) and his friend Tommy Robb at the Goodwood Festival of Speed, July 1999. The occasion was a gathering of former Honda works stars including Tommy, Luigi Taveri, Stuart Graham and Ralph Bryans. Mike was there in spirit, if not in person.

The unveiling of the Mallory Park Mike Hailwood memorial, summer 1998. From left to right: David Hailwood, Pauline Hailwood, Phil Read, Geoff Duke, Chris Meek (Mallory Park circuit owner) and Olga Malakh.

And that was exactly how, I'm sure, Mike saw life – enjoy yourself, make every minute count, life's too short.

And so Mike-the-Bike has passed from simply being part of motorcycle history to being a true legend – and for all the right reasons.

Appendices

Summary of motorcycle racing career

1957

Position	Class	Machine	Circuit	Date
11	150cc	MV Agusta	Oulton Park	22 April
4	125cc	MV Agusta	Castle Combe	27 April
5	250cc	MV Agusta 175cc	Castle Combe	27 April
3	200cc	MV Agusta 175cc	Brands Hatch	12 May
3	50cc	Itom	Blandford	10 June
1	125cc	MV Agusta	Blandford	10 June
5	175cc	MV Agusta 175cc	Blandford	10 June
Retired (crashed)	250cc	MV Agusta 175cc	Scarborough	14 June
2	250cc (race 1)	MV Agusta 203cc	Silverstone	6 July
2	250cc (race 2)	MV Agusta 203cc	Silverstone	6 July
3	125cc	MV Agusta	Snetterton	14 July
1	250cc	MV Agusta 203cc	Snetterton	14 July
2	200cc	MV Agusta 175cc	Brands Hatch	21 July
1	150cc	MV Agusta 125cc	Rhydymwyn	27 July
1	250cc	MV Agusta 203cc	Rhydymwyn	27 July
2	50cc	Itom	Oulton Park	3 August
3	125cc	MV Agusta	Oulton Park	3 August
Retired (crashed, collarbone)	250cc	MV Agusta 203cc	Oulton Park	3 August
1	200cc	MV Agusta 175cc	Brands Hatch	8 September
2	250cc	MV Agusta 203cc	Brands Hatch	8 September
3	250cc	MV Agusta 203cc	Scarborough	14 September

Crashed practicing for the Silverstone Hutchison 100 (20 September) and suffered a broken ankle, putting himself out for the remainder of the British short circuit season.

1	250cc	NSU	Pietermaritzburg SA	15 December
2	Handicap	NSU 250cc	Pietermaritzburg SA	15 December

6 victories, 6 seconds, 6 thirds

1958

Position	Class	Machine	Circuit	Date
1	250cc	NSU	Port Elizabeth SA	1 January (RL)
16	Handicap	NSU 250cc	Port Elizabeth SA	1 January
1	250cc	NSU	Pietermaritzburg SA	19 January (RL)
1	250cc	NSU	Pietermaritzburg SA	16 February
1	250cc	NSU	Pretoria SA	2 March
Retired (engine)	350cc	Norton	Pretoria SA	2 March
3 (remounted after crash)	250cc	NSU	Port Elizabeth SA	9 March
4	Handicap	NSU	Port Elizabeth SA	9 March
Retired (engine)	350cc	Norton	Port Elizabeth SA	9 March
1	250cc	NSU	Cape Town SA	29 March (RL)
2	Handicap	NSU	Cape Town SA	29 March
1	200cc	MV Agusta	Brands Hatch	4 April (RL)
2	250cc	NSU	Brands Hatch	4 April

Position	Class	Machine	Circuit	Date
1	200cc	MV Agusta	Crystal Palace	7 April (RL)
1	250cc	NSU	Crystal Palace	7 April
2	250cc	NSU	Mallory Park	13 April
5	350cc	Norton	Mallory Park	13 April
Unplaced	650cc	Norton 500cc	Mallory Park	13 April
1	125cc	MV Agusta	Silverstone	19 April
Retired	250cc	NSU	Silverstone	19 April
1	125cc	MV Agusta	Castle Combe	26 April
1	250cc	NSU	Castle Combe	26 April
6	350cc	Norton	Castle Combe	26 April
6	500cc	Norton	Castle Combe	26 April
1	200cc	MV Agusta	Brands Hatch	4 May
1	250cc	NSU	Brands Hatch	4 May
1	350cc	Norton	Brands Hatch	4 May
Retired (crash)	500cc	Norton	Brands Hatch	4 May
2	200cc	MV Agusta	Aintree	10 May
2	250cc	NSU	Aintree	10 May
1	200cc	MV Agusta	Cookstown NI	14 May
Retired (electrics)	250cc	NSU	Cookstown NI	14 May
2	250cc	NSU	North West 200	17 May
1	250cc	NSU	Brands Hatch	26 May
1	350cc	Norton	Brands Hatch	26 May
2	500cc	Norton	Brands Hatch	26 May
12	350cc Junior TT	Norton	Isle of Man	2 June
7	125cc Ultra-lightweight TT	Paton	Isle of Man	4 June
3	250cc Lightweight TT	NSU	Isle of Man	4 June
13	500cc Senior TT	Norton	Isle of Man	6 June
1	250cc	NSU	Mallory Park	8 June
1	350cc	Norton	Mallory Park	8 June
Retired (electrics)	500cc	Norton	Mallory Park	8 June
Retired (broken carb stub)	150cc	Paton 125cc	Scarborough	14 June
1	250cc	NSU	Scarborough	14 June
1	125cc	MV Agusta	Snetterton	15 June
1	250cc	NSU	Snetterton	15 June (RL)
1	350cc	Norton	Snetterton	15 June (RL)
2	500cc	Norton	Snetterton	15 June
1	500-mile	Triumph 650cc T110	Thruxton	21 June
	endurance unlimited (with Dan Shorey)			
10	125cc Dutch TT	Ducati	Assen	28 June
4	250cc Dutch TT	NSU	Assen	28 June
5	350cc Dutch TT	Norton	Assen	28 June
1	125cc	MV Agusta	Castle Combe	12 July
1	250cc	NSU	Castle Combe	12 July
1	350cc	Norton	Castle Combe	12 July
Retired (oiled plug at start)	500cc	Norton	Castle Combe	12 July
1	Handicap	NSU 250cc	Castle Combe	12 July
Retired (front brake problems)	250cc German GP	NSU	Nürburgring	20 July
4	350cc German GP	Norton	Nürburgring	20 July
2	350cc Swedish GP	NSU	Hedemora	26 July
3	250cc Swedish GP	Norton	Hedemora	27 July
1	125cc	MV Agusta	Crystal Palace	4 August
1	250cc	NSU	Crystal Palace	4 August
6	350cc	Norton	Crystal Palace	4 August
5	500cc	Norton	Crystal Palace	4 August
Retired (crash)	250cc Ulster GP	NSU	Dundrod	9 August

Position	Class	Machine	Circuit	Date
8	350cc Ulster GP	Norton	Dundrod	9 August
1	125cc	MV Agusta	Aberdare Park	23 August
1	250cc	NSU	Aberdare Park	23 August
3	350cc	Norton	Aberdare Park	23 August
2	200cc	Ducati	Brands Hatch	24 August
1	250cc	NSU	Brands Hatch	24 August
2	350cc	Norton	Brands Hatch	24 August
2	125cc	Ducati	Zandvoort	31 August
Retired	350cc	Norton	Zandvoort	31 August
1	250cc	NSU	Mallory Park	7 September
1	350cc	Norton	Mallory Park	7 September
1	500cc	Norton	Mallory Park	7 September
1	125cc	Ducati	Silverstone	13 September
1	250cc	NSU	Silverstone	13 September
Retired (ignition problems)	350cc	Norton	Silverstone	13 September
1	250cc	NSU	Cadwell Park	14 September
1	350cc	Norton	Cadwell Park	14 September
Retired	500cc	Norton	Cadwell Park	14 September
1	250cc	NSU	Scarborough	19-20 September
1	350cc	Norton	Scarborough	19-20 September
1	125cc	Ducati	Snetterton	21 September
1	250cc	NSU	Snetterton	21 September
1	350cc	Norton	Snetterton	21 September
1	500cc	Norton	Snetterton	21 September
1	125cc	Ducati	Aintree	27 September
3	250cc	NSU	Aintree	27 September
6	500cc	Norton	Aintree	27 September
Retired (clutch problems)	500cc	Norton	Mallory Park	28 September
1	125cc	FB Mondial	Crystal Palace	4 October
1	250cc	NSU	Crystal Palace	4 October
1	350cc	Norton	Crystal Palace	4 October
1	1000cc	Norton 500cc	Crystal Palace	4 October
2	200cc	Paton	Brands Hatch	12 October
1	250cc	FB Mondial	Brands Hatch	12 October
Retired(crash)	350cc	Norton	Brands Hatch	12 October
7	500cc	Norton	Brands Hatch	12 October
Retired (electrical problems)	Invitation	Norton	Brands Hatch	12 October
1	250cc	NSU	Cape Town SA	29 November (RL)
1	350cc	Norton	Cape Town SA	29 November (RL)
1	500cc	Norton	Cape Town SA	29 November (RL)
1	250cc	NSU	Pietermaritzburg SA	14 December (RL)
1	350cc	Norton	Pietermaritzburg SA	14 December (RL)
1	500cc	Norton	Pietermaritzburg SA	14 December (RL)

58 victories (many more in heats), 13 seconds, 5 thirds
Winner of the 125, 250 and 350cc ACU Stars.

1959

Position	Class	Machine	Circuit	Date
Retired (rag in carb)	500cc	Norton	Port Elizabeth SA	1 January
2	250cc	NSU	Pietermaritzburg SA	18 January
2	350cc	Norton	Pietermaritzburg SA	18 January
2	500cc	Norton	Pietermaritzburg SA	18 January
Retired (ignition)	250cc	FB Mondial	Mallory Park	22 March
1	350cc	Norton	Mallory Park	22 march

Position	Class	Machine	Circuit	Date
4	500cc	Norton	Mallory Park	22 March
2	200cc	Ducati 125cc	Brands Hatch	27 March
1	250cc	FB Mondial	Brands Hatch	27 March
5	350cc	Norton	Brands Hatch	27 March
6	500cc	Norton	Brands Hatch	27 March
3	1000cc	Norton 500cc	Brands Hatch	27 March
1	125cc	Ducati	Snetterton	29 March
1	250cc	FB Mondial	Snetterton	29 March
1	350cc	Norton	Snetterton	29 March
2	500cc	Norton	Snetterton	29 March
1	125cc	Ducati	Thruxton	30 March
1	250cc	FB Mondial	Thruxton	30 March
1	350cc	Norton	Thruxton	30 March
1	500cc	Norton	Thruxton	30 March
1	125cc	Ducati	Silverstone	18 April
1	250cc	FB Mondial	Silverstone	18 April
5	350cc	Norton	Silverstone	18 April
4	500cc	Norton	Silverstone	18 April
Retired (seized in heat)	250cc	FB Mondial	Mallory Park	19 April
Retired (seized gearbox)	350cc	Norton	Mallory Park	19 April
2	500cc	Norton	Mallory Park	19 April
1	125cc	Ducati	Castle Combe	25 April
1	250cc	FB Mondial	Castle Combe	25 April
2	350cc	Norton	Castle Combe	25 April
2	500cc	Norton	Castle Combe	25 April
1	250cc	NSU	Mallory Park	3 May
1	350cc	Norton	Mallory Park	3 May
3	500cc	Norton	Mallory Park	3 May
1	125cc	Ducati	Aberdare Park	16 May (RL)
Retired (crash)	350cc	FB Mondial	Aberdare Park	16 May
1	350cc	Norton	Aberdare Park	16 May
4	500cc	Norton	Aberdare Park	16 May
2	200cc	Ducati 125cc	Aintree	18 May
Retired (ignition)	250cc	FB Mondial	Aintree	18 May
1	500cc	Norton	Aintree	18 May
3	125cc Ultra-lightweight TT	Ducati	Isle of Man	3 June
Retired (engine)	250cc Lightweight TT	FB Mondial	Isle of Man	3 June
Retired (engine)	350cc Junior TT	Norton	Isle of Man	1 June
3	350cc Formula 1 TT	Norton	Isle of Man	30 May
Retired (crash)	500cc Senior TT	Norton	Isle of Man	6 June
1	250cc	FB Mondial	Mallory Park	7 June (RL)
5	350cc	Norton	Mallory Park	7 June
Retired (faulty front fork damping)	500cc	Norton	Mallory Park	7 June
3	125cc German GP	Ducati	Hockenheim	14 June
5	250cc German GP	FB Mondial	Hockenheim	14 June
1	250cc	FB Mondial	Scarborough	20 June (RL)
1	350cc	AJS	Scarborough	20 June (RL)
3	125cc Dutch TT	Ducati	Assen	27 June
4	250cc Dutch TT	FB Mondial	Assen	27 June
Retired (broken piston)	125cc Belgian GP	Ducati	Spa Francorchamps	5 July
Retired	350cc Belgian GP	AJS	Spa Francorchamps	5 July
13 (bike troubles)	500cc Belgian GP	Norton	Spa Francorchamps	5 July
1	125cc	Ducati	Castle Combe	11 July (RL)
1	250cc	FB Mondial	Castle Combe	11 July (RL)
Retired	350cc	Norton	Castle Combe	11 July

Position	Class	Machine	Circuit	Date
1	500cc	Norton	Castle Combe	11 July
1	Handicap	FB Mondial 250cc	Castle Combe	11 July
1	250cc	FB Mondial	Mallory Park	12 July
Retired (crash)	350cc	AJS	Mallory Park	12 July
3	500cc	Norton	Mallory Park	12 July
1	125cc	Ducati	Snetterton	19 July
1	250cc	FB Mondial	Snetterton	19 July
2	350cc	AJS	Snetterton	19 July
2	500cc	Norton	Snetterton	19 July
4	125cc Swedish GP	Ducati (twin)	Kristianstad	25-26 July
5	250cc Swedish GP	FB Mondial	Kristianstad	25-26 July
5	350cc Swedish GP	AJS	Kristianstad	25-26 July
4	500cc Swedish GP	Matchless	Kristianstad	25-26 July
1	150cc	Ducati 125cc	Oulton Park	3 August
1	250cc	FB Mondial	Oulton Park	3 August
Retired	350cc	AJS	Oulton Park	3 August
1	500cc	Norton	Oulton Park	3 August
1	125cc Ulster GP	Ducati	Dundrod	8 August (1st GP victory)
2	250cc Ulster GP	FB Mondial	Dundrod	8 August
Retired (broken valve spring)	350cc Ulster GP	AJS	Dundrod	8 August
1	125cc	Ducati	Aberdare Park	15 August
1	250cc	FB Mondial	Aberdare Park	15 August
1	350cc	Norton	Aberdare Park	15 August
1	500cc	Norton	Aberdare Park	15 August
Retired (oiled plug on start-line)	1000cc	Norton 500cc	Aberdare Park	15 August
1	125cc	Ducati	Silverstone	22 August (RL)
1	250cc	FB Mondial	Silverstone	22 August
3	350cc	AJS	Silverstone	22 August
4	1000cc	Norton 500cc	Silverstone	22 August
1	250cc	FB Mondial	Oulton Park	29 August
2	350cc	AJS	Oulton Park	29 August
2	500cc	Norton	Oulton Park	29 August
Retired	Handicap	n/a	Oulton Park	29 August
8	125cc Italian GP	Ducati	Monza	6 September
9	250cc Italian GP	MZ	Monza	6 September
Retired (valve gear trouble)	500cc Italian GP	Norton	Monza	6 September
1	250cc	FB Mondial	Cadwell Park	13 September (RL)
1	350cc	Norton	Cadwell Park	13 September (RL)
2	500cc	Norton	Cadwell Park	13 September (RL)
7 (carb fell off)	250cc	FB Mondial	Scarborough	19 September (RL)
1	350cc	AJS	Scarborough	19 September
Retired (clutch)	500cc	Norton	Scarborough	19 September
1	125cc	Ducati	Snetterton	20 September (RL)
1	250cc	FB Mondial	Snetterton	20 September (RL)
1	350cc	AJS	Snetterton	20 September
1	500cc	Norton	Snetterton	20 September (RL)
1	125cc	Ducati	Aintree	26 September
1	250cc	FB Mondial	Aintree	26 September (RL)
3	350cc	AJS	Aintree	26 September
1	Handicap	AJS 350cc	Aintree	26 September
Retired (puncture)	500cc	Norton	Aintree	26 September
1	250cc	FB Mondial	Mallory Park	27 September (RL)
2	350cc	AJS	Mallory Park	27 September (RL)
3	500cc	Norton	Mallory Park	27 September
3	Solo Championship	Norton 500cc	Mallory Park	27 September

Position	Class	Machine	Circuit	Date
1	200cc	Ducati 125cc	Biggin Hill	4 October (RL)
1	250cc	FB Mondial	Biggin Hill	4 October (RL)
1	350cc	AJS	Biggin Hill	4 October (RL)
1	1000cc	Norton 500cc	Biggin Hill	4 October (RL)
1	1000cc	Norton 500cc	Biggin Hill	4 October (RL)
Retired (crash)	200cc	Ducati 125cc	Brands Hatch	11 October
1	250cc	FB Mondial	Brands Hatch	11 October
2	350cc	AJS	Brands Hatch	11 October
1	500cc	Norton	Brands Hatch	11 October
2	Invitation	Norton 500cc	Brands Hatch	11 October

57 victories (many more in heats)
Winner of 125, 250, 350 and 500cc ACU Stars
3rd 125cc World Championship
5th 250cc World Championship

1960

Position	Class	Machine	Circuit	Date
1	125cc	Ducati	Silverstone	9 April
1	250cc	Ducati	Silverstone	9 April (RL)
2	350cc	AJS	Silverstone	9 April
2	500cc	Norton	Silverstone	9 April
1	200cc	Ducati 125cc	Brands Hatch	15 April (RL)
1	250cc	Ducati	Brands Hatch	15 April (RL)
2	350cc	AJS	Brands Hatch	15 April
2	500cc	Norton	Brands Hatch	15 April
2	1000cc	Norton 500cc	Brands Hatch	15 April
1	125cc	Ducati	Snetterton	17 April
Retired (crash)	250cc	Ducati	Snetterton	17 April
1	125cc	Ducati	Castle Combe	23 April (RL)
1	250cc	FB Mondial	Castle Combe	23 April
1	350cc	AJS	Castle Combe	23 April (RL)
3	500cc	Norton	Castle Combe	23 April
1	125cc	Ducati	Aberdare Park	30 April (RL)
1	250cc	FB Mondial	Aberdare Park	30 April (RL)
Retired (crash)	350cc	AJS	Aberdare Park	30 April
1	500cc	Norton	Aberdare Park	30 April
1	1000cc	Norton 500cc	Aberdare Park	30 April
1	250cc	FB Mondial	Mallory Park	1 May (RL)
Retired (slipped ignition timing)	350cc	AJS	Mallory Park	1 May (RL)
1	500cc	Norton	Mallory Park	1 May (RL)
1	250cc	FB Mondial	Scarborough	7 May (
1	350cc	AJS	Scarborough	7 May (RL)
2	500cc	Norton	Scarborough	7 May
1	150cc	Ducati 125cc	Aintree	14 May
1	250cc	FB Mondial	Aintree	14 May
1	350cc	AJS	Aintree	14 May
2	500cc	Norton	Aintree	14 May
1	200cc	Ducati 125cc	Brands Hatch	15 May
1	250cc	FB Mondial	Brands Hatch	15 May
1	350cc	AJS	Brands Hatch	15 May
2	1000cc	Norton 500cc	Brands Hatch	15 May
1	125cc	Ducati	Silverstone	28 May (RL)
1	250cc	Ducati	Silverstone	28 May
Retired (engine seizure)	350cc	AJS	Silverstone	28 May
1	500cc	Norton	Silverstone	28 May (RL)

Position	Class	Machine	Circuit	Date
Retired (crash)	Ultra-lightweight 125cc TT	Ducati	Isle of Man	13 June
Retired (broken throttle cable)	Lightweight 250cc TT	Ducati	Isle of Man	13 June
Retired (broken float chamber mounting)	Junior 350cc TT	AJS	Isle of Man	15 June
3	Senior 500cc TT	Norton	Isle of Man	17 June
1	250cc	FB Mondial	Mallory Park	19 June
1	350cc	AJS	Mallory Park	19 June
2	500cc	Norton	Mallory Park	19 June
8	125cc Dutch TT	Ducati	Assen	25 June
5	250cc Dutch TT	FB Mondial	Assen	25 June
5	500cc Dutch TT	Norton	Assen	25 June
6	125cc Belgian GP	Ducati (twin)	Spa Francorchamps	3 July
4	250cc Belgian GP	Ducati	Spa Francorchamps	3 July
4	500cc Belgian GP	Norton	Spa Francorchamps	3 July
1	125cc	Ducati	Brands Hatch	9 July
1	250cc	Ducati	Brands Hatch	9 July
1	350cc	AJS	Brands Hatch	9 July
1	500cc	Norton	Brands Hatch	9 July
1	125cc	Ducati	Castle Combe	16 July
1	250cc	Ducati	Castle Combe	16 July
3 (bent valves)	350cc	AJS	Castle Combe	16 July
1	500cc	Norton	Castle Combe	16 July
1	250cc	Ducati	Mallory Park	17 July
5 (valve problems)	350cc	AJS	Mallory Park	17 July
1	500cc	Norton	Mallory Park	17 July
1	125cc	Ducati	Snetterton	24 July
1	250cc	Ducati	Snetterton	24 July (RL)
1	350cc	AJS	Snetterton	24 July (RL)
Retired (misfiring engine)	500cc	Norton	Snetterton	24 July
1	125cc	Ducati	Oulton Park	1 August
1	250cc	Ducati	Oulton Park	1 August
Retired (engine problems)	350cc	AJS	Oulton Park	1 August
2	500cc	Norton	Oulton Park	1 August
2	Invitation	Norton 500cc	Oulton Park	1 August
4	250cc Ulster GP	Ducati	Dundrod	6 August
Retired (ignition)	500cc Ulster GP	Norton	Dundrod	6 August
1	350cc	AJS	Aberdare Park	13 August
1	500cc	Norton	Aberdare Park	13 August
1	1000cc	Norton 500cc	Aberdare Park	13 August
1	200cc	Ducati 125cc	Brands Hatch	21 August
1	250cc	FB Mondial	Brands Hatch	21 August (RL)
1	350cc	AJS	Brands Hatch	21 August (RL)
3	500cc	Norton	Brands Hatch	21 August
2	1000cc	Norton 500cc	Brands Hatch	21 August
1	250cc	FB Mondial	Snetterton	4 September (RL)
Retired (crashed in heat)	350cc	AJS	Snetterton	4 September
1	500cc	Norton	Snetterton	4 September
Retired (ignition)	250cc Italian GP	Ducati	Monza	11 September
Retired (rear wheel collapsed)	350cc Italian GP	Ducati	Monza	11 September
3	500cc Italian GP	Norton	Monza	11 September
2	200cc	Ducati 125cc	Brands Hatch	18 September
1	250cc	FB Mondial	Brands Hatch	18 September (RL)
1	350cc	AJS	Brands Hatch	18 September (RL)
1	500cc	Norton	Brands Hatch	18 September (RL)
1	1000cc	Norton 500cc	Brands Hatch	18 September (RL)

Position	Class	Machine	Circuit	Date
2	125cc	Ducati	Aintree	24 September
2	250cc	FB Mondial	Aintree	24 September
3	350cc	AJS	Aintree	24 September
2	500cc	Norton	Aintree	24 September
Retired (engine)	Aintree Century	Norton 500cc	Aintree	24 September
1	250cc	FB Mondial	Mallory Park	25 September (RL)
2	350cc	AJS	Mallory Park	25 September (RL)
1	500cc	Norton	Mallory Park	25 September
1	Race of the Year	Norton 500cc	Mallory Park	25 September (RL)
5	500cc	Norton	Oulton Park	8 October
3	200cc	Ducati 125cc	Brands Hatch	9 October
1	250cc	FB Mondial	Brands Hatch	9 October
1	350cc	AJS	Brands Hatch	9 October
2	1000cc	Norton 500cc	Brands Hatch	9 October
1	125cc	Ducati	Zaragosa	16 October
1	500cc	Norton	Zaragosa	16 October

60 victories (many more in heats), 18 seconds, 7 thirds
Winner of 125, 250, 350 and 500cc ACU Stars
5th 250cc World Championship
6th 500cc World Championship

1961

Position	Class	Machine	Circuit	Date
2	250cc United States GP	FB Mondial	Daytona	12 February
Retired (ignition)	500cc United States GP	Norton	Daytona	12 February
1	250cc	Ducati	Brands Hatch	31 March (RL)
1	350cc	AJS	Brands Hatch	31 March (RL)
Retired (crash)	1st over 350cc	Norton 500cc	Brands Hatch	31 March (RL)
1	2nd over 350cc	Norton 500cc	Brands Hatch	31 March (RL)
1	250cc	FB Mondial	Snetterton	2 April
1	350cc	AJS	Snetterton	2 April
2	500cc	Norton	Snetterton	2 April
1	250cc	FB Mondial	Thruxton	3 April
1	350cc	AJS	Thruxton	3 April
1	Commonwealth Trophy	Norton	Thruxton	3 April
Retired (black flagged)	250cc	Ducati	Silverstone	8 April
Retired	350cc	AJS	Silverstone	8 April
Retired (engine seized)	500cc	Norton	Silverstone	8 April
1	250cc	FB Mondial	Mallory Park	9 April
3	350cc	AJS	Mallory Park	9 April
1	500cc	Norton	Mallory Park	9 April
4	125cc Spanish GP	EMC	Barcelona	23 April (RL)
Retired (crash)	250cc Spanish GP	FB Mondial	Barcelona	23 April
Retired (stripped primary drive gears in practice)	125cc	EMC	Brands Hatch	30 April
1	250cc	Honda	Brands Hatch	30 April (RL)
Retired (crash)	350cc	AJS	Brands Hatch	30 April
Retired (crash)	500cc	Norton	Brands Hatch	30 April
Retired (fractured battery)	125cc German GP	EMC	Hockenheim	14 May
8	250cc German GP	Honda	Hockenheim	14 May
Retired	350cc German GP	AJS	Hockenheim	14 May
4	500cc German GP	Norton	Hockenheim	14 May
4	125cc French GP	EMC	Clermont-Ferrand	21 May
2	250cc French GP	Honda	Clermont-Ferrand	21 May
2	500cc French GP	Norton	Clermont-Ferrand	21 May

Position	Class	Machine	Circuit	Date
1	250cc	Honda	Castle Combe	27 May (RL)
Retired (broken frame after winning heat)	350cc	Ducati	Castle Combe	27 May
1	500cc	Norton	Castle Combe	27 May
1	Ultra-lightweight 125cc TT	Honda	Isle of Man	12 June
1	Lightweight 250cc TT	Honda	Isle of Man	14 June
Retired (broken gudgeon pin)	Junior 350cc TT	AJS	Isle of Man	14 June
1	Senior 500cc TT	Norton	Isle of Man	16 June
3	250cc	FB Mondial	Mallory Park	18 June
2	350cc	AJS	Mallory Park	18 June
Retired (crash)	500cc	Norton	Mallory Park	18 June
Retired (crash)	125cc Dutch TT	Honda	Assen	24 June
1	250cc Dutch TT	Honda	Assen	24 June (RL)
2	500cc Dutch TT	Norton	Assen	24 June
Retired (engine)	125cc Belgian GP	Honda	Spa Francorchamps	2 July
3	250cc Belgian GP	Honda	Spa Francorchamps	2 July
2	500cc Belgian GP	Norton	Spa Francorchamps	2 July
1	250cc	FB Mondial	Brands Hatch	9 July
4	350cc	AJS	Brands Hatch	9 July
Retired (crash)	Unlimited	Norton	Brands Hatch	9 July
1	250cc	FB Mondial	Castle Combe	15 July
Retired (engine)	350cc	Ducati	Castle Combe	15 July
1	500cc	Norton	Castle Combe	15 July
Retired (ignition)	125cc East German GP	Honda	Sachsenring	30 July
1	250cc East German GP	Honda	Sachsenring	30 July
2	500cc East German GP	Norton	Sachsenring	30 July
1	250cc	Honda	Oulton Park	7 August (RL)
Retired (ignition)	350cc	AJS	Oulton Park	7 August
3	500cc	Norton	Oulton Park	7 August
5	125cc Ulster GP	Honda	Dundrod	12 August
2	250cc Ulster GP	Honda	Dundrod	12 August
2	500cc Ulster GP	Norton	Dundrod	12 August
1	350cc	AJS	Brands Hatch	20 August
Retired (broken exhaust pipe)	500cc	Norton	Brands Hatch	20 August
1	350cc	AJS	Aberdare Park	27 August (RL)
1	500cc	Norton	Aberdare Park	27 August (RL)
2	250cc Italian GP	Honda	Monza	3 September (RL)
2	350cc Italian GP	MV Agusta	Monza	3 September
1	500cc Italian GP	MV Agusta	Monza	3 September
1	250cc Swedish GP	Honda	Kristianstad	17 September
7 (bent valves)	350cc Swedish GP	MV Agusta	Kristianstad	17 September
2	500cc Swedish GP	MV Agusta	Kristianstad	17 September
1	350cc	AJS	Mallory Park	24 September
2	500cc	MV Agusta	Mallory Park	24 September
2	Race of the Year	Norton 500cc	Mallory Park	24 September
1	250cc	FB Mondial	Aintree	30 September
1	350cc	AJS	Aintree	30 September
1	500cc	Norton	Aintree	30 September
1	Aintree Century	Norton 500cc	Aintree	30 September (RL)
1	250cc	FB Mondial	Oulton Park	7 October
Did not start	350cc	AJS	Oulton Park	7 October
1	500cc	Norton	Oulton Park	7 October
1	250cc	FB Mondial	Brands Hatch	8 October
3	500cc	Norton	Brands Hatch	8 October
Retired (crash)	125cc	MV Agusta	Zaragosa	15 October

Position	Class	Machine	Circuit	Date
1	500cc	MV Agusta	Zaragosa	15 October (RL)
1	500cc	Norton	Rosamund, Cal.	November

36 victories (many more in heats), 13 seconds, 3 thirds
250cc World Champion
2nd 500cc World Championship
6th 125cc World Championship

1962

Position	Class	Machine	Circuit	Date
Retired (seized big-end)	United States GP	Norton	Daytona	4 February
Retired (ignition)	250cc	MV Agusta (twin)	Modena	19 March
1	500cc	MV Agusta	Modena	19 March
1	250cc	Benelli	Mallory Park	1 April
Retired (ignition)	350cc	AJS	Mallory Park	1 April
1	500cc	Norton	Mallory Park	1 April
2	125cc	EMC	Silverstone	7 April
2	250cc	Benelli	Silverstone	7 April
2	350cc	AJS	Silverstone	7 April
1	500cc	Norton	Silverstone	7 April
Retired (ignition)	250cc	Benelli	Imola	15 April
5	500cc	MV Agusta	Imola	15 April
3	125cc	EMC	Brands Hatch	20 April
1	350cc	AJS	Brands Hatch	20 April
5	500cc	Norton	Brands Hatch	20 April
2	1000cc	Norton (500cc)	Brands Hatch	20 April
1	350cc	MV Agusta	Snetterton	22 April
1	500cc	MV Agusta	Snetterton	22 April (RL)
1	350cc	MV Agusta	Thruxton	23 April (RL)
1	500cc	MV Agusta	Thruxton	23 April (RL)
2	350cc Austrian GP	MV Agusta	Salzburg	1 May
1	500cc Austrian GP	MV Agusta	Salzburg	1 May (RL)
4	125cc Spanish GP	EMC	Barcelona	6 May
Retired (crash)	125cc French GP	EMC	Clermont-Ferrand	13 May
1	125cc Saar GP	EMC	St Wendel	20 May
Retired (engine)	500cc Saar GP	MV Agusta	St Wendel	20 May
Retired (engine)	Ultra-lightweight 125cc TT	EMC	Isle of Man	6 June
Retired (engine)	Lightweight (250cc) TT	Benelli	Isle of Man	4 June
1	Junior 350cc TT	MV Agusta	Isle of Man	6 June (RL)
12 (clutch and gearbox problems)	Senior 500cc TT	MV Agusta	Isle of Man	8 June
2	250cc	Benelli	Mallory Park	10 June
1	350cc	MV Agusta	Mallory Park	10 June (RL)
1	500cc	MV Agusta	Mallory Park	10 June (RL)
4 (after crashing)	350cc	MV Agusta	Brands Hatch	11 June
1	500cc	MV Agusta	Brands Hatch	11 June
Retired (loose handlebar)	250cc	Benelli	San Remo	18 June
5	125cc Dutch TT	EMC	Assen	30 June
2	350cc Dutch TT	MV Agusta	Assen	30 June
1	500cc Dutch TT	MV Agusta	Assen	30 June (RL)
4	125cc Belgian GP	EMC	Spa Francorchamps	8 July
1	500cc Belgian GP	MV Agusta	Spa Francorchamps	8 July
3	125cc West German GP	EMC	Solitude	15 July
3	350cc	AJS	Castle Combe	21 July
2	500cc	Norton	Castle Combe	21 July
Retired (engine)	350cc	AJS	Snetterton	29 July

Position	Class	Machine	Circuit	Date
Retired (heat, crash)	500cc	Norton	Snetterton	29 July
Retired (engine)	250cc	Benelli	Oulton Park	5 August
2	350cc	AJS	Oulton Park	5 August
3	500cc	Norton	Oulton Park	5 August
Retired (dropped valve)	350cc Ulster GP	MV Agusta	Dundrod	11 August
1	500cc Ulster GP	MV Agusta	Dundrod	11 August (RL)
2	250cc East German GP	MZ	Sachsenring	19 August (RL)
2	350cc East German GP	MV Agusta	Sachsenring	19 August
1	500cc East German GP	MV Agusta	Sachsenring	19 August (RL)
Retired (engine)	125cc Italian GP	EMC	Monza	9 September
Retired (crash)	250cc Italian GO	Benelli	Monza	9 September
1	500cc Italian GP	MV Agusta	Monza	9 September
Retired (crashed in practice)	125cc Finnish GP	MZ	Tampere	23 September
2	350cc	AJS	Swartkops SA	24 November
1	500cc	Norton	Swartkops SA	24 November
4	350cc	AJS	Bulawayo, S Rhodesia	2 December
1	500cc	Norton	Bulawayo, S Rhodesia	2 December
Retired (stone broke goggles)	350cc	AJS	East London SA	29 December
Retired (broken frame)	500cc	Norton	East London SA	29 December

22 victories, 11 seconds, 4 thirds
500cc World Champion
3rd 350cc World Championship
5th 125cc World Championship

1963

Position	Class	Machine	Circuit	Date
1	500cc	MV Agusta	Modena	22 March (RL)
1	250cc	Ducati	Mallory Park	31 March
Retired (blocked carb jet)	350cc	AJS	Mallory Park	31 March
2	500cc	Norton	Mallory Park	31 March
2	250cc	Ducati	Silverstone	6 April
1	350cc	AJS	Silverstone	6 April
4	500cc	Norton	Silverstone	6 April
Retired (crash)	350cc	AJS	Brands Hatch	11 April
3	500cc	MV Agusta	Imola	25 April
Retired (engine)	250cc Austrian GP	MZ	Salzburg	1 May (RL)
1	500cc Austrian GP	MV Agusta	Salzburg	1 May (RL)
Retired (engine)	Junior 350cc TT	MV Agusta	Isle of Man	12 June
1	Senior 500cc TT	MV Agusta	Isle of Man	14 June (RL)
2	350cc Dutch TT	MV Agusta	Assen	29 June
Retired (broken piston)	500cc Dutch TT	MV Agusta	Assen	29 June
1	500cc Belgian GP	MV Agusta	Spa Francorchamps	6 July (RL)
2	350cc Ulster GP	MV Agusta	Dundrod	9 August
1	500cc Ulster GP	MV Agusta	Dundrod	9 August (RL)
1	250cc East German GP	MZ	Sachsenring	16/17 August (RL)
1	350cc East German GP	MV Agusta	Sachsenring	16/17 August (RL)
1	500cc East German GP	MV Agusta	Sachsenring	16/17 August (RL)
1	350cc Finnish GP	MV Agusta	Tampere	1 September (RL)
1	500cc Finnish GP	MV Agusta	Tampere	1 September (RL)
Retired (engine)	350cc Italian GP	MV Agusta	Monza	15 September
1	500cc Italian GP	MV Agusta	Monza	15 September (RL)
1	500cc	MV Agusta	Mallory Park	29 September
1	Race of the Year	MV Agusta 500cc	Mallory Park	29 September (RL)
1	500cc Argentine GP	MV Agusta	Buenos Aires	6 September (RL)

Position	Class	Machine	Circuit	Date
1	350cc Casablanca GP	Kirby AJS	Casablanca	3 November (RL)
7 (after crashing)	500cc Casablanca GP	Kirby Matchless	Casablanca	3 November

25 victories, 10 seconds, 4 thirds
500cc World Champion
2nd 350cc World Championship

1964

Position	Class	Machine	Circuit	Date
1	500cc United States GP	MV Agusta	Daytona	2 February (RL)
5 (after crashing)	500cc	MV Agusta	Modena	19 March (RL)
1	500cc	MV Agusta	Silverstone	7 April
1	500cc	MV Agusta	Cesenatico	29 April
1	Senior 500cc TT	MV Agusta	Isle of Man	12 June
2	350cc Dutch TT	MV Agusta	Assen	27 June
1	500cc Dutch TT	MV Agusta	Assen	27 June (RL)
1	500cc Belgian GP	MV Agusta	Spa Francorchamps	5 July
1	500cc West German GP	MV Agusta	Solitude	19 July (RL)
Retired (crash)	250cc East German GP	MZ	Sachsenring	26 July (RL)
1	500cc East German GP	MV Agusta	Sachsenring	26 July
1	500cc Italian GP	MV Agusta	Monza	13 September
1	500cc	MV Agusta	Mallory Park	27 September
1	Race of the Year 500cc	MV Agusta	Mallory Park	27 September
5	250cc Japanese GP	MZ	Suzuka	1 November
2	350cc Japanese GP	MZ	Suzuka	1 November

11 victories
500cc World Champion
4th 350cc World Championship

1965

Position	Class	Machine	Circuit	Date
1	500cc United States GP	MV Agusta	Daytona	21 March
2	500cc	MV Agusta	Riccione	28 March (RL)
1	500cc	MV Agusta	Cervia	11 April (RL)
11	350cc	Kirby AJS	Brands Hatch	16 April
Retired	500cc	Mularney Norton	Brands Hatch	16 April
6	350cc	Kirby AJS	Snetterton	18 April
1	500cc	Mularney Norton	Snetterton	18 April
1	500cc	MV Agusta	Imola	19 April
2	350cc West German GP	MV Agusta	Nürburgring	24 April
1	500cc West German GP	MV Agusta	Nürburgring	24 April
Retired (broken valve)	500cc	MV Agusta	San Remo	23 May
Retired (engine)	Junior 350cc TT	MV Agusta	Isle of Man	16 June (RL)
1 (after crashing)	Senior 500cc TT	MV Agusta	Isle of Man	18 June
1	500cc	MV Agusta	Mallory Park	20 June
2	350cc Dutch TT	MV Agusta	Assen	26 June
1	500cc Dutch TT	MV Agusta	Assen	26 June (RL)
1	500cc Belgian GP	MV Agusta	Spa Francorchamps	4 July
Retired (engine)	350cc East German GP	MV Agusta	Sachsenring	18 July
1	500cc East German GP	MV Agusta	Sachsenring	18 July
Retired (big-end failure)	350cc Czech GP	MV Agusta	Brno	25 July
1	500cc Czech GP	MV Agusta	Brno	25 July (RL)
1	350cc	Kirby AJS	Silverstone	14 August
1	500cc	MV Agusta	Silverstone	14 August
1	Production	BSA (650cc)	Silverstone	14 August

Position	Class	Machine	Circuit	Date
Retired (crash)	350cc Italian GP	MV Agusta 3	Monza	5 September (RL)
1	500cc Italian GP	MV Agusta 4	Monza	5 September
1	500cc	MV Agusta	Mallory Park	26 September
5	Race of the Year	MV Agusta 500cc	Mallory Park	26 September
5	350cc	Kirby AJS	Brands Hatch	10 October
1	500cc	Kirby Matchless	Brands Hatch	10 October
Retired (crash)	Redex Trophy	Kirby Matchless	Brands Hatch	10 October
1	250cc	Honda 6	Suzuka	24 October (RL)
1	350cc	MV Agusta 3	Suzuka	24 October (RL)

18 victories
500cc World Champion
3rd 350cc World Championship

1966

Position	Class	Machine	Circuit	Date
1	350cc	Honda 4	Brands Hatch	8 April
4	1000cc King of Brands	Honda 4 350cc	Brands Hatch	8 April
Retired (crash)	350cc	Honda 4	Snetterton	10 April
1	350cc	Honda 4	Oulton Park	11 April
3	350cc	Honda 4	Imola	17 April
2	350cc	Honda 4	Cesenatico	24 April
1	350cc Austrian GP	Honda 4	Salzburg	1 May (RL)
1	250cc Spanish GP	Honda 6	Barcelona	8 May (RL)
1	250cc West German GP	Honda 6	Hockenheim	22 May (RL)
1	350cc West German GP	Honda 4	Hockenheim	22 May (RL)
1	250cc French GP	Honda 6	Clermont-Ferrand	29 May (RL)
1	350cc French GP	Honda 4	Clermont-Ferrand	29 May (RL)
1	1000cc	Honda 4 350cc	Brands Hatch	30 May
1	350cc	Honda 4	Mallory Park	19 June
1	250cc Dutch TT	Honda 6	Assen	25 June
1	350cc Dutch TT	Honda 4	Assen	25 June
Retired (crash)	500cc Dutch TT	Honda 4	Assen	25 June (RL)
1	250cc Belgian GP	Honda 6	Spa Francorchamps	3 July (RL)
Retired (exposure & gearbox problems)	500cc Belgian GP	Honda 4	Spa Francorchamps	3 July
1	250cc East German GP	Honda 6	Sachsenring	17 July (RL)
Retired (piston)	350cc German GP	Honda 4	Sachsenring	17 July
Retired (camshaft problems)	500cc East German GP	Honda 4	Sachsenring	17 July
1	250cc Czech GP	Honda 6	Brno	24 July (RL)
1	350cc Czech GP	Honda 4	Brno	24 July (RL)
1	500cc Czech GP	Honda 4	Brno	24 July
1	250cc Finnish GP	Honda 6	Imatra	7 August (RL)
1	350cc Finnish GP	Honda 4	Imatra	7 August (RL)
2	500cc Finnish GP	Honda 4	Imatra	7 August
1	350cc	Honda 4	Brands Hatch	14 August
Retired (crash)	Senior	Honda 4 (350cc)	Brands Hatch	14 August
1	350cc Ulster GP	Honda 4	Dundrod	20 August
1	500cc Ulster GP	Honda 4	Dundrod	20 August (RL)
6	Ultra-lightweight 125cc TT	Honda 5	Isle of Man	1 September
1	Lightweight 250cc TT	Honda 6	Isle of Man	27 August (RL)
Retired (broken exhaust valves)	Junior 350cc TT	Honda 4	Isle of Man	1 September
1	Senior 500cc TT	Honda 4	Isle of Man	3 September (RL)
1	250cc Italian GP	Honda 6	Monza	11 September (RL)
Retired (broken exhaust valves)	Italian GP	Honda 4	Monza	11 September
1	250cc	Honda 6	Cadwell Park	18 September (RL)

Position	Class	Machine	Circuit	Date
1	Invitation	Honda 6 250cc	Cadwell Park	18 September
1	250cc	Honda 6	Mallory Park	25 September (RL)
Retired (flat tyre)	Race of the Year	Honda 6 250cc	Mallory Park	25 September
Retired (broken con-rod)	Race of the South	Honda 6 250cc	Brands Hatch	9 October

28 victories
500cc World Champion
3rd 350cc World Championship

1967

Position	Class	Machine	Circuit	Date
Unplaced	350cc	Honda 4	Mallory Park	29 March
1	350cc	Honda 4	Oulton Park	30 March
1(crashed, remounted)	250cc	Honda 6	Oulton Park	30 March
1	250cc	Honda 6	Riccione	5 April (RL)
1	350cc	Honda 4	Riccione	5 April
2	250cc	Honda 6	Cervia	12 April
Retired	500cc	Honda 4 (350cc)	Cervia	12 April
1	250cc	Honda 6	Cesenatico	16 April
Retired (ignition)	350cc	Honda 4	Cesenatico	16 April
1	250cc	Honda 6	Imola	25 April (RL)
Retired (broken brake lever)	350cc	Honda 4	Imola	25 April
Retired (puncture)	250cc Spanish GP	Honda 6	Barcelona	3 May (RL)
1	350cc West German GP	Honda 297cc 6	Hockenheim	10 May (RL)
Retired (misfire)	500cc West German GP	Honda 4	Hockenheim	10 May
1	250cc	Honda 6	Rimini	17 May
2	350cc	Honda	Rimini	17 May
1	500cc	Honda Special 4	Rimini	17 May
2	250cc French GP	Honda 6	Clermont-Ferrand	24 May (RL)
1	250cc *	Honda 6	Brands Hatch	31 May
1	500cc *	Honda Special 4	Brands Hatch	31 May
1	750cc *	Honda Special 4 500cc	Brands Hatch	31 May
1	Lightweight 250cc TT	Honda 6	Isle of Man	15 June (RL)
1	Junior 350cc TT	Honda 297cc 6	Isle of Man	17 June (RL)
1	Senior 500cc TT	Honda 4	Isle of Man	19 June (RL)
1	250cc	Honda 6	Mallory Park	21 June (RL)
Retired (bent valves)	750cc	Honda 4 350cc	Mallory Park	21 June
1	250cc Dutch TT	Honda 6	Assen	28 June
1	350cc Dutch TT	Honda 297cc 6	Assen	28 June
1	500cc Dutch TT	Honda 4	Assen	28 July
2	250cc Belgian GP	Honda 6	Spa Francorchamps	5 July
2	500cc Belgian GP	Honda 4	Spa Francorchamps	5 July
Retired	250cc East German GP	Honda 6	Sachsenring	16 July
1	350cc East German GP	Honda 297cc 6	Sachsenring	16 July
Retired	500cc East German GP	Honda 4	Sachsenring	16 July
3	250cc Czech GP	Honda 6	Brno	23 July (RL)
1	350cc Czech GP	Honda 297cc 6	Brno	23 July
1	500cc Czech GP	Honda 4	Brno	23 July (RL)
1	250cc Finnish GP	Honda 6	Imatra	6 August
Retired	500cc Finnish GP	Honda 4	Imatra	6 August
1	250cc	Honda 6	Brands Hatch	13 August (RL)
1	250cc Castrol Challenge	Honda 6	Brands Hatch	13 August (RL)
1	750cc	Honda 297cc 6	Brands Hatch	13 August (RL)
1	750cc Castrol Challenge	Honda 297cc 6	Brands Hatch	13 August
1	250cc Ulster GP	Honda 6	Dundrod	20 August (RL)
1	500cc Ulster GP	Honda 4	Dundrod	20 August (RL)

Position	Class	Machine	Circuit	Date
1	250cc	Honda 6	Snetterton	27 August (RL)
Retired (engine)	350cc	Honda 4	Snetterton	27 August (RL)
Retired (engine)	250cc Italian GP	Honda 6	Monza	3 September
2	500cc Italian GP	Honda 4	Monza	3 September (RL)
1	250cc	Honda 6	Cadwell Park	10 September
1	350cc	Honda 297cc 6	Cadwell Park	10 September (RL)
1	750cc Invitation	Honda 297cc 6	Cadwell Park	10 September (RL)
1	250cc	Honda 6	Mallory Park	17 September (RL)
1	350cc	Honda 297cc 6	Mallory Park	17 September (RL)
1	Race of the Year	Honda 297cc 6	Mallory Park	17 September (RL)
1	250cc Canadian GP	Honda 6	Mosport	30 September (RL)
1	500cc Canadian GP	Honda 4	Mosport	30 September (RL)
1	350cc	Honda 297cc 6	Brands Hatch	1 October (RL)
1	Race of the South	Honda 297cc 6	Brands Hatch	1 October
Retired (misfire)	250cc Japanese GP	Honda 6	Fuji	15 October
1	350cc Japanese GP	Honda 297cc 6	Fuji	15 October (RL)
1	250cc Dickie Dale Trophy	Honda 6 250cc	Pietermaritzburg SA	26 December (RL)

* eventually excluded for riding 250 and 500cc Hondas instead of 350cc originally entered.
42 victories
250cc World Champion
350cc World Champion
2nd 500cc World Championship

1968

Position	Class	Machine	Circuit	Date
1	250cc	Honda 6	Killarney SA	14 January
1	350cc	Honda 297cc 6	Rimini	24 March
2 (after crashing)	500cc	Reynolds Honda 4	Rimini	24 March (RL)
Retired (crash)	350cc	Honda 297cc 6	Cesenatico	7 April
2	500cc	Reynolds Honda 4	Cesenatico	7 April
Retired (crash)	350cc	Honda 297cc 6	Imola	15 April
1	500cc	Reynolds Honda 4	Imola	15 April
3	350cc	Honda 297cc 6	Cervia	18 April
1	500cc	Reynolds Honda 4	Cervia	A8 April
1	350cc	Honda 297cc 6	Cadwell Park	19 May
4	500cc	Honda 4	Cadwell Park	19 May
1	350cc	Honda 297cc 6	Mallory Park	16 June
1	1000cc	Honda 297cc 6	Mallory Park	16 June
Retired (crash)	250cc Hillclimb	Honda 6	Monte Generoso (Swi)	7 July
1	350cc	Honda 297cc 6	Brands Hatch	11 August
1	Invitation	Honda 297cc 6	Brands Hatch	11 August (RL)
1	Invitation	Honda 297cc 6	Brands Hatch	1 September (RL)
1	350cc	Honda 297cc 6	Snetterton	1 September (RL)
1	500cc	Honda	Snetterton	1 September (RL)
1	1000cc	Honda 297cc 6	Snetterton	1 September
1	350cc	Honda 297cc 6	Oulton Park	2 September
1	500cc	Seeley G50	Oulton Park	2 September
Retired (crash)	500cc Italian GP	Benelli 4	Monza	15 September
1	350cc	Honda 297cc 6	Mallory Park	22 September
1	Race of the Year	Honda 297cc 6	Mallory Park	22 September
3	500cc	Benelli 4	Riccione	29 September
1	350cc	Honda 297cc 6	Brands Hatch	6 October
1	1000cc	Honda 297cc 6	Brands Hatch	6 October
1	350cc	Honda 297cc 6	Pietermaritzburg	26 December

20 victories

1969

Position	Class	Machine	Circuit	Date
1	1000cc	Honda 297cc 6	Cape Town	11 January
2	500cc	Honda 4	Riccione	30 March
3	1000cc	Seeley G50 500cc	Mallory Park	21 September
5	Race of the Year	Seeley G50	Mallory Park	21 September

1970

Position	Class	Machine	Circuit	Date
Retired (engine overheated)	Daytona 200	BSA Rocket 3 750cc	Daytona	15 March

1971

Position	Class	Machine	Circuit	Date
Retired (broken valve)	Daytona 200	BSA Rocket 3 750cc	Daytona	15 March
4	350cc	Yamaha	Silverstone	22 August
4	750cc	Yamaha 350cc	Silverstone	22 August
2	350cc	Benelli 4	Pesaro	29 August
4	350cc	Yamaha	Mallory Park	19 September
Retired	Race of the Year	Yamaha 350cc	Mallory Park	19 September

No racing on two wheels between 1972 and 1977.

1977

Position	Class	Machine	Circuit	Date
2	Classic Bike Event	Manx Norton 500cc	Amaroo Park, Sydney	January
3	Classic Bike Event	Manx Norton 500cc	Bathhurst, Australia	April
6	1000cc Six Hour Production Race	Ducati 748cc (shared with Jim Scaysbrook)	Amaroo Park, Sydney	23 October

Note: Mike also took part on the same Norton at two other meetings; results not known.

1978

Position	Class	Machine	Circuit	Date
9	750cc	Yamaha TZ750	Bathurst, Australia	26 March
7	1000cc Three Hour Production Race	Ducati 748cc (shared with Jim Scaysbrook)	Adelaide, Australia	7 April
1	Formula 1 TT	Ducati 864cc	Isle of Man	3 June (RL)
28	Senior 500cc TT	Yamaha TZR	Isle of Man	5 June
12	Lightweight 250cc TT	Yamaha TZ	Isle of Man	7 June
Retired (first lap)	Classic 1000cc TT	Yamaha TZ750	Isle of Man	9 June
1	Formula 1	Ducati 864cc	Mallory Park (Post TT)	11 June
Retired (crash)	Formula 1	Ducati 864cc	Donington Park	9 July
3	Formula 1	Ducati 864cc	Silverstone	12 August
Retired (crash, by Jim Scaysbrook)	1000cc Six Hour Production Race	Ducati 748cc (shared with Jim Scaysbrook)	Amaroo Park, Sydney	22 October

1979

Position	Class	Machine	Circuit	Date
4	Classic bike event	AJS 7R 350cc	Wigram, New Zealand	11 February
14	1000cc Three Hour Production Race	Honda CB900 (shared with Jim Scaysbrook)	Adelaide, Australia	25 March
5	Formula 1 TT	Ducati 864cc	Isle of Man	2 June
1	Senior 500cc TT	Suzuki	Isle of Man	4 June
2	Classic 1000cc TT	Suzuki RG500	Isle of Man	8 June
Retired (brake trouble)	Formula 1	Suzuki GS 1000	Mallory Park	10 June

Index

ND - #0345 - 270225 - C0 - 260/195/19 - PB - 9781780912141 - Gloss Lamination